MACMILLAN **EXAMS**

Ready for
IELTS
teacher's book

Sam McCarter

Liz Hunt

Rachael Roberts

Macmillan Education
Between Towns Road, Oxford OX4 3PP
A division of Macmillan Publishers Limited
Companies and representatives throughout the world

ISBN 978-0-2307-3222-3

Text © Sam McCarter, Liz Hunt and Rachael Roberts
2010
Design and illustration © Macmillan Publishers
Limited 2010

First published 2010

Note to Teachers
Original design by Andrew Jones
Page make-up by xen. http://www.xen.co.uk
Cover design by Barbara Mercer
Cover illustration/photograph by © Getty/Sean Davey

Authors' acknowledgements: Sam McCarter would
like to thank Debra Emmet and Jo Kent for their help
and expertise and Phil Vellender and Amanda
Holmbrook.
Liz Hunt would like to thank Clyde Fowle.
And finally, a special thank you goes to Alison Ross
and Amanda Anderson for their support, help and
humour.

The publishers would like to acknowledge and thank
the following students for supplying sample answers:
Wilonja Mutebwe, Abukar Haji Jimale, Darejan
Chitashvili, Kais Abdaly, Akram Moosavi, Nisreen
Shaker, Ibahim Almeriy and all the students at Reache
Northwest.

The authors and publishers are grateful for permission
to reprint the following copyright material:

Material from article 'Can the can' published in The
Economist 20.11.08, copyright © The Economist
Newspaper Limited, London 2008, reprinted by
permission of the publisher;
Material from article 'Just shut up, will you' published
in The Economist 4.12.08, copyright © The Economist
Newspaper Limited, London 2008, reprinted by
permission of the publisher;
Material from article 'Second life' published in The
Economist 15.1.09, copyright © The Economist
Newspaper Limited, London 2009, reprinted by
permission of the publisher;

Material from website www.ecotravelling.co.uk.;
Material from article 'The Legacy of Krakatoa' by
Roger Maynard, copyright © Roger Maynard 2008,
first published in The Independent 24.8.08, reprinted
by permission of the publisher;
Material from article 'The teenage brain: A scientific
analysis' by Steve Connor, copyright © Steve Connor
2006, first published in The Independent 5.11.06,
reprinted by permission of the publisher;
Material from article 'Study shows happiness 'is
contagious'' copyright © Independent Newspapers
2008, first published 5.12.08, reprinted by permission
of the publisher;
Material from article 'Learn what you want' by
Andrew Downie, copyright © Andrew Downie 2004
first published in The Telegraph 9.2.04, reprinted by
permission of the publisher;
Material from article 'Ancient trees found using 200
year old maps' by Paul Eccleston, copyright © Paul
Eccleston 2007, first published in The Telegraph
18.12.07, reprinted by permission of the publisher;
Material from article 'And the one in the middle is the
joker' by Olga Craig, copyright © Olga Craig 2007,
first published in The Telegraph 11.1.07, reprinted by
permission of the publisher.

Charts copyright © GALLUP. All rights reserved.
Reprinted with permission from www.gallup.com
pp150, 174:
www.statistics.gov.uk p189.

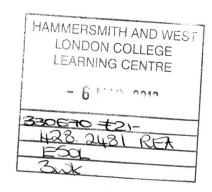

Printed in Thailand

2015 2014 2013 2012
10 9 8 7 6 5 4 3

Contents

Contents Map of the Coursebook

Introduction

The *Ready for IELTS* course consists of the following components:

- Coursebook (with and without key)
- Teacher's Book
- Five audio CDs
- CD-ROM containing interactive exercises
- Workbook (with and without key)

Coursebook

The Coursebook contains 14 units, each 10 pages in length with an additional two-page *Review*. The focus is on increasing the language competence of your students in the four main skills tested in the academic version of the IELTS examination (listening, reading, writing and speaking). In addition, there is a range of activities aimed at building your students' competence in vocabulary and grammar relevant to the IELTS exam. The two-page *Review* section at the end of each unit revises the language covered in that unit. You can use the *Review* section unit by unit as students progress through the Coursebook; and periodically as a quick revision tool along with the *Wordlists* and *Grammar reference* (see below); or in conjunction with the *Progress tests*.

There are four *Ready for ...* units after every third unit up to Unit 12, each dealing with one of the four main skills tested in the IELTS exam: *Ready for Listening, Ready for Reading, Ready for Writing* and *Ready for Speaking*. Each of these sections provides extra practice for the respective skills in the exam and may be used as they occur in the Coursebook. They may also be used as a whole or in part as an addition to a particular unit or units. Alternatively, you may want to keep them for revision purposes. They are meant to be used flexibly, so you can dip in and out of them and revisit as appropriate.

The *Wordlist* and *Grammar reference* are both closely linked to the 14 units in the book. Students refer to the *Additional materials* and *Listening scripts* for some exercises. The Coursebook is available with or without the answer key, which contains for most units examples of student writing marked by an examiner.

The following boxes providing tips and advice on performing various tasks are found throughout the Coursebook.

- **What to expect in the exam**: these contain information on what students should be prepared to see, hear or do in a particular type of task in the exam.

- **How to go about it**: these provide advice and guidelines on how to deal with different types of tasks and specific questions.

- **Don't forget!**: these remind students of certain procedures to follow as they perform a task.

Teacher's Book

The Teacher's Book contains teaching notes for all the activities in the Coursebook. A typical unit of the Teacher's Book provides you with:

- a summary of the contents of the unit, including the exam question types for each of the skills

- answers to the exercises along with sample answers for most of the writing tasks, with examiners' comments and scores

- guidelines for using the Coursebook along with suggestions for lead-ins and further activities

- transcripts of the listening tests with the part of the text relating to the answers underlined

- ideas for manipulating exercises.

At the end of the Teacher's Book there are also photocopiable exercises, five photocopiable *Progress tests* and a final test.

Photocopiable exercises

For each main unit, there is at least one photocopiable exercise relating to one of the language points taught in the main Coursebook unit. These may be used as further practice at the points indicated in the Teacher's Book, to supplement the corresponding exercise in the *Review* section at the end of each unit, or as revision exercises as your students progress though the units. You may also want to do the exercises as a revision aid before the students do the *Progress tests* at the end of the Teacher's Book. At the end of the photocopiable exercises there is an answer key.

Photocopiable *Progress tests*

These tests are intended to be used after your students have completed Units 1–3, 4–6, 7–9, 10–12 and 13–14. You can use them to assess the progress of your students as they move through the course. Each test contains practice in aspects of listening, reading and writing, along with revision of the language that is presented in the corresponding units in the Coursebook. Apart from the grammar and vocabulary tasks in each test, exam question types corresponding to the various modules are as follows:

Test 1: Listening Section 1 (form completion, note completion, selecting items from a list), Reading (matching paragraph headings, True/False/Not Given statements, global multiple choice), Writing Task 1 (describing a table)

Test 2: Listening Section 2 (labelling a map, multiple-choice questions, sentence completion), Reading (completing a flow-chart, sentence completion, multiple-choice questions), Writing Task 2 (causes and solutions)

Test 3: Listening Section 3 (note completion, answering questions, selecting items from a list), Reading (matching statements to paragraphs, classification, selecting items from a list), Writing Task 1 (map description)

Test 4: Listening Section 4 (table completion, selecting items from a list), Reading (table completion, summary with a word list and matching), Writing Task 2 (discussing views and giving opinions)

Test 5: Listening Section 4 (matching, summary completion), Reading (selecting items from a list, sentence completion, Yes/No/Not Given statements), Writing Task 1 (describing a table)

Final test

This is a full, photocopiable test, which contains all four modules with model answers for Writing Tasks 1 and 2. You can use the test near the end of the course (at about unit 12 onwards) as a final test before students take the IELTS exam.

At the end of the tests there is an answer key.

CD-ROM

The CD-ROM contains two full tests for the listening, reading and writing modules of the academic version of the IELTS exam.

Workbook

The Workbook contains 14 units and follows the general topics of the Coursebook. Each unit provides students with further practice, revision and extension of the language presented in the Coursebook, as well as examination practice. Each unit contains the following elements:

Listening

Each unit in the Workbook provides students with valuable additional practice in listening skills. An example of one of the sections in the IELTS Listening module is found in each unit. The section type and question type mainly follow those in the corresponding units in the Coursebook. Two full Listening tests are also found on the CD-ROM.

Reading

The reading practice in each unit mainly follows the question type in the corresponding Coursebook unit, so that students can refine their competence and techniques as they go through the course. The vocabulary of the reading passage is sometimes exploited in reading exercises. Two full reading tests are also found on the CD-ROM.

Writing

In each unit, there is writing practice either relating to Task 1 or Task 2 of the exam. There is ample practice of the range of data and diagram interpretation for Task 1, and of the range of question types covered in Task 2. The questions do not always correspond to the types of questions for each task in the Coursebook, but the task types do.

Vocabulary

The vocabulary practice in each unit follows closely the vocabulary practice in the Coursebook, with the exercise types being a combination of crosswords, puzzles and exercises similar to those found in the Coursebook (sentence completion, matching, note expansion, transformation, proofreading, etc.)

Language focus

This contains further practice of the grammar that the students have learnt in the Coursebook. You can refer them to the relevant section of the Coursebook and the *Grammar reference*.

Wordlist

The *Wordlist* at the back of the book contains a list of useful words. Space has been left to encourage students to write their own definitions of the words in the list, so they can build their own dictionary and hence their vocabulary. You can encourage students to complete the definitions for the words as they come across them in the course.

Using the course to prepare students for the academic version of the IELTS examination

The purpose of *Ready for IELTS* is to prepare students for the academic version of the International English Language Testing System (IELTS) examination. Students preparing for the General Training version of IELTS will find all the vocabulary and grammar practice, the listening practice and the speaking practice relevant. The Reading and the Writing modules in the General Training version are, however, different.

Listening

The range of listening practice in this course is a valuable resource for all students preparing for the IELTS examination. In all, there are five audio CDs to help develop your students' competence in listening (two to accompany the Coursebook, one for the Teacher's Book and two to accompany the Workbook). In addition, there is further listening practice on the CD-ROM which comes free with the Coursebook. In total, there are 49 sample sections relating to the IELTS exam. In the *Ready for Speaking* section there is also an example of the Speaking test, Parts 2 and 3.

Each unit contains one example of a section from the exam, with guidance in the *How to go about it/What to expect* boxes. The *Ready for Listening* section on page 42 contains an example of a full test with explanations. Throughout the Coursebook, there are valuable pre-listening and post-listening activities, with the listening providing a context for the vocabulary and the language in the unit.

As each section of the listening module in the exam is played only once, it is essential that students are well prepared in techniques that enable them to complete the listening module efficiently. To this end, the pre-listening activities and *How to go about it/What to expect* boxes provide ample advice and guidance. Students are encouraged to learn prediction techniques for general and specific answers, using the questions as a summary of the listening script. Some listening practices are followed by a discussion, to encourage the students to develop their critical-thinking skills.

The listening practice gives examples of a range of accents. Further listening practice is provided in the Workbook, the CD-ROM and in the *Progress tests*.

Reading

Each unit contains a reading passage. The *Reading for IELTS* section provides general information and further tips on reading, and a focus on True/False/Not Given and Yes/No/Not Given statements. The reading practices give students examples of the full range of question types that are tested in the exam. *How to go about it* and *What to expect in the exam* boxes focusing on reading generally and at least one new question type in each unit.

The texts are authentic and provide examples of the range of text types that occur in the exam, e.g., historical, argumentative, descriptive, process, classification, cause/effect, problem/solution.

As with the listening practice, pre-reading activities help students focus on various reading techniques like scanning, paraphrasing, content prediction, etc. After reading, students are encouraged to give their reaction to the text so that they can develop their critical-thinking skills. The reading texts throughout provide examples for the vocabulary and language focus exercises, so that the students can see the items they are practising in an authentic context.

Further reading practice is provided in the Workbook, on the CD-ROM and in the *Progress tests*.

Writing

Practice in either Task 1 or Task 2 is provided in each unit of the Coursebook with the *Ready for Writing* section on page 128 providing further practice. Each writing task is preceded by extensive practice with model or sample answers, so that students are familiar with the specific writing task covered in that unit before they attempt to write their own answer to a writing task at the end of the writing section. Practice is given in organization, planning, creating ideas, style/register and proof reading, as well as the specific vocabulary and grammar required to perform the various writing tasks.

At the end of the Coursebook, there is a Checklist for both Writing tasks to help students check their answers. Students are encouraged throughout the course to use the Checklist. For most of the Writing tasks in the main units, there is a sample answer in the answer key with comments and a score provided by an IELTS examiner.

In the *Ready for Writing* section a wide range of data interpretation is practised, with either good sample answers or models for students to check against. This section also contains information about the examiner's marking criteria.

The Workbook, the *Progress tests* and the CD-ROM contain further writing practice, as do several of the photocopiable exercises.

Speaking

At least one part of the three-part IELTS Speaking module is found in each unit. The speaking practice generally relates to the theme of the unit and helps practise the vocabulary and grammar presented in each unit. As the grammar and vocabulary in each unit have a context in the reading passage or the listening practice, students are constantly recycling language in different parts of the exam.

Within each speaking section, ample practice is given in the skills students will need to perform efficiently in the IELTS exam, e.g., organization, vocabulary use, creating ideas, developing ideas and speaking fluently with a natural rhythm. As with the writing tasks, speaking checklists are provided at the end of the Coursebook so students can monitor themselves and each other as they progress through the course.

The *Ready for Speaking* section is situated after Unit 12. You may, however, want to refer students to this section earlier in the course and use sections of it to supplement the speaking practice in the main unit. This section contains practice for Parts 2 and 3 of the Speaking test, with practice exercises.

Vocabulary

Every unit has at least one vocabulary or word building section. A context for the vocabulary is provided by either the reading passage or the listening practice in each unit. The purpose of the vocabulary section is to provide students with a wide range of words and collocations that they will find useful in all four skills in the exam. The exercises are designed to increase the students' competence in using the vocabulary, rather than just learning the words and phrases for their own sake.

The vocabulary items have been selected with a view to being used in a wide range of situations, not just in the contexts in the Coursebook. This should serve students well in all modules of the IELTS exam.

The two-page *Review* at the end of each unit provides further vocabulary practice. The *Wordlist* at the end summarizes the vocabulary items used in each unit. The Workbook provides further practice and the *Progress tests* provide an opportunity for testing the vocabulary.

Grammar

Like the vocabulary, the grammar in each unit is selected for its relevance in building students' competence in using language in the IELTS exam, in all four skills. Each unit contains at least one element of grammar in a *Language focus* section. The context for the grammar selected is found, as for the vocabulary, in either the reading passage or the listening practice. As well as specific speaking activities related to the grammar practice, the writing and speaking tasks provide a wide range of contexts for practising the grammar selected.

Sam McCarter

1 We are all friends now

Content overview

Themes

This unit is concerned with people, characteristics and relationships.

Exam-related activities

Reading

Topic	Networking sites
Question type	Matching headings
	Completing sentences
	TRUE/FALSE/NOT GIVEN

Listening

Topic	Applying for volunteer work
Section 1	Completing notes
	Completing a form
	Selecting items from a list

Writing

Task 1	Describing a line graph

Speaking

Part 2	Describing a person

Other

Language focus 1	Present simple, present continuous and past simple
Language focus 2	Likes and dislikes
Vocabulary 1	Describing people
Vocabulary 2	Verbs of movement

Vocabulary 1: Describing people Page 6

Lead-in

Before looking at the photographs, elicit adjectives to describe people's personalities. Collate them on the board under the headings 'positive characteristics' and 'negative characteristics'.

1 Students look at the photographs and discuss the questions in pairs, giving their reasons. Do the first photo together as an example.

2 Check understanding of the target vocabulary. Students then match the adjectives with the photos in pairs. Tell them they can use the adjectives more than once. Get feedback.

Answers
Possible answers
1 adventurous, sporty, dynamic
2 artistic, creative
3 wise, considerate, supportive, helpful
4 talkative, chatty
5 hard-working, conscientious

3 Start a whole class discussion. Discuss some situations where appearance and attitude may initially be important.

4 Students complete the answers. Check their spelling as you monitor the activity. Drill the pronunciation of both nouns and adjectives.

Answers
1 respected/respectful/respectable
2 ambitious
3 caring/careful
4 humorous
5 talented
6 generous
7 cheerful
8 sociable
9 calm
10 punctual
11 reliable
12 loyal
13 honest
14 patient

5 Students complete this exercise in their books. Check their answers quickly. Suggest they start a page in their vocabulary book or section in their files entitled 'People's characteristics' for self-study.

Answers	
1 humorous	7 respected
2 calm	8 generous
3 cheerful	9 loyal
4 talented	10 caring
5 ambitious	11 reliable
6 sociable	12 punctual

6 Students work in pairs. Write the following expressions on the board and encourage students to use them:

What's your friend like?

He/She's highly respected.

People respect him/her a lot because he/she …

For example, he/she …

First give them a model, using a student as an example. Check pronunciation and appropriacy as you go round the class.

7 As an extension of this activity, ask students to write three positive characteristics and three negative characteristics they have. This way they could look at making the negative forms of some of the target adjectives.

8 This could be in Part 3 of the Speaking test or a Task 2 question in the Writing test. Make this discussion as detailed as you want.

Further practice

This activity will help students get to know each other as well as develop the use of adjectives.

Ask students to work in groups and choose a famous person who is in the news at the moment. Alternatively you can bring in photos of famous people. Always be conscious of local sensitive issues. Give the materials at random to the groups. Or ask one person from each group to choose a photo from a batch of upside-down photos. Tell them they can swap their photo, but they shouldn't let other groups see who it is.

Give the students a time limit, e.g., 5–10 minutes, to prepare a description of the person, describing their personality and activities. You can encourage them to write down a few notes under the headings 'personality' and 'activities'. Then ask the group to show their photo to the class and describe the person. Or describe the person to the class and the others have to guess who it is.

A variation of this activity is to give each group two photos. They choose one person to describe and then when they present the description to the class they can ask the whole class to choose the appropriate photograph.

Reading
IELTS Reading Passage   Page 8

1–3 Follow the activities in the Coursebook. Go through the preparation stages carefully as it is vital to get the students into good training habits as early as possible. Emphasize the importance of initially surveying the title and sub-headings, then going on to look at the questions before reading anything in detail in the text. Don't let them start the reading yet. Once you are satisfied they are preparing effectively, let them do the reading. Time them for 20 minutes, but give extra time if necessary. At this stage, confidence-building is important and the extra time given in getting a correct answer can be slowly reduced over the duration of the course.

When going over the answers, it's helpful to project the text onto the board if possible so you can underline and indicate where answers are to be found. You can prepare this before class so you are sure of the answers yourself.

TRUE/FALSE/NOT GIVEN questions are one of the main areas of difficulty for students in the IELTS reading module, so time must be given in going over the answers and discussing them. The distinction between FALSE and NOT GIVEN must be carefully explained to students from the outset so that care can be taken in future units.

Make a grid with numbers 1–13 on the left. Each time the students do a reading exercise, get them to write their answers in the grid and keep it as a record. They should tick the questions they get right, and leave the ones they get wrong blank. This will help them analyze their reading performance to assist them in where to focus in their self-study. As in the exam, the reading passages vary in difficulty. As a rough guide, if students are aiming for a score of 6/6.5 in reading, they should aim to have around 9 out of 13 correct.

Questions 1–6

Go through the 'How to go about it' advice with the students, step by step. Analyze the form of the headings. They are often made up of general category nouns like *benefit*, *effect*, *solution*, etc. followed by a preposition phrase like *of...* . These general category nouns will usually be paraphrases of words in the passage, but not always. The nouns will summarize the content and the meaning or function of the sections in relation to the rest of the text. Generally speaking, it is useful to train students to recognize different section and paragraph types and where they would expect them to appear in a text.

Your students may be used to a reading approach where they read every word. But you gradually need to encourage them to skim and scan. Most of the time in the IELTS exam the students should be skimming to get the gist and scanning to locate information, and then stopping to read in more detail. Be very careful about overanalyzing a text and the questions. Gradually wean students off this as you go through the course, as it will slow them down in the exam.

Answers	
1	viii
2	vi
3	vii
4	iii
5	ii
6	i

Questions 7–10

Encourage students to use the headings to help locate the answers. As Question 7 is the first specific question, tell students that they will probably find it near the beginning of the text. Check if any of the questions relate in any way to the section headings. Use the scanning techniques described in **Ready for Reading** on page 84.

Answers
7 phenomenal level
8 university life
9 academic support
10 university friendships

Questions 11–13

Once again, students should use the headings to help locate the answers. As students find FALSE and NOT GIVEN statements particularly difficult, spend time analyzing the questions before they answer them. Look at examples of some common sentence types in **Ready for Reading** on page 86. Read the explanation there with the whole class for the difference between FALSE and NOT GIVEN.

Answers
11 FALSE. 'Virtual interviews' will not be the only research methodology used at Leicester. Section D: *This project will be using both an online questionnaire and virtual interviews.*
12 NOT GIVEN. Section D: no comparison is mentioned between the UK and other places.
13 TRUE. Section F: ... *or to bring together current and new students to provide peer support.*

Reacting to the text

Students discuss the questions in pairs or in small groups.

Language focus 1: Present simple, present continuous and past simple

Page 10

Photocopiable exercise on page 135.

1–3 Follow the instructions in the Coursebook. Elicit the form and function of the three tenses. Give a mini-presentation if there are any misunderstandings. Refer students to the Grammar reference on page 219 of Student's book if necessary.

Answers
1
1 Section D
2 Section A
3 Section B
4 Section D
2
1 raised – past simple
2 is running – present continuous
3 know, impacts – present simple
4 builds – present simple
3
a present simple
b present continuous
c past simple
d present simple

4–5 Follow the instructions in the Coursebook. Students check answers in pairs. In exercise 5, do the first one together as an example.

Answers
4
1 helps
2 participated
3 impacted
4 influenced
5 are now recruiting
6 feel
5
1 *help* is used as an infinitive (Section A) and in the present simple (Section B)
2 *participate* is used as a gerund after the preposition *with* (Section A)
3 *impact* is in the present simple (Section B)
4 *influence* is used as an infinitive (Section F)
5 *recruit* is used as an infinitive (Section A)
6 *feel* is in the same tense, the present simple (Section D)

Listening
IELTS Section 1   Page 11

1–5 Follow the instructions in the Coursebook. Go through the 'How to go about it' and 'What to expect in the exam' advice, as it is vital to get the students into good habits for listening tasks as early as possible.

Point out that IELTS exam candidates only hear the recording once in the exam, but students will hear it more than once at this early stage of the course. Play Section 1 through a second time. Students could fill in any answers they missed the first time with a different colour. Students compare their answers in pairs. Play Section 1 once more, pausing at each question so they can mark and hear where the answer is in the text.

As with reading tasks, encourage students to make a grid with numbers 1–40 on the left. Each time the students do a listening exercise, get them to tick in one colour those they get right on the first listening, and another colour for those they get right on the second listening. They should leave the ones they get wrong blank. This will help them analyze their listening performance so they know what to focus on in their self-study. Encourage them to keep a dated record of the listening answers together in their files so they can see their progress.

Answers

1

1 a name

2 a noun

3 a number

4 an adjective

5 a name

6 a name

7 a number

8 a noun

Questions 1–4

1 Andrews

2 July

3 8/eight

4 part-time

Questions 5–8

5 Davenport

6 Fordenham

7 8876451

8 morning

Questions 9 and 10

C, D in any order

1 We are all friends now

 1.1

(C = clerk; V = volunteer)

C: Hi. Charles Lewis speaking.

V: Hi. Am I through to Mr Lewis?

C: Yes, you are. How can I help you?

V: I'm, er, phoning about the notice I saw saying that you are looking for helpers for the charity event being held next month.

C: Yes, we are. We need a number of people. Em … we need about 20 volunteers to help out as guides, ticket collectors and to work on stalls, and some people to take charge of a range of children's events. The venue of the show will be Andrews Hall. I take it you're interested?

V: Yes, definitely. It says here the event will take place between Friday and Sunday on the 15th to the 17th of July. Is that correct?

C: Yes, it is. The event is open each day – Friday to Sunday at 10 am … and runs until 8 pm every evening that it's open.

V: OK. The times sound OK. Am I right in thinking you're only looking for part-time helpers?

C: Yes, that's right. We have lots of full-time volunteers, but we need part-time helpers to fill empty slots in the schedule.

V: I'd be interested in helping out part-time rather than doing the whole event anyway.

C: Yes, that's fine.

V: What do I have to do now?

C: I just need to take down a few details. Right … First of all, I need your name?

V: It's Andrea Davenport.

C: Is that D-E- … ?

V: No, it's em … , D-A-V-E-N-P-O-R-T.

C: Davenport. OK. And can I take some contact details?

V: Yes.

C: Let's start with your address?

V: It's 90 Fordenham Mansions, 62 Park Avenue.

C: Could you spell that for me?

V: It's F–O–R–D–E–N–H–A–M and then Mansions.

C: OK.

V: 62 Park Avenue. And that's London SW1 4PQ.

C: And a contact telephone number?

V: My home number is 887 6451. I work in the afternoons, so the best time to ring is in the morning.

C: Right. That's all that done.

V: Do I need to come along for an interview or anything?

C: Yes. We're seeing people at the moment. Can you come next Saturday from 9 am onwards?

V: Yes, that's fine.

C: Well Andrea, do you have any more questions about the work?

V: Em ... oh, can I just ask if experience is necessary?

C: No, but it certainly helps. We're just looking for people who get on with others and who are independent. For example, we need people we can leave in charge on their own if nobody else is available.

V: I think I can do that. I like working with other people, but I am able to work on my own without anyone around.

C: That all sounds really very useful and the sort of thing we're looking for. And we also need people who are always on time.

V: I think I'm OK with that.

C: Fine. I'll send you an event pack with all the event details, address, application form, etc. to go through. You can bring the completed application form along with you on Saturday.

V: OK.

C: I've got a slot at 9 am for an interview.

V: That's fine.

5 Students discuss the questions in pairs.

Language focus 2: Likes and dislikes
Page 12

1 Look at the sentence with the class and elicit the answer, referring back to **Language focus 1** if necessary.

Answers
She uses the -ing form after like as she is emphasizing what she enjoys from past experience of doing it. This is different from like followed by the infinitive with to, which indicates routine habit or duty as opposed to enjoyment.

2 Correct the sentences which have mistakes, ensuring students are clear why they are wrong.

Refer them to the Grammar reference on page 219 if necessary.

Answers
1 Correct
2 Correct
3 Incorrect – 'to join'
4 Correct
5 Correct
6 Correct
7 Incorrect – 'doing'

3–4 These exercises are a good opportunity to deal with any entrenched errors. Monitor students carefully and correct any errors as they work.

Answers
3
1 playing
2 to live
3 being/to be
4 to keep
5 taking
6 to be
7 socializing/to socialize, staying
8 playing
9 to see
4
1 I'd like to live in the countryside.
2 Nowadays people dislike doing certain sports.
3 Adrian likes cleaning/to clean the kitchen every morning.
4 She enjoys shopping enormously.
5 Pedro can't stand playing video games.
6 He likes people he knows to be honest.
7 She would prefer to see the film on DVD at home rather than in the cinema.
8 He really loves mingling/to mingle with other people at parties.

5 Before the students discuss sports in pairs, start a spidergram or word map on the board. Ask students to come up and complete it with vocabulary linked with sports, e.g., *yoga, fishing, aerobics, mountaineering, football, bowling, cycling, golf, judo, baseball*. They can then put this into their vocabulary books and extend it as they progress through the course, e.g., by adding collocations linked with actions and locations, and equipment used in each sport, e.g., *do, go, play*. (Answers: *do yoga, go fishing, do aerobics,* *go mountaineering, play football, go bowling, go cycling, play golf, do judo, play baseball*). Students then go into their pairs and discuss why they like or dislike the different sports.

6 Students discuss the questions either in small groups or as a whole class.

Speaking
IELTS Part 2   Page 13

Go through the 'What to expect in the exam' advice on Part 2 with the students. It is very important to stress that they only have one minute to make notes and that writing full sentences is not possible. Reading sentences out loud also leads to lack of fluency and will lose them marks in this criterion.

Making and taking notes are skills that need to be practised and are essential in academic settings. Judge the ability of your students in this area and focus on practice accordingly. An activity to assist them would be to set a general topic and give them one minute to make notes on it. Do this two or three times if necessary until the students have improved their skill.

1–6 Follow the instructions, carefully monitoring each stage and correcting the impulse to write sentences. Read through each point on the Topic card, writing an example on the board of one or two words or phrases for each point on the card. Remind them that each point must be covered.

Their notes should be as brief as possible. Eventually about 10 words will be ideal, but at this stage accept around 15 or 16. Ask the students to write the notes vertically as they are then easier to read quickly.

Write the following expressions on the board and encourage students to use them:

I like him/her a lot (because …)

I admire him/her enormously (because …)

What makes him/her special is …

What appeals to me most is that he/she …

Answers
1
Possible answers
1 supportive/considerate/helpful/wise
2 hard-working/conscientious/supportive/helpful
3 adventurous/sporty

4
who the person is – present simple
what they are generally like – present simple
what qualities this person has – present simple
and explain why you would like to be similar to this person – conditional

Vocabulary 2: Verbs of movement
Page 14

1 Students do the exercise in pairs. Check their answers carefully. If possible, put the graph on a transparency or project it through a computer so you can clearly indicate how each movement works on the page. It is very important to get these verbs right from the outset as they are essential for accurately describing line graphs.

Answers
1 h
2 d
3 b
4 g
5 j
6 i
7 a
8 e
9 c
10 f

2–4 Students follow the instructions in the Coursebook.

NB It is a good idea to encourage your students to take an interest in national and international affairs so that they have a general picture of current trends and topics to draw on. Give them access to news and current affairs journals and websites for them to look at once or twice a week. As this is the first such activity with them you might like to bring in one or two articles from a local English-language newspaper for them to draw ideas from.

Answers
2
1 fell and then levelled off
2 hit a peak
3 dipped
4 plummeted
5 rose gradually
6 remained flat/stable
7 fell gradually

8 fluctuated

9 hit a low

10 soared

3

a bottom out, a rocket, a soar, a plummet, a level off

4

1 There was a drop in the price of laptops followed by a period of stability.

3 There was a slight fall and then a quick recovery in the amount of money spent.

4 There was a plunge in visitor numbers to the website in the first quarter of the year.

5 There was a slow but sure increase in book purchases over the year.

6 There was stabilization in the number of students applying to the university over the period.

7 There was a steady decrease in attendance figures/attendances at the conference last year.

8 There were some fluctuations in the growth rate during the last year.

You cannot change sentences 2, 9 and 10.

Extension

Tell students to draw a mini-graph for each of the descriptions 1–10. Students work in pairs. Give five to one student and five to the other. Give each student empty grids and ask them to draw each one as their partner describes it.

Writing
IELTS Task 1   Page 15

Photocopiable writing exercise on page 134.

For both Writing tasks 1 and 2, it is a good idea to get the students to self-correct where possible. A marking scheme based on symbols can be devised whereby the teacher indicates the type of error on the piece of writing for the student to correct, e.g., *verb/subject agreement (v/s)* or *preposition (prep)*. The students can then fill out a grid indicating the three most commonly occurring errors for each piece of writing and work on them.

For Task 1 the students need to follow a basic pattern for all topics, substituting the detail in each task with synonyms and paraphrases. Encourage students to use a range of vocabulary and a range of complex sentences, and to avoid repetition. Make sure they write in paragraphs. Once they have a bank of trend language at their disposal, they can easily complete the task in the allotted 20 minutes. More marks are allocated to Task 2, so it's essential students do not spend more time than necessary on Task 1.

Give the students the procedure below to follow:

- Look at the topic of the graph/diagram in the title, axes (if a graph), headings or labels (depending on chart type).

- Analyze it by circling significant points only – contrasts, sudden movement, start and finish.

- Write the answer to the task, paraphrasing the instructions in the introduction, with two body paragraphs showing major trends and examples of specific data. One sentence for the conclusion or overview will be sufficient. The overview may sometimes be better at the beginning of the second paragraph.

It is very important that students do not try to describe everything in the chart or diagram in a linear fashion, as this does not demonstrate their ability to summarize the data.

1–2 Students follow the instructions in the Coursebook.

Answers

1

Introduction c is the best answer because it paraphrases the rubric. Note the change in words (*illustrates/hits/in the UK/on a weekly basis/over one year to March 2008*).

2

1 illustrates/shows

2 vary/varied

3 was

4 rose/climbed/increased

5 was/is

6 was/is

7 reached/hit

8 rose/climbed/increased (but avoid repetition)

9 fell/dropped

3 Students make notes and write their own answer to the question. If you want them to do the task at home, encourage them to time themselves and write the time on the essay. At this stage, taking longer than the required 20 minutes is natural. They can speed up later when they have more language at their command and more confidence in the layout, etc.

As you mark the students' answers, use the marking scheme as suggested before.

Review 1 answers Pages 16 and 17

Vocabulary

1

1 h
2 e
3 g
4 a
5 d
6 c
7 b
8 f

2

1 humorous
2 caring
3 punctual
4 respected
5 talented
6 artistic
7 patient
8 reliable

Present simple, present continuous and past simple

1

Sonja: 1, 4, 5
Wei: 3, 7, 8
Ahmed: 2, 10, 12
Tony: 6, 9, 11

2

1 c
2 c
3 c
4 b
5 a
6 a
7 a
8 b
9 b
10 b, a
11 b, c
12 b

Writing

1

1 noticeable
2 shows
3 fluctuated
4 surge

5 remained steady
6 plummeted
7 decline
8 downward
9 trend
10 breakdown

2

1 The trend in attendances is/was clearly upward.
   There is/was a clear upward trend in attendances.
2 There is/was an increase in student numbers over the year.
   Student numbers increased over the year.
3 Market share fell overall over/during the past decade.
   There was an overall fall in market share over/during the past decade.
4 Generally speaking, the trend in the cost of train journeys is/was flat.
5 The trend in prices is/was downward overall.
6 The miles covered by shoppers declined.
7 The price of grain rose steadily in the last six months.
   There has been a steady rise in the price of grain in the last six months.
8 There has been a clear downward trend in the number of flights abroad.

2 Technology–now and then

Content overview

Themes

This unit is concerned with the past, technology, and making things.

Exam-related activities

Reading

Topic	The Chinese Bronze Age
Question type	TRUE/FALSE/NOT GIVEN
	Classification
	Global multiple choice

Listening

Topic	Museum competition
Section 2	Multiple-choice questions
	Matching items

Writing

Task 2	Discussing both views and giving your own opinion

Speaking

Part 2	Describing something you have made

Other

Language focus 1	Past simple and present perfect
Language focus 2	Habit in the past
	Adverbs of frequency
Vocabulary	Verbs of cause and effect
Word building	Qualifying adjectives

Vocabulary: Verbs of cause and effect   Page 18

Lead-in

With books closed, ask students to list as many examples of technology as they can in two minutes. Encourage them to think of the past as well as the present, e.g., the wheel. Tell them that spelling doesn't matter nor even the language (the latter will illustrate that many of them are loan-words from English in their own languages). This will show you how wide their vocabulary is before starting the unit, and will prepare them for the unit topic.

1   In pairs, students discuss the first question. Monitor them, ensuring they know what the items have in common. After a maximum of five minutes, get whole class feedback. Individually, let them choose three items and discuss their choices in pairs. Draw two columns on the board entitled 'Items' and 'Reasons'. Ask students to come out and write their ideas on the board.

Answers

1 a wheel
2 an abacus
3 a telescope
4 a combustion engine
5 a laptop

They are all examples of technology which has changed the world.

2   Write an example on the board of each suffix, noting the schwa on /mənt/ and /ən/. Students then complete the exercise. When they have finished, elicit answers and write them on the board under the headings 'Verbs' and 'Nouns' to check spelling. Drill the pronunciation of both verbs and nouns.

Answers

1 improvement
2 destruction
3 shape/shaping
4 result
5 effect
6 harm
7 enhancement
8 promotion
9 damage
10 ruin/ruination
11 production
12 fostering
13 advance/advancement
14 deterioration
15 achievement
16 attraction

Affect does not follow any of the patterns.

3   Do the first one as an example and let the students complete the activity. Don't give them too long for this. Alternatively, you could just do the exercise orally around the class. Discuss any problematic items.

Answers

1 Positive
2 Negative
3 Neutral
4 Neutral
5 Neutral
6 Negative
7 Positive

8 Positive

9 Negative

10 Negative

11 Neutral

12 Positive

13 Positive

14 Negative

15 Positive

16 Neutral

4–5 Students complete the activity after doing the example as a whole class. They can do this individually, but careful checking needs to be done afterwards. Alternatively, they can work in groups of three or four with an OHT. Divide the sentences between the groups so that each group is responsible for three or four sentences. They can then be projected onto the board, if possible, for peer correction and discussion.

Answers

4

1 The demand for fuel is destroying the way of life of the inhabitants of rainforests.

2 People constantly debate whether television influences society positively or negatively.

3 The company restructuring will improve profits significantly.

4 Climate change has ruined many crops.

5 The fire did not harm the mountainside as much as people first thought.

6 Relations between the two countries deteriorated sharply as a result of the conflict.

7 The affair damaged his reputation enormously.

8 Artificial intelligence is impacting on the development of technology hugely.

9 Many people like Einstein and Newton shaped the world.

5

1 promotion

2 destruction

3 Improvements/Advancements

4 achievement

5 attraction

6 fostering/shaping

Listening
IELTS Section 2   Page 19

Go through the 'What to expect in the exam' advice with the students. Tell them that the 'How to go about it' section refers to Questions 11–15. Ensure that they have all grasped the importance of the pre-listening preparation in the exam. Remind them that in the exam itself they will only hear the recording once. It is especially important to highlight the point that they should leave a missed answer, as dwelling on that may cause them to miss the next couple of answers. Students can always make an intelligent guess once the task is completed.

Check students' underlining in the multiple-choice questions 11–15, and go over the synonyms suggested for A–F in questions 16–20. Play Section 2 right through and let them check their answers before listening for a second time. Using a different colour, the students should fill in any answers they missed the first time. They can then compare their answers in pairs. Play Section 2 again, pausing at each question so they can hear where the answer is in the text. Focus on any questions that were generally problematic for the class as a whole.

An additional listening activity to build your students' confidence before they listen to the recording is to ask the students to study all the questions and in groups describe as much information as they can about what they will hear. After they have done the listening exercise, ask students to listen and read the script on page 227 for self-study or read the script and locate the answers before listening again.

Answers

A big/not small
B not interesting/exciting
C handier
D thrilling/exhilarating
E well made/well put together
F trendy/in vogue

Questions 11–15

11 A

12 B

13 B

14 A

15 C

Questions 16–20

16 F

17 A

18 C

19 D

20 E

2 Technology–now and then

 1.2

Welcome to Radio South here in South London. My name is Darren Timpson, and I'm here with you for the next hour to bring you some local cultural news. Our first item is about a group of seven young people packing in the visitors of all ages at Penwood Museum. They have won first prize in the sixth summer show art competition, and their installation is on display along with the other four prize winners.

In case you don't know, the museum runs a competition as part of the yearly summer show. Each year the competition has a specific theme. The theme of this year's competition has been 'improving links between the local community and the museum'. The competition was open to groups of young people from organizations like schools and youth clubs, who were aged between 15 and 19 years of age on the final entry date for the competition, which was the 13th of May. While preparing their competition entry, the competitors were allowed to use the educational facilities at the museum and to look for help from local sponsors but were not allowed to buy any equipment.

The first prize was won by a group of youngsters from Tigers Community Centre, who called their entry *Technology – now and then. What use is it?* They took various exhibits from the museum's collection of equipment from the 1950s to the 1970s and arranged them with modern versions. The teenagers then recorded their own reactions and comments to the exhibits and did the same with the comments made by older people in their seventies and eighties. The prize-winning exhibits are having a big impact on Penwood Museum attendances, which have been up 45 per cent since the summer show opened.

Some of the video commentaries are very moving and some very funny.

....

I particularly liked seeing the recording of the reaction of several elderly people in their seventies when they talked about an early wooden-framed TV. They remembered the excitement of their first TV, which they thought still fitted in with today's trends. They remembered how they would sometimes all go round to someone's house to watch TV as a special treat. But they thought the modern

TV plasma screen with the remote was much easier to watch. As for the collection of old radios, it has to be seen. They are really huge old wooden frame radios in perfect working order and in perfect condition. The youngsters' reactions to the radios were very funny; they couldn't believe how big they were. And the older people, all of whom used to have one, said they liked them. But they also thought they were too big to fit into living rooms these days. A few more items worth looking at from the display are old kitchen items. The young people thought the cooker from the 1950s looked funny. The older interviewees nearly all used microwave ovens, which they thought were much handier. Seeing old typewriters on display next to slim laptops made them look weird and cumbersome. Even the older people preferred the laptops, which they thought were thrilling. The other electronic items on display were a collection of old and fairly recent cameras. The older people thought the older cameras were 'well made, and better than the newer ones'.

Reading

IELTS Reading Passage Page 21

Review the reading skills studied in Unit 1. Stress again that there is no time to read the texts in detail so selection of the significant sections of the text based on the questions is imperative.

Ask the students to discuss the statement and questions before reading in small groups and giving whole class feedback. Then go through the 'How to go about it' section carefully. Check their predictions and underlining choices carefully. Let them do the task, timing them and giving them a '5 minutes left' time check after 15 minutes. If after 20 minutes, many still haven't finished, give them an extra 5–10 minutes, but get them to put a mark against the question they were on after the initial 20 minutes. This way they can see how much time they need to cut by the time they do the actual exam.

In pairs, let them compare answers, and, if there are differences in their answers, go back to the text and examine it carefully to justify their answers. If they change their own answer based on this discussion, get them to write it in a different colour.

Go over the answers again by projecting the text onto the board if possible. Using the explanations in the answer key, check the TRUE/FALSE/ NOT GIVEN answers carefully. At this stage you can go over any difficult words in the text, pointing out that there is no glossary in the exam except for one or two words. Tell them it should be possible to predict the meanings from the context, and that precise dictionary definitions are not necessary in order to answer the questions.

> ## Answers
>
> 1 TRUE. Paragraph 1: *In the early stages of this development, the process of urbanization went hand in hand with the establishment of a social order.*
> 2 FALSE. Paragraph 2: *The Shang dynasty was conquered by the people of Zhou.*
> 3 FALSE. Paragraph 2: *... seven major states contended for supreme control of the country.*
> 4 NOT GIVEN. However, see paragraph 3: *Iron appeared in China towards the end of ...* . We do not know where it came from: inside or outside China.
> 5 FALSE. Paragraph 4: *Many versions include ...*
> 6 FALSE. Paragraph 5: *... the great patience and skill of the earlier period seem to be lacking.*
> 7 B
> 8 B
> 9 A
> 10 C
> 11 A
> 12 A
> 13 B

Reacting to the text

Discuss the question as a whole class.

Language focus 1: Past simple and present perfect   Page 23

1   Elicit the reasons for the tense choices from the reading passage. If there is still confusion, revise the differences between the past simple and the present perfect, and active and passive voices, eliciting as much as possible from the students. Refer students to the Grammar reference on page 220.

> ## Answers
>
> • Simple past. It is used because the text is talking about specific events in the past. The two examples of the present perfect relate to general/indefinite observations made at an unknown time.
> • Although the passive is used a lot, the active voice is more common when events are being mentioned.

2   Ask students to do exercise 2 in pairs or groups and check their answers at the end of the exercises.

> ## Answers
>
> 1 revolutionized
> 2 contributed
> 3 led
> 4 was first played
> 5 was invented
> 6 created, shaped, lived
> 7 travelled
> 8 influenced

3   Students discuss their answers in pairs.

> ## Answers
>
> 1 began
> 2 were, didn't have, have become
> 3 have started
> 4 transformed
> 5 went, have never visited
> 6 Have you ever seen
> 7 have improved
> 8 did, have not done, spent

4   Give students a time limit to write the five sentences and monitor for accuracy. Make sure they use some time phrases.

5   Encourage students to embellish their answers for the *wh-* questions asked by their partner. This is good preparation for the speaking component of the exam. Monitor for accuracy as they work together. Give them a time limit before they change roles. Question forms are often demanding for students and they may need extra practice. Also ensure that answers are given as fully as possible.

Word building: Qualifying adjectives

Page 24

Photocopiable wordbuilding exercise on page 136.

Elicit the concept of prefixes and suffixes referring back to the suffixes in the vocabulary section at the beginning of the unit. Note that some adjectives, like *necessary*, double the initial consonant to become *unnecessary*. Drill the vocabulary.

1–4 Follow the instructions in the Coursebook and check the answers. Drill the vocabulary. Explain why other alternatives are incorrect if necessary.

Answers
1
1 inconvenient
2 impractical
3 unimportant
4 unnecessary
5 insignificant
6 harmless
7 valueless
8 useless
9 ineffective
10 unappealing
11 unworthwhile
12 uninspiring
2
crucial, vital, essential, key, critical
3
trivial, insignificant
4
1 impractical
2 effective
3 convenient
4 worthwhile
5 harmless
6 inspiring

Language focus 2: Habit in the past

Page 25

1 Make any necessary clarifications. Elicit examples from the students for concept checking. Check with the Grammar reference on page 220 for the structure of questions and negatives with *used to*.

Answers
They remembered how they would all go round to ... b
all of whom used to have one ... c

2 In pairs, students discuss in detail what is wrong with some of the sentences and correct them. Bring together as class discussion.

Answers
1 Correct
2 Correct
3 *Used to* is used to talk about states (e.g. occupations), not *would*.
4 Correct
5 You don't say *would build* or *used to build his own car*, but *built*.
6 *Didn't go to* is needed, not *didn't use to*. The action is neither repeated nor a state.
7 Correct
8 Correct

Further practice

In pairs, students make sentences about their own childhoods. Each student says one to the rest of the class. Peer correct here where possible.

Adverbs of frequency   Page 25

1–2 Write the list 1–6 on the board. Students discuss the question as a class. Ask them to think of other words to add to the line.

Answers
1
sometimes, position 4
2
2 usually, normally, commonly

3 Fill the line in on the board as students come up with the answers. Drill the pronunciation of *occasionally, frequently, regularly,* and *rarely*. Do this as a class exercise. Monitor student responses for potential confusion and provide clear explanations if necessary. Refer them to the Grammar reference on page 220.

Answers	
Position 2	normally
Position 3	regularly, often, commonly
Position 4	occasionally, not often
Position 5	hardly ever, rarely

4 Students do the exercise individually. Get whole class feedback.

Answers
1 never read
2 usually/normally/regularly play
7 regularly used to watch

5 Monitor the accuracy of the students' written sentences, before they compare in pairs. Correct pronunciation and fluency of the spoken part of the activity. Ask two or three students to tell the whole class their sentences.

Speaking

IELTS Part 2   Page 26

1–3 Ask students to read the task card and make notes. Remind them that they only have one minute so notes must be brief (refer them back to the practice in Unit 1). Monitor their notes and ensure each point on the card is covered. Encourage them to keep within the time for notes and for the speaking itself, with students timing each other in their pairs or groups.

Writing
IELTS Task 2   Page 26

1 When planning an argument essay, several simple stages need to be followed. Once students get used to this basic structure, they can follow this for all Task 2 questions. Encouraging them to plan in this way will give them more confidence in the basic skills and will allow more time to reflect on the detail required of the essay title.

Give students the following simple guidelines:

- Analyze the question carefully. Underline key words and pay attention to the focus of the topic. What kind of argument/discussion is required?

- Brainstorm ideas and write them down on a piece of paper as they occur to you. Write two headings on the board: 'technology – taking control' and 'technology – positive developments.' Elicit ideas to put in each list. From this the students can see the structure of the essay and where their viewpoint lies. Note that one list may have the most points, but there may be one very strong argument in the other list which outweighs all of them.

- Put one or more of the ideas from list 1 in Paragraph 2. Paragraph 3 contains one or

more ideas from list 2, with paragraph 4 giving your own opinion. Then write the introduction.

- Ensure each paragraph in the body (paragraphs 2–4) has a topic sentence followed by one or two supporting ideas with reasons and examples.

- Check for cohesive devices so your ideas are linked together.

Planning is essential, so ensure in all writing practices that the students hand in their plan as well as the essay. In timed practice sessions, 4–5 minutes for Task 2 planning, and 2–3 minutes for checking are reasonable.

After going through the 'How to go about it' section with the class, students answer questions 1–10.

Answers
1 You will lose marks if you write less than 250 words, as you will not have completed the task properly.
2 The instructions ask you to discuss both views so it is important to support your ideas with reasons and examples. As in Speaking Part 3, the ideas and examples should be abstract and about people in general, not about what happened to you.
3 Yes. You can support your ideas and reasons by showing the results, causes and effects and express any reservations or doubts you may have.
4 There is no specific limit, but ideally aim to write an introduction, three main paragraphs in the body of the essay, and a conclusion. As this is formal writing you will lose marks if you do not write in paragraphs.
5 There are three parts: a discussion of the first view – 'some people fear that technology is gradually taking over control of our lives'; a discussion of the second view – 'while others think that it has led to many positive developments in all aspects of their lives'; and your own opinion.
6 Three main ideas – one per paragraph. However, you could have two ideas in some paragraphs. Avoid listing ideas without developing them by giving reasons and examples.
7 Yes you can and then support it.
8 If you write around 30 words each for the introduction to the essay and the conclusion, this leaves a minimum of 190 words to write for the body of the essay, roughly 65 words per paragraph. Note these are just rough estimates. So learn how much 60/70 words is in your own handwriting so you can estimate how much to write. Even draw a line on your writing paper which represents

an approximation of 250 words in your handwriting and aim to cross the line as you are writing.

9 There is more than one way of writing any essay. Try to follow the way described here and then develop different ways of writing an essay.

10 Complex sentences are sentences with more than one clause. Or in other words a sentence with more than one idea linked by a connecting word. For example, a statement like *Technology is beneficial because it ... , resulting in ...* has three ideas: statement/opinion–reason/result. Use a mixture of simple and complex sentences and avoid the overuse of the connecting word *and*.

2–3 Follow the instructions in the Coursebook.

Answers

2

3 and 4. 1 is not suitable because it doesn't deal directly with the questions asked. 2 is not suitable because it copies the rubric.

3

4

4–5 Stress the importance of linking words in writing to gain marks in the cohesion criteria of the marking key. Suggest students build up a table as they work through the book and add in new linkers in the appropriate function box as they encounter them. This way they can build up a bank of cohesive devices to draw on.

Do the activities as a whole class, monitoring accuracy in interpreting the functions of the linkers.

Answers

4

	Adverb	Conjunction	Other
Example	for example, for instance		like, such as
Reason		because	
Result	As a result		
Additional information	Moreover		
Purpose		in order to	
Contrast	However		

5

a good example is .../the best example is .../ take .../ take ... for example/instance/As far as ... is concerned .../Where the impact of ... is concerned/namely

6 Students do the exercise in pairs so they can discuss the usage of the alternatives. Check answers with the whole class.

Answers

reason: since/as

result: consequently/so (conjunction and adverb)/therefore/accordingly/and so (conjunction)

additional information: similarly/furthermore/what is more/also

purpose: to

contrast: but, although (conjunctions)/despite (preposition)

7 Students write the essay. If you want them to do it at home, encourage them to time themselves and to write the time at the end of the essay. At this stage taking longer than the required 40 minutes is to be expected. They can speed up later when they have more language at their command and more confidence in the layout, etc. As you mark the essays, use the marking scheme suggested in Unit 1.

Sample answer

Although technology has brought many benefits to our lives, it has some drawbacks like entering into people's privacy which has become a cause for concern for some people.

It is true that due to advances in technology, our privacy is increasingly violated with our personal details being constantly exposed in public. Take for example cameras which are found in the UK on the streets, in shops or in different premises. These devices working around the clock record pictures of all individuals passing in their visual field and they can be watched at any time for various purposes. This seems to be offensive to some people who fear that their pictures may be used in some unacceptable practices. Furthermore, most supermarkets like Sainsbury's provide loyalty cards to their customers offering them discounts according to points they gain when they purchase goods. As these cards contain customers' personal details, shops know what people consume therefore they can continuously control our lives.

However, besides these drawbacks there are numerous advantages resulting from technology in various aspects of the life, namely in education, banking, security or employment. For example these cameras found at the corner of the streets are used to tackle criminality. Once a crime is committed in an area, images are analysed by police to find the offender. Regarding communication for example, the internet has transformed the world into a small village. A person from Congo living in the UK can exchange with their family e-mails, photos or videos, they can even chat what was not possible some decades ago.

To sum up, I think that despite some violations of our privacy which are unavoidable, the advantages of technology are still greater. Therefore its utilisations should be encouraged but the authorities in charge of the community should protect people's privacy as much as possible and personal details or their images should only be disclosed in case of crime investigations.

Word count: 315

Possible score: 8.0

Examiner's comment:

A well-balanced and coherently presented response, with relevant examples being adduced in support of the chosen standpoint. Any grammatical errors do not impede communication, and the conclusion rounds the essay off effectively. Good range of vocabulary and sophisticated and well controlled use of language.

Review 2 answers Pages 28 and 29

Vocabulary
1 affected
2 achievement
3 shape
4 result/impact/effect/consequence
5 affected/influenced/enhanced/improved
6 development/improvement/achievement
7 improving/affecting/ruining/damaging/harming/destroying
8 further/advance/enhance/improve

Word building
1
1 convenient
2 significant
3 uninspiring
4 necessary
5 worthless
6 appealing
7 harmless
8 ineffective
9 crucial
10 inconvenient/important/insignificant

2
1 harmless
2 useful
3 inspiring
4 impractical
5 crucial
6 necessary

Past simple and present perfect
1 played, haven't played
4 have affected, made
6 designed, have designed

Habit in the past
1 Correct
2 Correct
3 I knew
4 Correct
5 Correct
6 used to attend
7 Correct
8 Correct
9 Correct
10 used to rain
11 it never seemed
12 just carried on

Spelling check
1 convenient
2 worthwhile
3 appealing
4 ineffective
5 useful
6 unnecessary
7 impractical

3 Thrill seekers

Content overview

Themes

This unit is concerned with seeking thrills, sports, and the benefits of sports.

Exam-related activities

Reading

Topic	Thrill seekers
Question type	Matching statements to paragraphs
	TRUE/FALSE/NOT GIVEN
	Global multiple choice

Listening

Topic	A sports club
Section 3	Multiple-choice question
	Completing notes
	Completing a table

Speaking

Part 1	Discussing sport
Part 2	Describing a sporting activity
Part 3	Discussing the benefits of sport

Writing

Task 1	Describing a table/chart

Other

Language focus 1	Comparison
Language focus 2	Adjectives with prepositions
Vocabulary	Sports
Word building	Adjectives ending in -ing/-ed

Vocabulary: Sports   Page 30

Lead-in

Ask the class what the title of the unit means. Elicit the meaning of *extreme sports* and the connection with the unit title.

1 In pairs, students describe what is happening in the photos. Discuss the questions as a whole class. Sort out any problems with the target vocabulary and ensure the students are clear about the usage.

Answers

1 wingsuit flying
2 white water rafting
3 playing Wii
4 snowboarding

2 Give the class a few minutes to do the activity. Check answers with the whole class. Drill the pronunciation of new vocabulary. (Tell them that they may see *racquet* as *racket* in US spelling.)

Answers

1 football, rugby
2 boxing
3 running
4 bodybuilding, weightlifting
5 swimming
6 scuba-diving
7 tennis, squash
8 golf

3 Ask students to start a mind map in their vocabulary books, classifying the sports by name, equipment and place. They can add to it as the unit progresses. Encourage them to date the entries so they can look back and see what they have learnt.

Answers

Possible answers
1 Formula 1 racing, motocross
2 hunting, fishing
3 water-skiing, swimming, windsurfing, water polo, sailing, surfing
4 martial arts, judo, fencing
5 tennis, squash, badminton
6 show jumping, horse-riding
7 skiing, snowboarding
8 squash, basketball
9 rugby, running
10 football, basketball, hockey, cricket

Listening
IELTS Section 3   Page 31

Ask students to skim the questions and tell you what the listening test is about. Look especially at question 21 and the headings for the table. This section of the listening can include tables, graphs and charts. Go over the strategies for this section, emphasizing the number of words required in the instructions. Point out that they need to check the type of language that is required for questions 22–30. See if they can predict any of the answers and whether the answer is likely to have a plural or singular noun. Remind them that spelling is important. As this is the first time the students have done this section, you may prefer to stop and check their answers after each group of questions.

Question 21

Before playing the first part of the listening for multiple-choice question 21, discuss the topic and setting and look at the type of word(s) that will be necessary to complete the information. What does the question tell the students about the content of the listening test? Play the recording once, monitoring potential problems. Students compare their answer in pairs.

Questions 22–25

Next, ask students to look at questions 22–25. Play the recording a second time all the way through, monitoring self-correction. Finally, play it a third time, pausing at the answers and showing where to find them and the clues in the text.

Questions 26–30

Now turn to the table and ensure they look carefully at the headings and layout for the questions. Look at the word form for the gap and ask students to try to predict the word if possible. Students may be able to get a feeling for some of the missing words, but not the exact word. Follow the procedure as for the previous part.

Ask them to count their correct answers for the first listening, and for the second.

Answers
21 C
22 freelance workers
23 173 people
24 more details
25 representatives
26 individuals, companies
27 travelling/traveling expenses
28 (the) coaching
29 full potential
30 dedication

3 Thrill seekers

 1.3

(T = Tutor; M = Marcello; V = Vicky)

T: Right, Vicky and Marcello. We arranged this tutorial so you could give me an update of your joint project, the, er … case report on the work you've been doing at a local sports club. Is that right?

M: Yes. That's it. Mmm … it's Stars Club – the one that's been in the news a lot lately. It's not that far from the Kennedy Campus.

T: Right … Yes, I have it here. Fire away.

M: Well, at first we were going to look only at the management structure of the club, but, em … we decided to include what's made it more successful than other local clubs. The club's success has not just come from its many sporting achievements: it's also attracting so many young people. Mm … we talked to staff and members and …

T: How many people did you talk to?

V: There're just over 600 members overall and 23 staff, including freelance workers. So far we've talked to mm … ooh, about 173 people.

T: Didn't you think of giving a questionnaire to everyone?

V: We decided against it.

T: Why was that?

V: Well, we thought that face-to-face interviews, however brief, would be better as we'd be able to probe people gently to give us more details if need be.

T: And your findings so far?

M: The club's actually very well run. The managers're very focused and work well together. And the management team also includes representatives from the various teams at the club.

V: This means that when decisions're made, they're not taken in isolation of the members, as so often happens in other organizations. The management team's in touch with the members and vice versa.

T: You seem to have learnt a lot so far.

M: I agree. It's a really exhilarating experience being there. I can't wait to go in every day.

....

T: OK. Would you like to tell me a bit about the reasons behind the success of the club? Vicky, would you like to go first?

V: OK. Mmm … well … when we asked the people we questioned to say what they thought were the most important reasons for the club's success, many people gave loads of reasons without being prompted, but it was clear that there were three factors that stood out from all the others.

T: Can you say something more about each of these specific points? Marcello, would you like to go on?

M: Well, as Vicky said, we isolated three main factors; though some are more important than others. We found that for most people having financial help from the government, private <u>individuals</u> and <u>companies</u> was absolutely crucial. They felt that it was important to … have money to pay for facilities, em … for <u>travelling expenses</u> and, em, for any absences from their job.

T: Yes. That doesn't sound surprising considering the costs the athletes incur. We can't expect them all to be rich amateurs. And the next factor?

M: Mmm … I personally thought the quality of facilities would come next but a close second was the quality of <u>the coaching</u>, which is more professional.

V: Like Marcello, I expected facilities to come next, and …

M: And most people said the club managed to attract some really top-quality people working as coaches. And the coaches saw their job as pushing athletes to realize their <u>full potential</u>. The most influential coaches were those preparing athletes for the track events, swimming, weightlifting and climbing. They also had coaches for more esoteric areas like rock climbing and rowing.

T: And the other items? … Vicky?

V: Er … the next factor is the motivation and <u>dedication</u> of the athletes themselves, which has been necessary for them to become the best in their field. It was really thrilling to see this in action.

T: And success breeds success.

M: Yes, definitely.

T: It sounds as if you've got a lot out of this experience.

M: It's the sort of place I'd like to work after I've graduated.

V: Me too. I'd like to train as a coach there.

T: Brilliant. And have you started writing up the case study yet?

M: Yes, we've done quite a bit and …

Language focus 1: Comparison   Page 32

1 Students answer the questions. A quick review of the format of comparatives and superlatives can be done on the board, eliciting the rules from the students. Remember to point out:

comparative + *than*
the + superlative

Refer students to the Grammar reference on page 220.

Answers
a adjective
b noun
c verb

2 In pairs, students complete the table. Check their answers with the whole class. Review any spelling changes, e.g., *y* to *ier/iest*; double the final consonant on single-syllable adjectives such as *wet*.

Answers		
Adjective	**Comparative**	**Superlative**
bad	worse	the worst
good	better	the best
noisy	noisier/more noisy	the noisiest
wet	wetter	the wettest
tasty	tastier	the tastiest
cheap	cheaper	the cheapest
lively	livelier	the liveliest
appetizing	more/less appetizing	the most/least appetizing

3 Monitor the exercise for form and spelling. Get whole class feedback, and write the answers down the left side of the board.

Answers	
1	easier
2	more popular
3	the most energetic
4	happier

5 more difficult

6 the least/most stressful

7 more/less important

8 the fittest

4 In pairs, students refer back to exercise 3 and think of the noun forms for each adjective. Write these on the board next to the adjectives.

Answers

1 ease

2 popularity

3 energy

4 happiness

5 difficulty

6 stress

7 importance

8 fitness

5 Do the first one with the students as an example. Then let them write the rest in their books. You could also ask them to write the answers on the board as they finish.

Answers

1 Places to do specialist sports can be found with more ease outside cities and towns.

2 Activities like bowling enjoy more popularity among older age groups.

3 Which sport do you think requires/needs the most energy (of all)?

4 People who do some physical activity are supposed to experience more/greater happiness than less active people.

5 People have greater difficulty/more difficulties organizing their lives around leisure activities nowadays.

6 Do people experience greater stress in their work nowadays than before?

7 Does mental activity have less/more importance than physical activity?/Is mental activity of lesser greater importance than physical activity?

8 People don't realize that racing drivers have a greater level of fitness than many other individuals in sport.

6 Students rewrite the questions that are incorrect. Get whole class feedback, checking spelling.

Answers

1 ... more exciting than ...

2 Correct

3 ... more dangerous than ...

4 ... fitter ...

5 ... the most exciting ...

6 Correct

7 ... the richest ...

8 Correct

9 Correct

10 ... more tiring than ...

7 Depending on the size of your class, do the questionnaire as a whole class or in two groups. Make sure they actually ask the questions and don't just point at them or say the number! If you have time you may like to collate their answers on the board.

Word building: Adjectives ending in *-ing/-ed* Page 33

Photocopiable wordbuilding exercise on page 136.

The adjective endings *-ing* and *-ed* are a common cause for confusion with learners. Look at the example with the students. Point out or elicit that the adjective with *-ing* tells you what the experience is doing to you – it's *exhilarating* you – and that *exhilarated* tells you how you feel if you have an *exhilarating* experience: *I was exhilarated*.

1 Students do this exercise on their own and compare in pairs. Get whole class feedback.

Answers

1 thrilling

2 irritated

3 interested

4 motivating

5 exciting

6 annoying, annoyed

7 challenging

8 invigorated

2 Students ask and answer the questions in pairs. Suggest they choose different questions. Monitor to ensure they elaborate on their answers (which is a good link for Speaking Part 3), and are accurate with the target language. Use one or two good pairs of students to model to the whole class.

3 The students do this exercise first on their own and then compare in pairs. Get whole class feedback.

Answers
1 electrified
2 challenged
3 interesting
4 fascination
5 motivated
6 exciting
7 refreshed
8 excitement

Speaking

IELTS Part 1   Page 34

1 Do the first question as an example on the board. Ask students to write the others in their books, getting them up to write on the board as they finish.

Answers
1 What kinds of sports are popular in your country?
2 Are they as popular as they used to be in the past?
3 Are the same games as popular as in the past?
4 Do young people do more physical activities like extreme sports now than in the past?
5 What makes these games interesting to people?
6 Are sports more challenging now than they were in the past?
7 Are young people challenged more nowadays than in the past?

2 Elicit the adjectives that could be used with each question. Monitor the pairs as they ask and answer the questions to ensure they answer as fully as possible.

Reading

IELTS Reading Passage   Page 34

Go through the 'What to expect in the exam' and the 'Don't forget' advice with the students. Expand on the points regarding patterns in texts, and give examples of what is meant by cause and effect, etc. This is very important as

understanding this concept can help students to use the lexical cues given in the text to indicate these patterns.

Encourage students to make a habit of first looking at the multiple-choice question with the alternative headings before reading the text. This encourages them away from the vertical–linear approach to texts and questions. Give the students time limits for each step so they become aware of the time they will have in the exam. Remind them of the technique of underlining key words in the questions.

Questions 1–6

Do the questions in groups, starting with 1–6. Go over the answers focusing on the links between the words in the questions and the text. Show synonyms, e.g., *impact*, *auditory – effects*, *inner ear*. Compare this type of question with matching paragraph headings. There are two types of phrases: referring to a specific piece of information in a paragraph and summarizing a whole paragraph.

Answers
1 D
2 H
3 B
4 H
5 F
6 I

Extension

After students have finished the reading test, ask them to focus on the phrases in questions 1–6 and decide whether they refer to part of or the whole of the paragraph. Point out the general category nouns in the questions, like *impact*. Ask them to write the words in their vocabulary records and add to the list as they go through the course. They could look back at the headings in the reading passage in Unit 1 and add general category nouns from there as well. Ask if any of them are the same, or if there are any synonyms of general category nouns. Point out that they will meet these words again and again in all components of the IELTS exam.

Questions 7–12

Do the same as for questions 1–6 with the TRUE/FALSE/NOT GIVEN questions, eliciting the differences. Check them carefully, ensuring full comprehension before moving on.

Answers

7 NOT GIVEN. Paragraph A: Computer games and fairground rides are mentioned but there is no comparison.

8 TRUE. Paragraph D: *the brain struggles to make sense of conflicting and changing signals from the senses.*

9 NOT GIVEN. Paragraph F: The number does not tell you how many people are involved. Always watch out for words of quantity like *all/a few/little/most* and make sure they match the meaning in the text.

10 FALSE. Paragraph G: *The human body cannot tolerate much more of a G-force than the latest rollercoasters, ...*

11 NOT GIVEN. Paragraph H: The text does not mention anything about the balance of men and women.

12 TRUE. Paragraph I: *Equally, the next generation of rides will sense when too many people feel nauseous and wind down accordingly. In short, they will be able to distinguish terror from titillation.*

Question 13

Do question 13 with the class. After doing questions 1–12 they should be able to answer this without further referral to the text.

Answer

13 B

Reacting to the text

Students discuss the questions in small groups.

Language focus 2: Adjectives with prepositions Page 36

1–4 Follow the instructions in the Coursebook. Students do the exercises in pairs and check as a class. Ask them to make a note of these patterns in their vocabulary reference books. There are no hard and fast rules and familiarity through use is the only way to consolidate them. Refer them to the Grammar reference on page 221.

Answers

1

1 on

2 to

3 about

4 in

5 with

6 to

7 about

8 of

9 about

10 of, about

2

1 b/c/f

2 c

3 e

4 d

5 b/f

6 g

7 a

Speaking
IELTS Part 2   Page 37

1 Elicit the strategies for this section and remind students of the need to make brief notes to work from. Give them a one-minute time limit to make their notes. When they have finished, ask students to show their notes to their partner. Go round and make a quick check that they are short enough. Stop the students from writing sentences, and show them how to reduce sentences to nouns and adjectives and verbs. Encourage them to write the notes vertically to make them easier to read as they speak.

2 Time the pairs as they discuss the topic, and make sure they swap over after just under two minutes. Do the same for the second partner. Use a stopwatch to train the students to stick to the time limit and check for students who stop early. Encourage the pairs to give each other feedback. Give general feedback on any problems you heard with regard to relevance of the topic, pronunciation, structure, and vocabulary.

Speaking
IELTS Part 3   Page 37

Elicit ideas for how the previous topic might be expanded on in Part 3.

1 Follow the instructions in the Coursebook. Take whole class feedback.

2 Check the underlined words as a class. Give them time to write their own sentences. Monitor and encourage originality. Check the accuracy of the target language.

Answers

1 to
2 so
3 so that
4 in order to
5 so as to
6 in order to

3 Do this as a class activity. Give them time to write down the alternatives.

Answers

Possible answers

1 because they want/like to keep fit
2 because they would like/want to lose weight
3 because they would like/want to make friends
4 because they like/want to relax
5 because they want an adrenaline rush
6 because they like to escape from the real world

4 Students read the questions and select two main questions. Tell them to ask each other the questions they chose and check the answers using the expressions of purpose. Consolidate this section with the 'How to go about it' advice.

Writing
IELTS Task 1   Page 38

Lead-in

Do a quick spot-check review of how we make comparisons.

1 Elicit the main points to note in the table (e.g., topic, year, subjects, sports). Ask students to answer the questions on the table in pairs. Check as a class with them telling you where they found the information.

Answers

1

1 No. Fewer men than women went swimming.
2 No. There was a greater proportion of men than women involved in walking, but not a far greater proportion.
3 No. Women were less likely to take part in sporting activities.
4 No. Nearly twice as many men as women went cycling.
5 Yes. The table compares information about male and female involvement in a selection of activities in the United Kingdom in 2002.

6 Yes. Ten per cent of men played football while no women played.
7 Yes. Compared to males, more than twice as many women went to keep fit/yoga classes.
8 Yes. Football was the least popular activity overall.
9 Yes. Overall males were more involved in physical activity than females.

2 Students work in pairs. Get feedback with reasons for their answers.

Answers

a the introduction: 5
b the overview: 3 and 9
c specific data: 1, 2, 4, 6, 7, 8

3 Tell students to add the comparison words to their list of appropriate phrases for Task 1 in their reference books.

Answers

1 fewer ... than
2 a far greater proportion of ... than
3 less likely to
4 twice as many ... as
5 compares data about ...
6 while
7 Compared with ... more than twice as many ...
8 the least popular
9 more involved in ... than ...

4 Students rewrite the sentences individually and check in pairs. Do whole class feedback, ensuring they are all clear about the choices made.

Answers

1 The rugby match was attended by a third of the number of spectators at the football match.
2 The sports department was visited by five times the number of shoppers in February 2008 when compared to February 2009.
3 More than 40% of the competitors were from the main city.
4 A smaller proportion of players were home-grown rather than from overseas.
5 Three-quarters of the members of the sports club paid by credit card rather than cash.
6 The team won just over 50%/half of the games they played last season.

5 Look at the writing task and go through the 'Don't forget!' advice with the class. Do this task in class as a timed essay. You can give them more than 20 minutes at this stage, but get them to make a note of where they are once that time has passed. When the time is up, ask them to go through the checklist on page 209. Encourage them to use this every time they do a Task 1 question. Discourage them from going straight into writing without preparation.

Sample answer

The table gives information about an involvement of 11–14 years age teenagers in five different types of Extreme sports by both sexes in 2003.

Overall, with the exception of Rollerblading the participation of boys in Extreme sports exceeds the involvement of girls. For example, the proportion of boy participants in Mountain biking is much grater (22.7%) than the percentage of girl participants (13.3%). On the other hand, the percentage of males (27.5%) involved in Skateboarding is almost double the proportion of females taking part on it (13.8%). The same pattern is seen when we look at Snowboarding (male 8,1 % and female 4.%).

Regarding [the] Mountain climbing there was nearly same proportion of both gender participants (10.6% male and 9.3% female). The exception was Rollerblading where the girls outstrip the boys, 31.7% and 21.7% respectively. It is clear that, the proportion of males involved in Extreme sports is much higher than the percentage of the females.

Word count: 156

Possible score: 6.5

Examiner's comment:

The response is well organized, fluently written and identifies the main trends. The lexical resource is evident. However, elementary errors persist, reducing effectiveness overall. *Greater* is misspelt and rules regarding capitalisation, prepositions (*on*) and articles (first sentences paragraphs 1 and 3) are ignored. The response also employs inappropriate sign posting (*on the other hand*).

Review 3 answers Pages 40 and 41

Vocabulary

1

1 golf: outdoor
2 snowboarding: outdoor
3 boxing: indoor
4 squash: indoor
5 football: both
6 baseball: both
7 rugby: outdoor
7 running: both

2

1 squash, football, baseball, rugby
2 squash
3 golf
4 football
5 football, rugby
6 skateboarding, snowboarding
7 boxing
8 squash
9 baseball
10 running

Comparison

1

1 Is windsurfing more expensive than ordinary surfing?
2 I find watching sport more appealing (to me) than taking part.
3 Which sport is the most challenging?
4 Which sport is the safest?
5 As they are old, the facilities are less valuable than those at other clubs.
6 The club is more successful than similar organizations.

2

1 India is not as big as Africa./India is not bigger than Africa.
2 The Pacific Ocean is wider than the Atlantic Ocean.
3 Mountaineers do not earn as much as footballers.
4 Football matches attract far great numbers than squash tournaments.
5 Parkour seems to be much riskier/more/less risky than skateboarding.
6 Many sports demand more/less stamina than intellect.

7 An active life is considerably less harmful than a sedentary lifestyle.

8 Private cars (don't) make as much noise as lorries.

Adjectives with prepositions

1 keen

2 interested

3 capable

4 addicted

5 indifferent

6 enthusiastic/fanatical

7 bored

Word building

1

1 fascinated, correct

2 motivating, incorrect – *motivated*

3 thrilled, correct

4 irritated, incorrect – *irritating*

5 interesting, incorrect – *interested*

6 excited, incorrect – *exciting*

7 annoyed, correct

8 challenging, incorrect – *challenged*

2

1 e

2 c

3 b

4 d

5 a

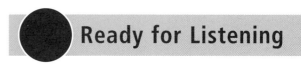

Ready for Listening

IELTS Listening Module	
Section 1	Completing a form
	Completing sentences
Section 2	Matching items
	Multiple-choice questions
Section 3	A multiple-choice question
	Selecting items from a list
	Completing a table
Section 4	Multiple-choice questions
	Completing a diagram

This is the first of four 'Ready for …' units. You may use these units in the order they come in the book or at any time during the course, as revision or as an introduction to one of the four modules in the IELTS exam.

Introduction Page 42

Elicit the types of questions the students will encounter in the listening test and ask them to read the Introduction themselves. Allow the students to ask you any questions for clarification.

Optional lead-in

Before the students open the Coursebook, ask them the following questions about the Listening test:

1 How long does the Listening test last?

2 How many sections are there?

3 What sort of situations are Sections 1 and 2 related to?

4 What sort of situations are Sections 3 and 4 related to?

5 How many times do you hear the recordings?

6 Where do you write your answers during the test?

7 How long do you have to transfer your answers onto the answer sheet at the end of the recording?

8 Why do you have to be careful when you transfer your answers?

Answers
1 40 minutes (30 minutes for the test and 10 minutes to transfer answers)
2 Four
3 (More) general/social situations
4 Academic
5 Once

6 In the question booklet and then transfer to an answer sheet

7 10 minutes

8 Because it's easy to make mistakes, especially spelling mistakes, and leaving off the *s* at the end of words.

Section 1 Page 42

1 Get the students to predict what is required for questions 1–10: nouns, adjectives, numbers, etc.

Students listen and follow the instructions. Ask them to transfer their answers to a sheet of paper or to an answer sheet after the listening is finished. Note that you can do all four listening sections as a full test. If you do, remind the students to look ahead as they listen rather than going back over the section they have just done. Remind them they have ten minutes at the end to transfer their answers.

Answers
1 *The Judgement*
2 Wight
3 691-08879-9
4 North America
5 biographical
6 17
7 54 65 36
8 mandy
9 90
10 special offers

Ready for Listening

Section 1

 1.4

S = sales person; C = customer

S: Good morning, Jackson's Bookstore. You're through to the book search department. How can I help you?

C: Hi. Mm … I'm looking for a book. I've found the title on the Internet, but I can't find a copy of it anywhere. I understand you undertake a book search to locate copies of books.

S: Yes, we do. Can I just take down a few details of the book title, etc?

C: Yeah sure.

S: First of all, what's the title and the author?

C: It's called *The Judgement* by Dayne Wight.

S: *The … Judgement*. OK. That's typed in. Hmm, I'm afraid the computer's being a bit slow this morning.

C: They're always causing problems.

S: And the author is Dayne Wight?

C: Yes, that's it. It's Dayne Wight. That's W–I–G–H–T not W–H–I–T–E.

S: OK. Wight. Em … this computer is being really slow. And, er … the ISBN number?

C: 978-0-691-08879-9. And it's a paperback, not hardback.

S: … 08879-9 and a paperback. OK. Em … I can see from the computer that it has never been in print in this country. It's only been published in North America, but it's out of print now.

C: Yes. I read part of it at a friend's house a while back, but couldn't find a copy of it. I'm not sure what you'd put it under, but I suppose you could call it … er … biographical fiction, if such a category exists.

S: Hmm … the computer's showing that we don't have any copies in our own collection of second-hand books or our overseas books either.

C: Ah, OK.

S: But I can do a book search for you through other collections and try distributors in the United States, but it might take some time.

C: I see. How much will that cost?

S: Well, it depends on the search. We offer two types: gold or silver.

C: OK.

S: For the gold we search around the world, and for the silver we only look in America, Europe and in this country. The gold search is £25.

C: £25. That's more than the book costs!

S: Yes, probably, but it depends on how much you want the book. And the silver is £17.

C: OK. I'll go for the silver. How long will it take?

S: I can't say. With this service we go on until we come up with something, but I can't guarantee that we'll find anything.

C: No. I realize that.

S: Right. I'm afraid the computer's not working. I'll write everything down by hand and copy it in later. OK, I need your contact details.

C: The best way is probably by mobile or email.

S: OK … your mobile number?

C: 08967 54 65 36

S: 54 65 36. And … your email address?

C: And my email address is mandythompson9z … all one word … @yahoo.fr. All lower case.

S: OK. Is that mandy with a 'y' and thompson9z?

C: Yes, that's it.

S: And, er … I need to take a home address for our records.

C: It's 90 Chaucer House, Ludlow Park Drive, Richmond, SW20 9RL.

S: OK. And do you want to receive notification by email about special offers?

C: I'd rather not.

S: OK. I'll just tick this box …

---

2 Follow the instructions in the Coursebook.

3 Follow the instructions. Elicit strategies from the main units in the book to help with the problem areas they identify.

Section 2 Page 43

1–3 Follow the instructions in the Coursebook.

Answers

1

The parts of the cinema (items 11–16) as they will normally be introduced first, followed by details about what happened to them.

2

Possible answers

A enlarged: extended, bigger, more spacious

B replaced: changed, taken the place of; instead of/in place of

C still closed: not open yet, still being renovated, work still being done/carried out

D thoroughly cleaned: spotless, the dirt removed, as good as new, looks like new

E split up: divided, partitioned, made into 2/3/4 smaller …

F brightened up: made brighter, less dull, cheered up

G moved: shifted, transferred, relocated, not in the same place as before

3

17 open

18 group/free/tickets/first week

19 Wednesdays/reduction/members

20 new development

4 Monitor the students as they do the task and troubleshoot any queries or misunderstandings. Remind them that in the test, they will hear the items in the order they appear in the questions, but that the options (A–G) are jumbled.

Play the recording. If you are doing this as a separate section and not as part of a whole test, ask the students to transfer their answers to a sheet of paper or an answer sheet. Remind them to be careful as the answers are all letters of the alphabet so it is easy to get them mixed up.

Answers

11 D
12 E
13 A
14 B
15 C
16 G
17 A
18 C
19 B
20 C

5 Follow the instructions in the Coursebook.

Answers

11 D thoroughly cleaned: all the dirt has been completely removed

12 E split up: partitioned

13 A enlarged: made bigger

14 B replaced: where there was … there is now …

15 C still closed: will be opening shortly

16 G moved: no longer beside … it is now next to …

Ready for Listening

Section 2

 1.5

Hi everyone, and welcome to the local evening news. I'd like to start with an exciting new development on this side of the city – the redevelopment of the old Regal Cinema on Duncton Street. Last night was the official opening of the new Regal Cinema Complex, as it is now known.

And what a transformation! The venue has changed from being a rundown, depressing building to a state-of-the art cinematic experience, and it's wonderful to see so many of the original features still intact. The building which housed the old cinema has been completely renovated, while managing to incorporate some of the old features of the cinema like the façade, which is still there, but all the dirt has been completely removed with a few modern touches added. Multicoloured glass panelling has been added to the facade so the entrance now looks really snazzy.

The old auditorium, which was like a huge cavern and not particularly welcoming, has been partitioned to create three screens. This means that there is now one large cinema screen – 'Screen 1' – which has a capacity of 500 people. The two smaller screens – Screens 2 and 3 – have a capacity of 175 and 150. There are fewer seats overall compared to the old cinema – about 150 actually – but there is now a greater variety of shows to choose from.

The foyer to the cinema has been totally brought up-to-date and made bigger with a much larger ticket office and machines for collecting tickets that have been booked in advance. People will no longer have to stand outside in the rain as they had to in the past while they were waiting to buy tickets. And, where there was a bar serving coffee and cold drinks with a few stools and high tables, there is now a restaurant.

The roof terrace, which used to have just a few benches and seats, will be opening shortly with a landscaped garden with a bar which is open all year round. This will be a welcome addition to the centre.

The basement, which leads out into a garden at the back, has been totally renovated and turned into a members' room with a bar–restaurant and a small display area for artwork

or stalls. The cinema shop is no longer beside the ticket office; it is now next to the entrance to the restaurant. It doesn't just sell sweets, as it did before, but cinema-related memorabilia including programmes and books, DVDs, CDs, posters …

....

And I've got a leaflet here about the programme for the opening week of the newly refurbished cinema, em … which is the week beginning the 14th of July. As it's during the school holidays, there will be a special promotion. For the matinee performance each day the cinema is offering free tickets to the first 100 children up to and including 16 years of age, and to all pensioners. And there will be special rates for cinema goers who book a meal in the restaurant as well. Plus there will be special nights where there are child-free performances, and also each Wednesday tickets will be half-price for members of the cinema. I see here the membership is only £30 a year and gives you access to member-only previews and to the members' restaurant in the basement.

But, perhaps the biggest innovation at the cinema is the monthly programme of lectures where not just actors and actresses, but producers and writers, will be involved in delivering talks about a particular film. This is certainly a major development which will definitely pull in many cinema enthusiasts, and hopefully revitalize the area.

Section 3   Page 45

1–3 Ask the students to refer to their vocabulary books for any synonyms they might have already recorded. Follow the instructions in the Coursebook and monitor as before. Remind them that these strategies should be employed automatically when doing listening tests.

Answers

1

Possible synonyms:

talk: seminar/lecture
electronic gadgets: devices/gizmos/appliances

2

Nearly all of them could be undecided with the aims being the most likely to be decided upon.

Possible synonyms:

A length of the questionnaire: survey

B pictures to use: photos/illustrations/drawings/ images

C volume of data: amount of information/statistics/
facts and figures

D duration of interviews: length of questioning

E period of research: investigation/study

F age of interviewees: people to be questioned/
asked questions to/participants

G exact aims: objectives

3

Numbers: Questions 27, 28, 30

Plural: Question 25

4 Tell the students to listen and follow the
instructions as for the first two sections.

Answers

21 C

22–24 A, F, G in any order

25 emails/e-mails

26 browsing the Internet

27 8

28 5

29 everything

30 10

Ready for Listening

Section 3

  1.6

Z = Zahra; T = Tim

Z: Hi Tim.

T: Zahra, hi. So, have you decided yet what
you're going to do your tutorial paper on?

Z: Yes, actually I have. I agonized over it for
ages, as you well know. You had to listen to
me.

T: Well, that's true, but you've had to listen to
me too! ... So, what's it on?

Z: Electronic gadgets, but from a particular
angle: 'must-carry' gadgets. You know,
<u>gadgets that people cannot leave the house
without</u>, er ... like mobile phones, etc. It's
not particularly original.

T: That's really very neat.

Z: Oh. Do you think so?

T: Yes, actually I do.

Z: I thought it was really quite ordinary.

T: And how are you going to do the research
for the paper?

Z: I thought of interviewing people in the
age groups 20–25 and 50 plus, so I can ask
students for the first group and I'll have
to ask lecturers and people in the street or
people working on campus for the other
group. <u>But I haven't made up my mind yet
which groups to choose</u>.

T: Em ... and what are you setting out to
show?

Z: I'm not sure at this stage, but something
along the lines of ... er ... the idea that we
are making ourselves more stressed, and
it has reached such a stage that we are so
dependent on the gadgets that leaving the
house without them makes us ill. I'm just
thinking on my feet here. <u>I haven't really
thought it right through to the end</u>.

T: What about your questionnaire?

Z: Mmm ... , yes that's another thing. <u>What
I'm not really decided about is the length
the questionnaire should be</u>.

T: The best thing is to keep it short.

Z: Maybe. But I'll finalize the length when I
sit down to type it up.

....

Z: I need to find someone to try out my
questions on. I've got some already written.

T: I can be your guinea pig if you want.

Z: Great!

T: Fire away!

Z: First ... question number one. What
electronic gadgets are you carrying with
you now?

T: Let's see. I've got my mobile phone, ... my
iPod, my laptop.

Z: Which do you carry with you every day?

T: All of them!

Z: What do you use your mobile phone for
generally?

T: Em ... apart from phoning, mostly for
texting and downloading music. But I also
use it for video-phoning, sending <u>emails</u> ...
and I talk to my family now using the video
on the phone.

Z: On a scale of 1–10, where 1 is not at all
difficult and 10 very difficult, how difficult
would you find it to leave your mobile at
home for a whole day?

T: Very difficult, so 10. I'd be completely lost without it.

Z: And what about the laptop? What do you use it for?

T: I use it for em … writing up assignments, <u>but mainly for browsing the Internet</u>.

Z: Using the same scale, what about your laptop?

T: Well, let's see … It's not as essential as my mobile phone, but it's still important. A score of … <u>8</u>. This one's not heavy, but I can do without it, if necessary. I seem to use my mobile for most of the things I used to use the laptop for. Soon I probably won't need it.

Z: What about the iPod?

T: I can use my mobile for music as well, so it's not essential, but I carry it everywhere with me because it's light and it's got my whole music collection on it that I can listen to on the move. And, mmm … well, for that, I'd give a score of <u>5</u>.

Z: Is there any gadget you intend to get in the near future?

T: Yes. I'd like to get a newspaper reader when they become lighter and cheaper and more readily available. <u>I think I'll end up using it for everything</u>, even to replace the mobile.

Z: Do you think so?

T: Oh yeah. They'll be perfect for video messaging.

Z: And the score?

T: Definitely <u>10</u>. And I'd like a pair of …

5 Students work in pairs and answer the question.

Section 4 Page 46

Emphasize the importance of transferring questions accurately. Point out that if they miss a number, they should put a mark by it so they can return to it later. They need to make sure they don't fill in the space with the next answer which would mean that all the subsequent answers are wrong. Encourage them to fill in all the boxes as they lose nothing by a wrong guess but can get no marks for an empty space.

1–2 Follow the instructions in the Coursebook.

Answers

1

Words in the stem:

31 bore holes

32 in the past/induce rain

33 proof/increases rainfall

34 not support

35 country/keen

Possible paraphrases in the alternatives:

31
A employed/utilized in factories
B on farms/to water fields
C drinking and washing

32
A mystical/magical methods/ways
B burning (something)
C ritual (dancing)

33
C a quarter

34
A advantages of cloud seeding
B price of the equipment/equipment is expensive/costly/not cheap
C impact/outcome/result

3 Ask the students to listen and follow the instructions.

Answers

31 B

32 A

33 A

34 C

35 B

36 chemical/silver iodide

37 water freeze

38 generator

39 fuel tank

40 cloud level

Ready for Listening

Section 4

 1.7

Good morning everyone. The topic of my seminar paper this week is a rather unusual method of bringing water to drought-ridden regions of the world. The methods people most think of, or read about in newspapers and or see on TV, mmm … are preventing deforestation and encouraging reforestation to prevent water run-off from barren land and hence to stop flooding. Another method is … er … drilling bore holes to bring water from aquifers deep in the ground <u>to irrigate the land</u>.

But the method I would like to talk about today is the production of rain through *seeding clouds*. For those of you who are not familiar with this practice, it is basically a process where nature is *coaxed*, as it were, to produce rain. In many places in the world attempts have been made throughout history to produce rain in times of drought <u>through magic</u>, but from the latter part of the last century scientists've been endeavouring to come to the rescue by chemical means. And in some places they've been trying not just to produce rain but also to divert it so that it does not rain on special days, such as national or international ceremonies.

Cloud seeding has been carried out since the middle of the last century, but no scientist can confirm that the practice is actually responsible for cloud seeding and not nature itself. Because who can confirm that the clouds would not let loose a deluge anyway? Having said that, there is some evidence that seeding clouds to produce rain can lead to <u>a 15% increase in rainfall</u>.

But what would happen, for example, if the actions of cloud seeding in one place led to a disastrous deluge in another? It would also be tricky to prove that any damage was the responsibility of cloud seeders. Some people are understandably against the practice of cloud seeding as <u>we do not really know the consequences of interfering with nature</u>.

Cloud seeding has apparently been used by Californian officials to replenish reservoirs. In other parts of the US, electricity utility companies are especially fond of seeding to bring more water to hydroelectric plants. And the practice is also popular with authorities in Russia and China too. For years the Russian air force has tried to coax moisture out of clouds to ensure sunshine on national holidays. <u>But no country is more committed to researching weather modification than China,</u> with a national budget in the tens of millions of dollars and thousands of miles flown by rain seeding aircraft every year.

Last year the university agricultural and meteorology departments were given a 20 million dollar grant, funded in part by the government and various companies in the food and agricultural industry, to conduct research into cloud seeding to increase precipitation. While the research is aimed primarily at the US, it is hoped that the benefits accrued will have far-reaching consequences for other drought-ridden regions of the planet.

Now … let's see, mmm … if we look at this slide here, we can see how cloud seeding works. There are two basic methods: from the air and from the ground. Looking first at seeding from the air, we can see that <u>an aeroplane flies above the clouds from where it fires silver iodide into clouds by dropping chemical flares</u> in order to increase precipitation. <u>Silver iodide crystals then attach themselves to water droplets which makes the water freeze and fall as rain or snow</u> over high ground. If we now look at the diagram showing cloud seeding from the ground, we can see that there is a <u>ground seeding generator</u> here on the right of the slide, which has a tall chimney, and em … next to this is on the left is a … em … this structure here which is <u>a fuel tank containing propane</u>. <u>Heat generated from the burning of the propane lifts the silver iodide crystals up to cloud level</u> again leading to precipitation.

4 Follow the instructions in the Coursebook.

4 Global problems and opportunities

Content overview

Themes

This unit is concerned with world problems and possible solutions.

Exam-related activities

Reading

Topic	Sea pollution
Question type	Summary with a wordlist
	YES/NO/NOT GIVEN

Listening

Topic	Birth of the railways in the UK
Section 4	Completing a table
	Selecting items from a list

Speaking

Part 1	Discussing a country's resources
Part 2	Describing an incident
Part 3	Discussing world problems/news and events

Writing

Task 2	Giving reasons and examples

Other

Language focus 1	Countable and uncountable nouns
Language focus 2	Making suggestions
Vocabulary 1	General category nouns
Vocabulary 2	Developing ideas by expanding the meaning of adjectives

Vocabulary 1: General category nouns   Page 48

1 Check any vocabulary problems and ask if there are any such places in students' own countries and where. Students then discuss the questions.

2 Elicit the word *problem* for the two example sentences. Students do the exercise individually then check in pairs. Go over the answers with the class and clarify any misunderstandings in the shades of meaning here. Tell them that unfortunately, there are no hard and fast rules for collocations, although you may be able to make some connections between positive and negative adjectives, e.g., *golden + opportunity*. *Event*, *situation* and *occasion* will be problematic and may need extra clarification.

Answers

2

problem can be used in both gaps

1 b
2 c
3 a
4 g
5 h
6 f
7 d
8 e

3 Students complete this individually. Point out the necessity for plurals with some nouns. Check the answers with the class, explaining any problematic choices.

Answers

1 incident
2 possibility
3 dilemma
4 events
5 problem
6 issue
7 impression
8 outcome

4 Ask students to match the sentences. Point out that the nouns in a–f will help them link the sentences. You may want to ask the students to add the nouns in this section to the list of general category nouns they created in Unit 3.

Answers

1 f
2 d
3 e
4 b
5 c
6 a

5 Put students into pairs and give them two minutes to prepare notes. Monitor that they are using the vocabulary correctly and logically. Elicit the tenses they will be using before they start. Point out the relevance to IELTS Speaking Part 2.

On a general note, point out the importance of general category nouns in all parts of IELTS. When you come across them throughout the course, draw them to the students' attention.

Listening
IELTS Section 4   Page 49

Go over the 'What to expect in the exam' and 'How to go about it' advice for section 4, answering any questions that come up. For the third point in 'How to go about it', tell the students they may have to consider more than one question at a time if they come close together. Emphasize that they should not worry about a big gap which might come at the beginning as well as in the middle. Also advise them that sometimes the information given in the questions and the information that students need to listen for in order to complete answers are not in the same order that they occur in the recording. For example, students might hear: *The dog bit the man* and be asked to complete *The man was bitten by* _____ .

Remind students that they need to pay attention to singular and plural nouns.

Questions 31–37

Ask your students to predict the types of words that will come in each gap and look at the topic of the table and what kind of information is already given. Elicit the signal words for the information in the test. Play the recording once or twice and then a second or third time to go over the answers. Remind students that the recording is played only once in the exam.

Answers
31 public railway
32 unnoticed
33 steam locomotive
34 coal
35 passengers
36 passenger traffic
37 Canals

Questions 38–40

Students should underline the key words and elicit the type of information they are about to hear. Play the recording once and then a second or third time to go over the answers. Make sure they all understand the rationale for the answers before moving on.

Answers
C, D, F in any order

Some teachers like to ask students to look at the listening script section at this point. For Section 4 this can be useful if the students are having

difficulty. However, if you do this, be careful not to create over-reliance on the written text rather than the spoken text as students could end up focusing on irrelevant details.

At the end of the exam itself, students are given ten minutes to transfer all their answers onto the answer sheet. During the transfer it is easy for students to create mistakes in spelling, put answers with letters in the wrong order and to leave off the *s* in plural nouns or add an *s* to nouns in the singular. Encourage students to practise transferring information onto an answer sheet even if it is only a list of numbers for the questions they have done themselves. Ask them to date the exercise and keep it for reference.

4 Global problems and opportunities

 1.8

Good morning. Last week we had a broad overview of the development of early forms of transport up to the late 18th century in Europe, and also looked at how the problems faced by various communities provided new opportunities for innovation and progress. Now, this week we are going to continue with this theme as we examine a number of significant events in the evolution of modern railways – events which took place in England in the first four decades of the 19th century.

If you look at the timeline here on the left of the screen, mmm … you can see the first significant date is the year 1803. This was the year an engineer called William Jessop opened the first public railway in south London, England – to carry industrial goods. Although the railway was horse-drawn and not really what we would consider a railway today, nonetheless it's still regarded as the world's first public railway. The railway was constructed as a cheaper alternative to building a canal, then a common means of carrying freight.

The first railway steam locomotive was built in 1804 by an English engineer, Richard Trevithick, to whose work later pioneers like George Stephenson are seriously indebted. Richard Trevithick died a poor man, and what he had achieved went largely unnoticed. His engines were not commercially successful, partly because the locomotives he built were too heavy for the railway tracks of the time.

Wars in Europe led to an increase in the cost of feeding the horses which pulled the coal on horse-drawn railways like the Surrey Iron

Railway. With this and the cost of using the canals, which were run by private companies, the time was now right to introduce a locomotive that was economically viable.

In the year 1812, <u>the first commercially successful steam locomotive, the Salamanca,</u> appeared on the scene at Middleton in Yorkshire in the north-east of England. Apparently, the Salamanca was even visited by Tsar Nicholas 1.

But probably the most important year was 1825 when the engine *Locomotion*, created by George Stephenson, ran on the Darlington to Stockton Railway. <u>The line was initially built to connect inland coal mines to Stockton, where coal was loaded onto boats.</u> Initially the Railway was to be horse-drawn, but permission was granted to use locomotive or 'moveable' engines. <u>Provision for transporting passengers was made, although at the time they were regarded as being of little importance.</u>

....

The year 1831 saw the opening of the successful Liverpool to Manchester line with Stephenson's locomotive *The Rocket*. The Liverpool to Manchester Railway is thought of as the first modern railway. <u>The reason for this is that both goods and passenger traffic were carried on trains according to a scheduled timetable.</u> After the success of the Stockton to Darlington Railway, money poured into the north-west of England as the region went through a period of rapid industrialization, with the railway linking the rich cotton manufacturing town of Manchester and the thriving port of Liverpool.

Up to now the <u>canals, which were constructed in the previous century, were felt to be making too much profit from their fees on trade using the canals and thereby to be hindering the development of the conurbations in the region.</u>

And the effect of the opening of the Liverpool and Manchester Railway? It was quite dramatic. <u>By 1834 nearly half a million passengers were being carried each year, a significant increase. Also, more merchandise, including cotton, coal and other goods, was transported between the two cities</u> using the railway. The age of the railway as a means of ferrying people from one place to another had arrived. <u>The increase in passenger numbers and in the movement of goods led to a drop in toll prices on the roads, as well as a decrease in charges for the use of canals.</u>

It's hard for us to appreciate the opportunities these early pioneers seized in the face of

difficulties in construction and in changing people's attitudes. Perhaps we can end for today with a brief quote from Dr Larder, author of the *Steam Engine Familiarly Explained and Illustrated* in 1823, 'Rail travel at high speed,' he said, 'is not possible, ... because passengers, unable to breathe would die of asphyxia.' Next time you take a train ...

Language focus 1: Countable and uncountable nouns   Page 51

Photocopiable language focus exercise on page 137.

Lead-in

Give a quick review of countable and uncountable nouns and elicit some examples from the students.

1–2 Follow the instructions in the Coursebook. Suggest they transfer exercise 2 straight into their vocabulary books. The uncountable nouns listed here make good headings for lexical sets. Refer them to the Grammar reference on page 221.

Answers
1
Countable: forms, opportunities
Uncountable: development, transport, innovation, progress, evolution
Note: *innovation* and *development* can also be countable
2
1 b (tables, shelves, desks ...)
2 a (shoes, sweaters, hats ...)
3 j (bags, rucksacks ...)
4 f (notes)
5 c (apples, bananas, lemons ...)
6 d (houses, hotels, cabins ...)
7 h (newspapers, television/radio programmes ...)
8 e (products)
9 g (thefts, robberies, shootings ...)
10 i (cans, packets, cigarettes ...)

3 Point out the instruction regarding making changes to the verb as this is of key importance here. Go over the exercise when the students have finished, ensuring accuracy and understanding.

Answers

1 Litter is …
2 Machines are …
3 The behaviour of football hooligans costs …
4 Information …
5 Robberies and thefts are …
6 Musical instruments are played …
7 Suggestions … are …
8 Language … follows …

4   Ask students to do this exercise in pairs. Pre-teach the phrase *in decline* which they will need for question 3.

Answers

1 Many businesses now demand a lot of work from (their) employees.
2 People expect good weather when they go on holiday.
3 Theatre audiences are in decline generally, but the audience for the new musical was extremely small last night.
4 Increased use of public transport like buses and trains is good for the environment.
5 With the increase in the price of paper, books and newspapers are becoming expensive.
6 Coffee and tea are commodities which saw a fall in value recently.
7 Entertainment like horror and violent films should be banned.
8 Electronic goods like refrigerators cause considerable harm to the planet.

5   Students complete this exercise individually and check their answers in pairs.

Answers

1 equipment, computers
2 weather, storms
3 Information, details
4 Business, businesses
5 luggage, cases
6 Furniture, wood, trees
7 Waste, litter
8 jobs, work, money

Speaking
IELTS Part 1   Page 51

Point out to students that they may be asked to talk about a wide range of general subjects in Part 1. They might be asked about flowers, plants, trees, the weather, etc. in their country, not just hobbies and family. However, reassure them that the subjects require no in-depth knowledge.

1   Put the students into groups to discuss the answers to the questions. If you have a multi-cultural group, put them into groups according to their country or region for maximum effect in the brainstorming. With a mono-cultural group, it might be an idea to do some research yourself before the lesson to help with ideas. Students should underline the countable and uncountable nouns as they go along.

Answers

1 Countable: types, resources, country
2 Countable: goods, country
3 Countable: types, country
   Uncountable: food
4 Uncountable: produce
5 Countable: country
   Uncountable: food
6 Countable: commodities, country
7 Countable: shops, country
   Uncountable: merchandise
8 Countable: crops, country

2   Pair students up with someone from another group for this activity.

Reading
IELTS Reading Passage   Page 52

Look at the pre-reading discussion and check that students understand what they are being asked to do.

Go over the 'How to go about it' section for Questions 1–9. Students should read the instructions for the summary carefully. For Questions 10–13, make sure they are clear about the differences between YES/NO/NOT GIVEN and TRUE/FALSE/NOT GIVEN tasks. These initial stages are crucial in getting the students used to the strategies for each part of the reading test and applying the tips as soon as possible. See Ready for Reading on page 63.

Questions 1–9

Tell students to look at the photograph and at the title of the text, checking they understand the use of *scourge*. Ask them what they think the title means and what kind of information they expect to find in the passage. Let them complete the summary and go over it, asking how many of their initial predictions were correct or close.

Questions 10–13

Move on to questions 10–13, getting the students to underline the key words they will need to find the answers and where they think they will find them in the text. Ask them to check their answers in pairs, justifying their answers with reference to the text. In whole class feedback, ensure they understand why any errors they had were made.

Answers
1 B
2 G
3 D
4 A
5 E
6 P
7 N
8 K
9 I
10 YES. Paragraph 2: *The vast expanse of debris – in effect the world's largest rubbish dump.* The phrase *in effect* and the fact that the information is between dashes tells you this is what the writer thinks – it is his/her claim, not a statement of fact.
11 NO. See the information given by Marcus Eriksen in paragraph 3. Then look at the beginning of the next paragraph: The *soup* is actually two linked areas ... The word *actually* tells you what the writer claims is true.
12 NOT GIVEN. The writer does not make any predictions about this, even though Mr Moore warned in Paragraph 7: *unless consumers cut back on their use of disposable plastics, the plastic stew would double in size over the next decade.*
13 YES. Paragraph 13: *Plastic is believed to constitute 90 per cent of all rubbish floating in the oceans.* Note that the writer is claiming what is believed to be true.

Reacting to the text

Students discuss the questions in pairs or small groups.

Language focus 2: Making suggestions
Page 54

1 Ask students to discuss which they think is the best suggestion to solve the problem.

2 Give an example of a strong and a tentative suggestion. You may want to point out that *should* and *ought to* are interchangeable to many people, but that *should* carries the speaker's/writer's opinion and that *ought to* is neutral. Compare them with *must* and *have to*. Refer students to the Grammar reference on page 221.

Answers
1 could
2 The most important ... is ...
3 should
4 ought to
Suggestions 2, 3 and 4 are strong suggestions; 1 is tentative.

3 Students discuss the possible solutions in pairs.

4 Give a quick review of the modals and where they occur on the possibility/probability line. Look at the example and point out the changes that have been made to accommodate the modal in the sentence. Let the students do the exercise and write their answers on the board. Encourage them to correct each other, and give feedback.

Answers
a Governments ought to try to encourage people to return to the countryside.
b Banks could cancel the international debts of poor countries.
c Governments should provide poorer countries with the skills to feed themselves.
d Rivers could be oxygenated and fish reintroduced.
e Protection orders can be put on all wild animals.
f Water desalination plants might work in some regions.
g More trees should be planted.

5 Students do this individually and check in pairs. Give whole class feedback.

Answers
a 6
b 2
c 1
d 4
e 5
f 7
g 3

6 Ask the students to write their suggestions in pairs and then change partners. Students should share their ideas as a whole class.

Vocabulary 2: Developing ideas by expanding the meaning of adjectives
Page 54

1 Students do this exercise individually and then compare their answers in pairs. Encourage them to discuss their answers if they differ, in order to really understand the differences in the two meanings within the context of the sentences. Ask the students to add the words to their vocabulary books.

Answers
1 pleases
2 encourage
3 frightened
4 trouble
5 attracts
6 fascinated
7 stunned

2 Go over the example and let the students do the exercise individually. Put the sentences on the board when they have finished in order to peer correct and discuss the answers.

Answers
1 Some people find buying consumer goods very pleasing. Sometimes, it is just the act of purchasing which satisfies them.
2 Positive health education on TV can be encouraging. It can motivate people to improve their lifestyle.
3 The results were frightening. They alarmed the government so much they actually took some action.
4 The news on TV is sometimes so troubling. It can worry people all day long.
5 Disaster movies are very attractive to many people. It is the fact that they feel comfortable and safe themselves as they watch that appeals to them.
6 I found the festivities really fascinating. They interested me so much that I had to read more about them.
7 The scale of crime in some cities has been so stunning it has shocked even the police.

Writing
IELTS Task 2   Page 55

1 Tell students to read the rubric carefully so they are aware of exactly what is being asked of them. Go through the text and elicit what kind of linker will be required for each gap.

Answers
1 reason
2 contrast
3 result/conclusion
4 example
5 purpose
6 result
7 concession

2 Students do this in pairs. Feed back as a whole class, ensuring they understand what each linking device represents. It is a good idea to get them to classify their linkers on their writing hints pages under the types, e.g., contrast, addition, example, etc. Or create a page for linking devices in their vocabulary books or folders.

Answers
1 because
2 Yet
3 therefore
4 For example
5 in order to
6 then
7 Although

3 Do the first one as an example with the whole class and let them do the rest in pairs. Go over the answers as a whole class.

Answers		
Adverb	**Conjunction**	**Both**
however	although	though
even so	but	yet
nevertheless	even if	
nonetheless	much as	
still	while	
	despite the fact that	
	in spite of the fact that	

4 Ask students to choose the correct words individually, before checking in pairs.

Answers
1 However. You will see *But* used as an adverb in some texts.
2 but/although
3 While/Although
4 Even if/Though
5 Even so/Nonetheless

5 Students read the Task 2 question and make a list of ideas in pairs. Check as a whole class, dealing with any difficulties as they arise.

6 Put the ideas up on the board and make connections between similar ideas. (This can act as a larger-scale example for when the students sort their own ideas in the exam.) Ask the class to put linking words with the relevant ideas and to identify which paragraph they could go in.

Go over the 'How to go about it' section step by step, and stress that this is good practice even under the pressure of exam conditions.

7 Follow the instructions in the Coursebook. Check back with the class.

Answers
7
A causes
B examples
1 c
2 f
3 d
4 e
5 a
6 b

8 Students write their answers to the question. Emphasize the importance of using the checklist on page 209. Ask them to look at the sample answer opposite and to compare it with their own answer.

Further practice

Put the students into pairs or groups and give them a copy of the sample answer or a sample answer that you have collected yourself from a previous class. If you are using a different essay question, give the question as well. Ask students to decide whether the ideas are developed well and to state the approximate score band the essay would achieve in the exam. Expect a wide variation of answers and lots of discussion. Students will probably focus on the mistakes and not the overall text. Do this exercise periodically throughout the course for both Tasks 1 and 2.

Sample answer
Recent decades have witnessed a significant increase in the amount of rubbish produced by people around the world, causing a serious threat to all living things. It has been pointed out that changes in lifestyle and the industrial revolution are the main causes for this rise. However, there are many steps that can be taken to halt this problem.
After the industrial revolution there was a huge growth in the number of products available for people. Most of the producers try to attract consumers by using different types of packaging materials. Sometimes, the size and the amount of these materials are bigger than those for the products themselves. Also the production of new versions of different equipment, such as mobile phones, increases the waist.
Moreover, while most people, in the past, used their own bags when they went for shopping, nowadays, they depend on the disposable bags offered by shops, which are mostly made from plastic. In addition to that, the consumption of prepared food has experienced a crucial increase as a result to the rise in the number of working women. These foods are covered by different types of packaging material leading to increase in the amount of rubbish produced per capita.
Not only does the increase in the amount of rubbish threaten our lives by different pollutants, but it also causes depletion of valuable resources. For this reason there should be a new movement to decrease the amount of waste to its lowest level, and to use less harmful materials like biodegradable ones. Governmental and social organizations, like schools and media, should contribute to this process by explaining to people the important of conserving our environment and resources.
Word count: 280

Possible score: 7.0

Examiner's comment:

A reasonably successful response that deploys both ideas and supporting evidence quite coherently. The sentence structures are varied, although some errors are evident. Overall, the response exhibits a fair level of precision and flexibility. Ambitious writing results in some grammatical inaccuracy, but this does not impose undue strain on the reader.

Page 57

1–2 Follow the instructions in the Coursebook. Students should stay in the same pairs as in the previous exercise.

Page 57

Go through the 'How to go about it' advice, expanding with examples where necessary. Remind the students that Part 3 is their chance to show the examiner their range of vocabulary and structures.

1 Put students in pairs and explain the two parts of the task given. Students discuss possible answers in groups to the questions. You could divide the questions out among the groups. Select one from each section to discuss as a whole class.

Answers

1

News and events

influence: affect/have an impact/impact on

encourage: persuade

change: adapt/modify

achieve: realize/accomplish/attain

issues: matters/problems

concern: worry

World problems

tackle: deal with

discarded: thrown away

waste: rubbish

mankind: human beings

dilemmas: problems

2 Students choose the questions not covered as a whole class and practise in pairs with timings and making the notes as suggested. Monitor and make notes yourself with suggestions to feed back when the students have finished.

Review 4 answers Pages 58 and 59

Vocabulary

1

1 dilemma

2 issue

3 event

4 opportunity

5 incident

6 impression

2	**3**
1 Correct	1 shocking, stunned
2 incident	2 interesting, fascinates
3 Correct	3 appealing, attracts
4 situation	4 satisfying, pleases
5 Correct	5 alarming, frightened
6 incident	6 motivating, encourage
7 occasions	7 worrying, troubled
8 Correct	
9 Correct	

Countable and uncountable nouns

1 litter	6 accommodation
2 clothing	7 furniture
3 cash/money	8 crime
4 luggage/baggage	9 media
5 fruit	

Writing

1

1 Nevertheless/Yet/Still

2 Despite the fact that

3 yet

4 Much as/Although

2

Possible answers

a The general topic is water shortages. The question presents you with two separate opinions and asks for your opinion. You can follow one opinion or you can agree with parts of each one.

b The general topic is water shortages. The question asks you to describe the causes. It does not ask you for solutions. You can give examples of about three situations or problems around the world. Then you can give the cause for each. Although you are not asked for any solutions, you could mention one or two by way of conclusion.

5 The future

Content overview

Themes

This unit is concerned with the future, predictions and robotics.

Exam-related activities

Reading

Topic	Robotics
Question type	Summary without a wordlist
	Multiple choice
	Short answers

Listening

Topic	Robotics exhibition
Section 1	Completing notes

Speaking

Part 3	Discussing robots/the world in the future

Writing

Task 1	Describing a pie chart

Other

Language focus	Ways of looking at the future
Vocabulary 1	Adjective/noun collocations
Vocabulary 2	Verbs of prediction
Word building	Forming adjectives from nouns

Language focus: Ways of looking at the future   Page 60

Lead-in

Put students in groups and ask them to predict the major changes of the future. You could divide the changes into the near future, e.g., the next five years, and the distant future, e.g., fifty years. Monitor the tense forms they use as you go round, as a diagnostic exercise.

1–2 Follow the instructions in the Coursebook.

3–4 Work through these exercises, ensuring the students know the differences between *predictions* and *plans*. Pay close attention to the answers for exercise 4. Refer students to the Grammar reference on page 222 and look at the form of the tenses.

Answers

3

1 Plan
2 Plan
3 Prediction
4 Prediction
5 Prediction

6 Fixed schedule

4

a 2
b 1
c 5
d 3
e 4
f 6

5–8 Follow the instructions in the Coursebook.

It is important that students understand the differences in usage of these future forms. A good score in Part 3 of the Speaking can depend on the correct manipulation of these forms. They may also be required in task 2 in Writing and Listening.

Answers

5

1 we're flying – a
   shall I arrange – c
2 going to spend – b
   it'll do – c
3 we'll have completed – e
   it'll be working – d
4 are going to be – b
   it won't last – c
5   she arrives – f
   she'll be carrying – d

6

1 will they really enjoy it/be enjoying
2 I'll be sitting
3 I'll meet you
4 is going to happen/will happen
5 will have thus improved

7

1 The present simple is not possible. It is used for a timetable.
2 Society will not have changed dramatically by 2030.

   not going to shows this is a prediction about what is not going to happen based on present information.

   The future perfect shows this will not have happened before the date mentioned.
3 The present continuous is not possible.
4 The world is certainly going to change for the better by then.

   The future perfect shows that it will have happened before the date mentioned.

going to shows this is a prediction about what is going to happen based on present information.

5 The human race will live in more closely knit communities in the future.

The future continuous predicts what will be happening in the future.

The simple future makes a straightforward prediction.

6 *going to* is not possible. Both are predictions. However, the simple future is a spontaneous reaction and *going to* is used after looking at present information.

Vocabulary 1: Adjective/noun collocations   Page 61

1 Ensure the students have chosen the correct adjectives before moving onto exercise 2.

Answers

1 modern
2 agricultural
3 dominant
4 thriving
5 general
6 urban
7 governing
8 indigenous

Extension

Put students into four groups and give them two of the phrases each to put into a new sentence.

2 This activity looks at the vocabulary and revisits the structures from the language focus section. Monitor for correct usage and range of structures.

Answers

1 general public
2 modern civilization
3 agricultural societies
4 urban populations
5 dominant culture
6 governing elite

3 Students discuss the questions in small groups.

IELTS Part 3   Page 62

1 Ask students to focus on the **Useful expressions** before eliciting example sentences around the class. Check the concept and pronunciation.

Answers

Possible answers

In 10/20/50/100 years' time, people will be living in very high skyscrapers as in the film, *Blade Runner*.

Over the next century, the population on the planet will grow enormously.

Before the end of the century, the human race will have settled on the moon and other planets outside the solar system.

By the time we reach the end of the century, war will have disappeared.

In the coming decades, the advances in communication will be very rapid indeed.

2 Students work in pairs and discuss the example questions about robots. Briefly check the meanings of *pessimistic* and *optimistic* and their noun forms. Continue with the example questions about the world in the future. Try to encourage realistic answers and correct use of the target structures.

It might be an idea to run through the checklist criteria on page 210 to make sure they understand what each question is looking for.

IELTS Section 1   Page 62

1 Do the pre-listening activity and discuss what other contexts the words and phrases might be used in.

Answers

1 booking office: a place where tickets are booked, bought and collected
2 preview: a chance to see a show, film or play before it opens to the general public
3 the week after next: two weeks from now
4 restrictions: limitations
5 sign up for: register for
6 come up: appear
7 register: enrol/join
8 range: variety/scope

Read the 'Don't forget!' advice and reiterate the importance of predicting answer types. Monitor the students carefully as they do this preparation.

Questions 1–10

Play the listening all the way through for both sections twice: the first time to see how many answers the students get, and the second time to see what else they can pick up.

- Question 4: they need to check to see if they need any extra practice with the alphabet and/or numbers.

- Question 9: as you check the answers, take the opportunity to drill the difference between 17 and 70, 16 and 60, etc. so students are aware of the potential confusion between the numbers 13 to 19 and 30, etc. up to 90.

- Check the plurals and stress the importance of accuracy here.

Ask the students to transfer their answers to an answer sheet. Remind the students to fill out their listening checklist.

Answers
1 day passes/tickets
2 Thursday
3 Tuesday, Friday
4 SF6733
5 3/three
6 special promotions
7 60
8 45 minutes
9 70
10 17

---

5 The future

 1.9

M = Marcus; C = Customer

M: Good morning, exhibition booking office. Marcus speaking. Can I help you?

C: Is that the booking centre for 'Robots: the end of <u>modern civilization?</u>'

M: Yes madam, that's correct. How can I help you?

C: Well, mmm … I'm attending the exhibition and I'd just like to check a few details if that's OK.

M: Yes, sure.

C: OK. I understand the exhibition opens the week after next on the Tuesday, and … the preview is on Monday.

M: Yes, that's right. There is a preview on Monday, but the exhibition is not open to the general public on that day. But for the rest of the week it is.

C: OK, I see. That's fine. I've got <u>two complimentary day passes</u> for the exhibition; can you tell me if I can use the <u>tickets</u> on any day?

M: Well, I'm not sure if there are any restrictions, … let's see … Yes, here we are.

C: Yes?

M: You can use them on any day including the preview day, except Saturday. But you need to sign up for the days you want to attend in advance.

C: Oh, I see. I haven't decided what days to attend yet.

M: Mmm … well … Saturday you can't attend with the tickets you have, and <u>Thursday</u> is already completely booked. I think the other days'll book up fairly quickly now as there's a lot of interest in the exhibition.

C: You mean I won't be able to attend on Saturday even with a free ticket.

M: I'm afraid not. So it's better to book your days now.

C: OK. I suppose, mmm … I'll attend on the <u>Tuesday and Friday</u>. Do you need my name?

M: No, I just need to take a reference number with the day passes. Your name will come up with the number; it'll be the same number on each one. I'll register them for both days, and then when you use one it'll automatically cancel.

C: OK, the number is <u>S–F–6–7–3–3</u>.

M: … 3–3. Thank you, I've got that.

C: What about services like cafés and so on?

M: Oh, there are 15 restaurants in all, that's <u>three</u> cafés and the rest are different types of dining areas round the Exhibition Centre. Some restaurants around the centre will be doing <u>special promotions</u> at the Exhibition Centre itself, so you won't go hungry.

....

C: Is there somewhere nice to stay nearby?

M: Oh yes. There're rooms at the nearby halls of residence, which are part of the university. They're just across the road from the Exhibition Centre.

C: How much are they?

M: A single room is £30 per night, which includes breakfast in the cafeteria. And there are some very pleasant hotels in the area. They range from around £30 to about £60. It depends how much you want to spend really.

C: What about getting there? Has the Exhibition Centre got good transport links?

M: Yes. We're very well located – about 20 minutes' walk at most from the station, and about 45 minutes from the airport. There are lots of buses; the best one, which stops just by the Exhibition Centre's main entrance, is bus 17. No, sorry, it's bus 70. I keep getting them mixed up. It only costs £3 from the station.

C: And taxis? Just in case.

M: Er … you'll pay a maximum of £17.

C: Mmm … well that all sounds OK.

2 Arrange the students in groups to discuss the questions after the Listening test. Ask each group to select one person to give feedback to the class.

Word building: Forming adjectives from nouns   Page 64

1 Tell students that this exercise is not simply a matter of adding the suffix to the existing word, as some letters need to be dropped, some added, and others changed. Put the three columns on the board. When students finish, ask them out to write up the adjectives. Check for spelling.

Answers

Adjectives ending -al	
usual	traditional
technological	national
agricultural	industrial

Adjectives ending -ous
luxurious
populous
spacious
dangerous
industrious

Adjectives ending -ful
useful
successful
beautiful

Extension

Ask students to collocate the adjectives with a noun. These can then be transferred into their vocabulary books.

Answers	
Possible answers	
usual suspects	populous nation
technological age	spacious classroom
agricultural community	dangerous situation
traditional costume	industrious student
national treasure	useful exercise
industrial society	successful outcome
luxurious goods	beautiful game

2 Follow the instructions in the Coursebook. Note the preposition *at* with *successful*.

Answers
1 spacious
2 technological
3 beautiful
4 traditional
5 national
6 Luxurious
7 populous
8 successful

3 Tell students to use the negative form as well if it is more appropriate. Monitor for accuracy of meaning and for logical examples.

Reading

IELTS Reading Passage   Page 64

Follow the instructions for the pre-reading questions in the Coursebook. Make sure students are clear about the clues they found to help with the five points. Elicit the meaning of *pragmatics*.

Questions 1–13

Review the strategies needed to complete summaries on page 53 of Unit 4. Ask what is different about the instructions for the task in

Unit 5 and the one in Unit 4 (the words from Unit 4 are taken from a wordlist; in this question type the words are taken from the passage).

Go through the 'How to go about it' advice carefully step by step. The advice about checking to see if the summary is based on part of the passage or the whole passage is particularly relevant. They can look at the first and last sentence and one in the middle to gauge this, but remind them that usually summaries without a heading cover the whole reading passage. At this stage, don't be too concerned about timing, unless the students are taking too long, as they will get used to applying the strategies automatically.

You can ask the students to answer all the reading questions in the time limit or you can break it up into sections. Do the summary (give them a time limit now of around 10 minutes) and check it carefully together. Then give them another 10 minutes to do the remaining questions. They should check answers in pairs before whole class feedback, discussing any problem areas.

Answers

Possible answers

  robot developments

  types of robots

  examples from two countries

  cost

  different markets

- students' own answers
- pragmatics: practical applications

1 receptionist

2 vacuum

3 different approaches

4 human beings

5 pragmatic

6 the elderly

7 technological revolution

8 B

9 A

10 C

11 A

12 (undisputed) leader

13 $210 million

Reacting to the text

Students discuss the questions in small groups.

Vocabulary 2: Verbs of prediction
Page 67

1–2 Elicit the four verbs that cannot be used in this context and discuss context and appropriacy issues. Illustrate the differences if necessary. Go over the noun and verb forms and remind the students that using a variety of structures as well as a wide range of vocabulary helps to increase their chances of a better score.

Answers

1

prophesy, assume, foretell, foresee

2

prediction, predicted/predictable; forecast, forecast(ed); projection, projected; estimation, estimated; anticipation, anticipated; expectation, expected

3 Look at the example and focus on the changes to the verbs. Ask the students to look out for similar necessary changes in the other sentences. Remind them also of the subject *it* and how it is used for referencing, again showing an ability to use cohesive devices efficiently. Students come up to the board to write their sentences when they have finished. Point out that using a variety of structures like this will improve the style and coherence of their writing.

Answers

1 By the year 2030 it is estimated that the population will have increased to nearly 70 million.

2 Spectator numbers are forecast to rise dramatically towards the end of the year.

3 It is projected that sales next month will be lower than this month.

4 The forecast is for a substantial increase in passenger numbers./The forecast is that passenger numbers will increase substantially.

5 Sales are predicted to climb at the rate of 20 per cent a year./It is predicted that sales will climb at the rate of 20 per cent a year.

6 Attendances are anticipated to decline gradually in the next two years.

7 It is expected that advances in technology will not slow down in the coming years.

8 Ticket purchases are estimated to recover in the third quarter.

Further practice

To help increase students' flexibility with these structures, ask them to work in pairs. One student reads out one of the sentences from the exercise, and the partner transforms the sentence without looking at the exercise. Encourage them to do the transformation both ways. When you see that the students are getting faster, do a quick check around the class. Once you are happy that the students are able to do the transformations easily, ask them to close their books. Dictate some of the sentences which the students then have to transform and write down. Check answers with the whole class. You can use this checking sequence with other transformation exercises.

Writing
IELTS Task 1   Page 68

Photocopiable writing exercise on page 137.

1 Ask the students to read the rubrics and say what the topic of the task is and how the information is measured. Then discuss how the charts are divided and what each one refers to. Circle or mark on the charts what they consider to be significant similarities and differences. Emphasize that this is good practice and that they should automatically do this with Task 1 questions.

Students work through the model answer and check in pairs. Elicit the tenses and why they are used. Ask which indicators in the charts show the most appropriate tense to use.

Answers		
1 show	7	is anticipated
2 is	8	will fare
3 is expected	9	represented
4 is predicted	10	is
5 will shrink	11	compares
6 will see	12	is expected

2–3 Follow the instructions in the Coursebook. Point out that when using referencing pronouns in their own writing, they must be clear as to *what* or *who* they are referring to; otherwise, cohesion breaks down.

Answers
2
Then, By contrast, While, but

3
Second paragraph: *It* refers to 'traffic volume from high-speed transport'.
Third paragraph: *This* refers to the whole sentence 'The former represented …'.
Third paragraph: *The former* refers to 'railways'.

4 Students choose the linkers. Check answers with the whole class, ensuring they understand the difference in meanings if they chose the wrong ones. If they haven't already done so, ask students to add these linkers to their page of cohesive devices in their vocabulary/writing notebooks.

Answers
1 By contrast, By comparison
2 By contrast, Meanwhile
3 but, whereas
4 Meanwhile, By contrast
5 whereas, whilst

5 Do the first one together, indicating the changes that have to be made to some of the words and the information that has to be added in. Students can do this individually and then on the board for class feedback. Check for structure and accuracy of data.

Answers
1 High-speed transport accounted for 9% of traffic volume in 1990 while in 2050 it is forecast to represent 41%.
2 It is estimated that the proportion of the traffic volume of automobiles will fall to 35% in 2050 in contrast to 53% in 1990.
3 In 1990 automobiles made up the bulk of passenger kilometres (53%), but by 2050, this is forecast to drop to 35%.
4 In 1990 out of a total traffic volume of 23.4 trillion pkm, automobiles accounted for 53% compared to buses, railways and high-speed transport 29%, 9% and 9%, respectively. By comparison, by 2020 it is anticipated that high-speed transport will jump to 41% with automobiles, buses, railways making up 35%, 20% and 4% respectively.

6 Give the students a time limit, e.g., two minutes, to highlight key points from the charts. Depending on their performance on this, you can go over this with them before they write. Give them pointers as to the significant details or ask them to go straight onto the writing stage without your input. You can do the remainder as a timed writing in class, getting them to mark where they are when a further 18 minutes is up, or as a writing at home. If the latter, ask them to work out how long it takes them and to write it on their Task 1 answer.

Encourage them to use the checklist on page 209 to check their answer. Tell them that, in addition to checking for summarizing and selecting information, you will be looking for correct usage of the linking devices and referencing pronouns in the text.

Sample answer

The pie chart depicts different proportions of fuel type that generate energy in Florida 2007 compared with the forecast for 2017.

Overall, it is clear that Natural gas is the main energy generator both years, while Renewables and Oil come at the bottom of the list. For example, the energy generated by Natural gas increased from 38.8% in 2007 to 54.4% in 2017. Next comes the energy production by Coal which accounts for 29.3% of the energy market in 2007, followed by a drop of 5.6% in the forecasted year of 2017. As for Nuclear, although it represents the third energy generator in Florida for both compared years, the trend here is upwards reaching 15.9% at the estimated period.

In contrast, there is a significant drop in the energy production for both Oil and Other sources in the two separate years from 6.7% to 1.1% for the former and 11.1% to 3.4% for the latter. As for the Renewables, the decrease in fuel generation over the period is less dramatic.

Word count: 178

Possible score: 7.5

Examiner's comment:

A generally sound response with the main areas of the prompt covered and the main trends and counter trends identified. A sophisticated range of vocabulary is employed and the rubric is neatly paraphrased, although just occasionally the register and phrasing are slightly uneven. Errors in capitalization throughout.

Review 5 answers Pages 70 and 71

Vocabulary

1

1 Do you think that modern civilization will change much over the next century?

2 Should we try to protect the remaining agricultural societies?

3 Are urban populations under threat from increasing violence?

4 Will the dominant cultures always be in control?

5 Are indigenous peoples under threat?

6 Do the governing elites have any idea what the lives of ordinary people are like?

7 Do thriving communities in inner cities have a beneficial impact on society in general?

8 Does the opinion of the general public influence governments?

Word building

1 Electronic dictionaries are useless/not really very useful, because …

2 Certain south-east Asian countries are much more technological, because …

3 This country has many beautiful buildings, because …

4 Bangladesh is populous, because …

5 Agricultural jobs are very demanding, because…

6 A luxurious life is not open to all of us, because …

7 It is dangerous when astronauts go out into space, because …

8 Traditional skills are going out of fashion, because …

Ways of looking at the future

1
1 leaves, 'll be sitting
2 will have landed
3 will lead
4 will rise, will certainly disappear
5 will be, will live/will be living, will be done, will be

2
2, 3, 4, 5
Extract 1 is personal, the others are more abstract.

Proof reading

1 will have increased/will increase
2 … , whereas …
3 shows
4 passenger numbers
5 Traffic
6 dramatically
7 made up
8 The most striking feature
9 … . By contrast, …
10 predicted

6 Fruits and seeds

Content overview

Themes

This unit is concerned with nature, conservation, and describing processes.

Exam-related activities

Reading

Topic	The life of a pomegranate
Question type	Matching statements to paragraphs
	TRUE/FALSE/NOT GIVEN
	Completing a flow-chart

Listening

Topic	Describing a place
Section 2	Multiple choice
	Labelling a map
	Completing sentences

Speaking

Part 2	Describing a park that you like/something you have grown

Writing

Task 1	Describing a process

Other

Language focus	Transitive and intransitive verbs
Vocabulary 1	Conservation
Vocabulary 2	Describing sequences

Reading

IELTS Reading Passage   Page 72

Lead-in

As an awareness-raising exercise, you could elicit language the students know about the lifecycle of plants and the part insects play in this. This could develop into a discussion about the survival of species in general.

1 Look at the photographs and ask the students to describe them to each other in pairs. You may need to pre-teach *lavender*, *germinate*, *bloom* (n & v), *pollinate* and *cocoon*.

2–4 Discuss the vocabulary that helped them to match the photos with the texts and check for logical links. Ask the students to put new words under a heading in their vocabulary books or folder.

Answers

2

a 4

b 1

c 3

d 2

Text e relates to the making of a juice drink.

3

a flowered, fruit, produced, seeds, fall, ground, carried, birds, animals, wind, drop, wait, spring, germinate, grow, process, repeats

b blooms, crop, picked, taken, factory, oil, extracted, distilled, essence, perfumes, toiletries

c lays, egg, leaves, plants, eggs, hatch, caterpillars, eat, leaves, form, cocoon, insect, emerges

d plants, produce, flowers, open, attract insects, pollinate, plant

4

e fruit, ripens, collected, taken, factory, crushed, extract, juice, packaged, sent, shops, sold

Questions 1–13

Go through the 'How to go about it' advice step by step. Check that students are using the right strategies to find the answers. Tell them they should always skim the questions before reading through the text. Remind them that when reading the passage, they must learn to skim at high speed for gist and scan to locate information.

Give the students 20 minutes to do the reading test. After this time, get them to make a note of which question they've reached and then continue. Depending on how the majority are coping, give them no more than another five minutes. Remember, the timing excludes the preparation time.

For the flow-chart in questions 9–13 point out the title, the word limit and the fact that the text is in note form. Tell students that sometimes the information in the flow-chart and the reading passage may not be in the same order. Ask the students what the grammatical form of most of the words in the flow-chart is and predict what they think the form of the missing words is. Relate this to the pre-reading exercise focus on nouns and verbs.

Ask the students to check their answers in pairs and then as a whole class. You need to make sure they have located the correct answers in the text before moving on.

Answers

1 C The phrase relates to the whole paragraph.

2 G The phrase relates to part of the paragraph: *but certain types are grown in home dooryards ...*

3 B The phrase relates to the whole paragraph.

4 D The phrase relates to part of the paragraph: *The pomegranate tree is native from Iran to the Himalayas in northern India ...*

5 FALSE. Paragraph B: *... and extremely long-lived, some specimens at Versailles known to have survived two centuries.*

6 NOT GIVEN. The flowers are mentioned in paragraph B, but there is no mention of whether they are particularly enticing to bees and birds or not.

7 FALSE. Paragraph C: *The seeds represent about 52% of the weight of the whole fruit.* Note how the answer to number 1 helps you locate the answer for number 7.

8 TRUE. Paragraph G: *The plant favors a semi-arid climate and is extremely drought-tolerant.*

9 pits

10 stem

11 tips

12 development

13 suckers

Reacting to the text

Students discuss the questions in small groups.

Extension

To show students how they can increase their speed, ask them to underline the nouns and verbs in a–e in exercise 2. Then read the nouns and verbs to the students as they look at the text and ask them if they can understand generally what is being talked about. Get them to do the same in pairs. One student reads the noun/verbs underlined and the other student without looking at the text listens and says what is being talked about. The students will probably be quite surprised by how much they understand.

Alternatively, choose a paragraph on growing olive oil or nuts, beans or a common plant. Dictate the nouns and verbs in sequence and ask the students to write them down or just listen. You can ask them to say what they think is being talked about as you dictate or ask them to wait till the end and then ask them. Get them to give you the evidence from the words they have. Give the students the paragraph to read quickly on an OHT/electronic whiteboard or on paper. Discuss

the process and get them to see how quickly they can read for gist by reading the nouns and verbs only. Repeat this process regularly – don't leave it to the students to do it on their own. Maybe spend 5–10 minutes on it once a week.

Speaking

IELTS Part 2   Page 75

1 Monitor carefully for correct usage and efficient note-making. Elicit the tenses the students will need to make the descriptions and tell them to use the phrases in the **Useful expressions** boxes. These can be added to the speaking section of their notebooks.

Tell students not to waste time trying to imagine something to describe. Ask them to think about or visualize a place they know well, something they are familiar with in their garden at home or that they know about. Point out also that it is not a test of whether they are telling the truth.

2 Students give their descriptions to their partner. Using the criteria from the previous unit, their partner then uses the checklist to give feedback when they have finished. They can focus on one or more points chosen by the person who speaks. Or the person who role-plays the examiner can choose which criteria to give feedback on. At all times encourage students to begin with constructive feedback.

3 Get them to check their notes and see if they can be improved. If so, let them reword their notes and try again, specifying to their partner one or two of the criteria points for particular focus. Self/peer-assess and note any improvements on the second turn.

Extension

Bring in photographs of various plants, enough for the whole class. Or ask each student to bring in a photo. Students work in pairs and choose a photo for their partner to talk about. Students have one minute to prepare what they are going to say using the first topic in exercise 1. Or put the students into groups and ask each group to choose a picture for another group to prepare. If it is group work, ask them to make sure they agree on what is going to be said. They will need longer to discuss. Give the students a time limit. In both cases tell them they must prepare a vertical list of notes; each student must have the list in the groups. Then ask them to describe the item as per the task in 1.

Vocabulary 1: Conservation Page 76

1 Let the students attempt this exercise without any input from you. They can do it in pairs if they are having difficulty. When you check their answers, discuss the context of the alternatives that are not used to clarify why they would be inappropriate in these sentences.

Answers
1 e, c
2 c, a
3 e, b
4 b, d
5 e, a
6 b, a
7 d, b
8 c, a

2 You can do this in groups, giving them two sentences each to put on an OHT or the board. When students have finished, project the answers and discuss the choices they have made through peer correction.

Answers
1 views
2 lungs
3 stretches, area, spoilt
4 sights
5 safeguarded
6 Conservation, areas

3 Look at conservation schemes in the students' own countries or areas and get them to describe them to others in their groups. As a lead-in you could bring in some information on a conservation scheme that is going on locally, nationally or internationally, and explain the methods that are being employed and the reasons. Go through the other questions, noting the use of speculation for question 3.

Language focus: Transitive and intransitive verbs Page 77

1 Check that the students understand the difference between the two types of verbs. Ask them to look up three Transitive and three Intransitive verbs in their dictionaries. You can point them to the symbol denoting each type of verb. Point out that Intransitive verbs cannot be used in the passive, so they need to learn to distinguish between them. Refer them to the Grammar reference on page 222.

Answers
a Transitive
b Intransitive

2 Students look back at text **a** in exercise 2 on page 72. Ask them to focus only on the verbs. Tell them that they need to comment on the usage of the verbs in this context, and that some of the verbs could have a different use in a different context. If the students have underlined the text already, ask them to put a box around the verbs.

Answers
Intransitive: flowered, becomes, fall, drop, wait, germinate, grow
Transitive: produced, carried, repeats
NB *become* can be transitive and intransitive in some circumstances

3 Let them fill in the table, monitoring that they are on track and then go over the exercise. The students may need some examples of those in the 'Both' column.

Answers		
Transitive	**Intransitive**	**Both**
make	look	grow
produce	happen	decrease
collect	rise	smell
sow	flow	roast
harvest	emerge	increase
lay	occur	weave
pick	disappear	become
crush		

4 You could put the students into pairs for this exercise. Alternatively, do the exercise as a quiz with two teams. Ask them to put their answers on the board one by one; the first team to write them all accurately wins. Or you could do it as a running dictation-type activity, but instead of writing the question, they just write the answer on a piece of paper, one for each team.

Answers
1 the sun
2 cereals
3 tea
4 cotton
5 a butterfly
6 flowers

5 Elicit or point out that the sentences are in the active and in the passive. Put an example on the board. Students write the rest in groups on a large piece of paper. When they have finished, ask them to leave their sentences on their table and go around looking at each other's sentences. Tell them to peer correct if necessary. Monitor this process and make a note of any consistent errors for whole class feedback.

Answers

Possible answers

1 The sun rises and goes down every day.
2 Cereals are reaped/gathered to make bread.
3 Tea leaves are harvested to produce a hot drink from China.
4 Cotton is white and is utilized to create a very light cloth.
5 A butterfly comes out of a cocoon to become a flying insect.
6 Flowers are colourful, bloom in gardens and look and smell very nice.

6 Do this exercise as a whole class activity, giving examples where necessary.

Answers

become bigger, grow tall, blossom, appear, come out, fall

7 Get the students to write the matching items on the board to show the relationship between the action and the nature of the noun. Ask them to put these collocations into their vocabulary books.

Answers

seeds: sprout, eat, disperse, sow, plant, transplant, fall

saplings: become bigger, grow tall, sprout, appear

branches: become bigger, grow, prune, sprout, bear

tree: become bigger, grow tall, blossom, appear, bear, grow, transplant, prune, cultivate, plant, sprout

buds: appear, open up

flowers: become bigger, grow tall, blossom, appear, open up, pollinate, grow, cultivate

fruit: become bigger, appear, bear, grow, ripen, fall, harvest, eat, cultivate

8 Ask the students to match the nouns and verbs with the sections of the diagram. This can be done by putting the diagram onto card

which has been cut into sections. The vocabulary can also be put on separate cards. The students then match the parts of the diagram with the appropriate verbs and nouns. Students can now describe the diagram to each other. Monitor them for pronunciation and accuracy.

9 Ask students to complete the text individually. Get whole class feedback.

Answers

1 seeds
2 are planted
3 transplanted
4 pruned
5 trees
6 become bigger
7 leaves
8 pollinate
9 fruit
10 ripen
11 harvested

Listening
IELTS Section 2   Page 78

Lead-in

Set the scene and talk a little bit about the topic. You might like to discuss how conservation projects get funding to introduce the ideas of people paying to stay, donations, being self-sufficient through selling produce or crafts, etc.

Questions 11–20

Go through the 'How to go about it' advice step-by-step, explaining and expanding where necessary. Ask the students to look at the map and locate the entrance first, then each of the letters. Elicit other sequencers they might hear, and also the other points of the compass and where they are. As well as looking at the words in questions 14–17, encourage students to mouth them to help with recognition, but tell them not to say them aloud as they listen, especially in the exam. Look at any other buildings or features that are included in the map. Point out that the places in 14–17 are in the order that they occur in the listening practice. For questions 18–20, remind students to be careful with singular and plural nouns.

Play the recording all the way through once. Then play it a second time, but get them to make any corrections or additional answers in another colour so they can rate their initial performance.

Check by playing the recording and pausing at the relevant places for the answers. Ask students to add up their scores for the first listening and the second listening, reminding them that in the listening practice they only hear it once. They then transfer their answers to a separate sheet of paper or an answer sheet.

Students sometimes find this type of exercise tricky. Play the section relating to the map once again after they have the answers and invite questions.

Answers
11 B
12 A
13 C
14 G
15 B
16 J
17 A
18 views
19 landscape
20 seeds, flowers

6 Fruits and seeds

 1.10

Good morning and welcome to the Fairbridge Countryside and Woodland Centre. I'd like to give you some information about the centre and the short programmes we run for young people on woodland therapy. We're actually a centre run by volunteers, and we were set up 15 years ago to educate people of all ages and backgrounds about nature. And for the past two years we have been taking groups of youngsters in their teens on educational programmes on Fridays, Saturdays and Sundays, em … from schools mainly from around the area, … but some have come from much further afield. Initially the youngsters are not very impressed by the setting because there is no way for them to get in touch with friends, etc. as there is no mobile phone signal, so it throws them quite a bit. But almost without exception, by the end of the three days they're here the young people don't want to leave and want to come back again. In fact, two of the workers here came with student groups five years ago, and when they left school they came straight to work for us.

The centre is self-sufficient due in part to the sales from the nursery and we also get donations, but the bulk of our income is now from running the educational courses.

This is a basic map of the centre. We are here at the entrance to the centre, and you can see the cabins run along the east side of the path as you go north. The first cabin, Oak Lodge, is for students. It's quite large and can accommodate 16 students in bunk beds. Then the next four cabins are for families, and the cabin after that, Ash Lodge, is for teachers, which can hold up to six adults. On the west side of the path, directly opposite the student cabins, are the educational facilities. They are quite up-to-date with all the latest wizardry. And next to that is the cafeteria, which is shared with visitors to the centre. Just beside the cafeteria is a picnic area with climbing frames for children. We don't allow open-air cooking here, because of the trees. The plant nursery is that complex you can see that runs all the way along the north part of the map.

………………………………………………………………

If you go over here, between the picnic area and the nursery, the path leads to the woodland itself. As we are on a hill here, we are quite high up and so you have quite breathtaking views of the countryside. You can see the river stretching for miles through rolling countryside. Fortunately the whole woodland is safeguarded, so nobody can chop down any trees. The landscape here has not changed for hundreds of years. Some of the trees have been growing here a rather long time, and the aim of the centre and the volunteers is to keep it that way. We advise people to stick to the paths, as it's very easy to get lost. As you walk through the woodland you will see workers removing dead wood and chopping down trees. I would ask everyone not to remove anything like seeds or flowers from the woodland so we can conserve it for future generations.

Vocabulary 2: Describing sequences
Page 79

1 Students identify the linking word or phrase which is not used to describe sequences.

Answer
at last

NB *Where* is used to describe what happens at a point in a sequence. The word *when* can also be used in this way.

2 Once students have located the linking words and phrases, get them to put the sentences in order. You could put the sentences on strips and give these to students in groups so they can see the text as a whole in front of them.

Answers
1 If
2 and, then
3 Once
4 then
5 First
6 After that
7 At the same time
The lifecycle of a mobile phone is being described.
5 First, the various internal components like the chip are manufactured in one place.
7 At the same time, the case and the SIM card are produced.
4 These are then shipped to a different factory for assembly.
6 After that they are dispatched to a central warehouse for distribution.
3 Once a device is broken, it is either thrown away or sent for recycling.
1 If it is the latter, the broken components are mended
2 and the phone is then sent for sale.

3 Ask students to identify the transitive verbs and count them for the comparison.

Answers
The manufacturing process

4–6 Again, this is more visually helpful if it is done by matching strips. The words in exercise 5 can then be stuck up on the side. Elicit the verb form for each noun and write it up in a final column. Give the students time to record this in their notebooks.

Answers
4
1 d
2 a
3 c
4 f
5 e
6 b

5
3 c storage
4 f delivery
6 b pasteurization
1 d harvesting
4 f assembly
5 e packaging
6
storage: store
delivery: deliver
pasteurization: pasteurize
harvesting: harvest
assembly: assemble
packaging: package/pack

Writing
IELTS Task 1   Page 80

Photocopiable writing exercise on page 138.

1 First, get the students to match the vocabulary to the relevant parts of the diagram. Let them decide which linking words they will use and where, and elicit what tense they will use. They should then describe the process to each other in their groups. Monitor and check for accuracy and use of vocabulary.

2 Students complete the text with linking words from Vocabulary 2. You might want to see if they can recall the vocabulary without looking back at the section. Remind them to discuss the use of as many alternatives as possible. Check their answers and suggest any possibilities they may have forgotten. Elicit or point out the tense and the active and passive forms.

Answers
1 Once/When/As soon as/After
2 Then/Next/After that
3 where
4 then/next/after that
5 then
6 where

3 Elicit alternatives for the word *step*. Go over any other vocabulary they may not know.

Answers
phase/stage

4 Go over the 'How to go about it' and 'Don't forget!' sections on page 81 step by step. Students write the introduction and the overview for the text in exercise 2. Pay particular attention to the overview as students often leave this out when describing processes. Monitor and get good examples written on the board as a model.

Answers

Possible answer

Introduction: The pictures show how glass is recycled/the recycling process for glass.

Overview: It is clear that during recycling glass goes through a number of stages.

5 Use strictly controlled writing techniques for this stage. Tell them what you will be looking for in particular, e.g., linking words, especially those indicating sequences and logical processes. Give them two minutes to look at the rubric and the diagram and to make notes, including the vocabulary they will use to familiarize themselves with the task, the tense, the verbs, transitive or intransitive, active or passive. Next give them two minutes to write an introduction and an overview, and 14 minutes to write the process. They should spend another two minutes checking and correcting any 'silly errors'.

Ask the students to use the checklist on page 209 to check their answers. Also ask them to look at the marked sample answer.

Collect the students' answers and mark them, focusing on the linking devices, and the transitive and intransitive verbs.

Sample answer

The picture shows how pencils are produced from logs and leads.

On the whole, the process is not only efficient, because all parts of the tree are used but also ecofriendly. First, the seeds are cultivated in nurseries before being planted four months later. After three years the plantation is thinned facilitating the growth and improving the quality of the wood. Once the trees are fourteen years old, they are now ready to be used for the manufacturing of pencils and so are cut down to make logs.

The wood obtained is cut into thin pieces, treated to become dry, and then left sixty days before being used for the production of pencils. At this stage, a groove is cut into the slat and a special

glue is injected. After that, a black lead is put into the slat followed by the placement of an empty slat on top to form a sandwich, which is heated and hard-pressed. By this action the two slats are converted into one piece which is then cut to produce individual pencils which in turn are finally printed, sharpened and stamped before reaching the consumers.

Word count: 192

Possible score: 9.0

Examiner's comment:

This is an extremely fluent and well-realized response. The process is clearly presented. Occasional punctuation choices and overuse of markers slightly diminish clarity, but without impeding communication. A sophisticated range of vocabulary and grammatical structures are both in evidence, demonstrating near-first-language speaker competence.

Review 6 answers Pages 82 and 83

Vocabulary
1 unspoilt
2 conservation
3 dominate
4 scenery
5 panoramic
6 sights
7 spaces
8 protected
9 disappear

Transitive and intransitive verbs
Language focus:

1

Transitive: absorbed, extracted, reducing, carry, collected, provide, needed, sent, treated, purified
Intransitive: falls, runs off, is, rises, occurs

2
Possible answers
1 The sun shines.
2 Rice is harvested and then cleaned, after which it is stored and then sold.
3 Cotton is grown to make cloth. When it is picked, it is woven and made into clothes.
4 Once the fruit is picked and squeezed, it is either diluted or concentrated and then bottled.
5 When a mobile is sold it is used. As soon as it becomes worn out, it is thrown away.

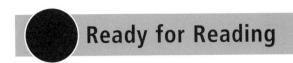
6 The butterfly lays its egg. The caterpillar eats the leaves and makes a cocoon. The butterfly emerges from the cocoon, lays eggs and the cycle repeats itself.

Listening

1

1 We start off here at the bottom of Theed Street.

2 The tour takes us past Wren House on the **left**.

3 We then turn left into Chatham Street.

4 We go past Brompton Palace which is on the north side of the street on our **right**.

5 Just after the palace we immediately turn right into Manor Way, where we stop and look at the building of the College of Music, which is on our left.

6 We then turn **right** into Weston Avenue to look at the old City Hall, which is on the north side of the street.

7 We continue to the end of Weston Street where we go **north**.

8 We then turn left and finish our tour on the north side of the Old City Hall.

Proof reading

1 germinates

2 atmosphere

3 shows

4 lungs

5 seeds

6 countryside

7 Pomegranates

8 part

9 steps

IELTS Academic Reading Module

Scanning a text

Skimming a text

Understanding 'TRUE/FALSE/NOT GIVEN' statements

Understanding 'YES/NO/NOT GIVEN' statements

Reading passage:

    Topic: coastal erosion

    Matching headings

    Multiple-choice questions

    Summary without a wordlist

Recognizing and understanding basic text relationships

Introduction   Page 84

Lead-in

Before students open their books, elicit what they know about the IELTS Reading test. You can ask the following questions:

1 How many sections are there in the Reading test?

2 What kinds of sources are used for the texts?

3 What kinds of skills do you need to employ to answer the questions?

4 Do you need knowledge of specialist vocabulary to do the Reading test?

5 Where should you write your answers as you do the test?

6 What should you do if there are any unknown words that you need to know to answer the question?

Answers
1 three
2 books, magazines, journals, newspapers (any two)
3 skimming, scanning, reading for gist, predicting, reading for detail (any three)
4 no
5 (the) answer sheet
6 guess (from context)

Elicit the question types they expect to find in the Reading test.

Go through the introduction in the Coursebook with the class. Remind them of the importance of not reading the whole text in detail. Tell them that the average native speaker would find it hard to complete the test in the time limit if they did this. Show the links with the strategies employed here and those needed for academic study, if relevant.

Scanning a text   Page 84

Practise the scanning activities, emphasizing their eye movements and likening them to physical muscle exercises. Go on to do the word search in the text. Give them a time limit.

Skimming a text   Page 85

Link the skimming exercises to the skills employed when we first open a newspaper and skim the headlines and sub-headlines.

Understanding 'True/False/Not Given' statements   Page 86

1–2 Go over the TRUE/FALSE/NOT GIVEN activities and elicit any other techniques for answering these questions. Remember that it is the FALSE and NOT GIVEN statements which cause the most confusion.

Answers

1

1 more than (i)

2 more for weapons than (i)

3 only (b)

4 is said to (h)

5 ten (f)

6 destroyed (g)

7 simpler (d, i)

8 all (c)

9 are connected (j)

10 had an impact on (a)

2

1 TRUE. ... *between about 2000 and 771 B.C.*

2 NOT GIVEN. There is no comparison of weapons and ritual objects.

3 FALSE. ... *speak of a series of ancient rulers who invented agriculture, writing, and the arts of government.*

4 TRUE. ... *founding the Xia dynasty.*

5 FALSE. ... *Yu also cast nine sacred bronze vessels.*

6 FALSE. ... *these were passed on to subsequent dynasties.*

7 FALSE. ... *the archaeological record reveals a more complicated picture of Bronze Age China.*

8 FALSE. *Archaeological investigation has confirmed much of the legendary history of the dynasty following the Xia – the Shang.*

9 TRUE *Chinese scholars generally identify Xia with the Erlitou culture, ...*

10 TRUE ... *that greatly influenced material culture in the Shang and subsequent Zhou dynasties.*

Understanding 'Yes/No/Not Given' statements   Page 86

Students discuss the function of the underlined words in pairs.

Answers

1 Comparison

2 Comparison

3 Recommendation

4 Generalization

5 Tentative proposal/possibility

6 Possibility

7 Qualifying adjective

8 Qualifying word

9 Comparison

2 Follow the same procedure for the YES/NO/NOT GIVEN statements as in the previous section. Point out the differences in the language between statements that check the writer's views and claims and the TRUE/FALSE/NOT GIVEN statements.

Answers

1 YES. *Some adults are clearly intimidated by the environment of libraries and bookshops in a way that children are not.*

2 NOT GIVEN. The writer does not pass judgement about which way is the best.

3 NOT GIVEN. The writer does not give any opinion about this.

4 NOT GIVEN. The writer does not pass judgement about any building.

5 YES. *So maybe there is a place for teaching library managers marketing skills.*

6 YES. *This however may be a step too far for some people.*

7 YES. The writer states his opinion by saying: *all of which are worthwhile activities for attracting readers.*

8 NO. The writer states his opinion by saying: *all of which are worthwhile activities for attracting readers.*

9 NOT GIVEN. The writer does not pass judgement.

Reading
IELTS Reading Passage   Page 88

Follow the instructions in the Coursebook. Go through the 'Don't forget!' advice with the students.

Answers

1 viii

2 i

3 xi

4 iv

5 vi

6 ix

7 B. Paragraph A: *There is little doubt that rates of coastal change will escalate with enhanced rates of sea level rise and increasing storminess.*

8 D. Paragraph B: *These techniques are used to determine coastal topography, coastal erosion, and shoreline position with high accuracy.*

9 A. Paragraph D: *Three national agencies (English Nature, the Conservancy Council for Scotland and the Countryside Council for Wales) are responsible for preserving flora, fauna and geological features, including those along the coast.*

10 widespread consultation. Paragraph F: *These decisions cannot be made without widespread consultation.*

11 Coastal managers. Paragraph G: *Coastal managers have to consider not only which parts of the coast they should attempt to defend ...*

12 traditional constructions. Paragraph G: *using traditional constructions, such as sea-walls, dykes, groynes and breakwaters.*

13 isolation. Paragraph H: *Whatever approach is used, no section of coast should be studied or managed in isolation.*

Recognizing and understanding basic text relationships   Page 91

Before you do this section, let the students quickly discuss in pairs the different types of text they know, and the kinds of relationships we can find in each one. Emphasize the importance of recognizing these connections, i.e. problem/solution, cause/effect and looking for synonyms within the text and between question and text.

Answers

1 The text is about cause and effect.

2 Cause

3 viii (methods–solutions); vi (techniques–methods/solutions); ix (integrated approach/solution). Note paragraph A (X factors–causes)

4 No. They use other words. See the words in brackets in 3.

5 It is the effect. B is the cause.

6 It is the cause.

7 The word *answers*.

8 It is based on cause/effect and problem/solution.

9 It is historical.

10 Possible answers: classification, argumentative, explanation and process.

Content overview

Themes

This unit is concerned with work, training and educational assessment.

Exam-related activities

Reading

Topic	Assessing MBA students
Question type	Matching names and statements
	Completing sentences
	Global multiple-choice

Listening

Topic	A presentation
Section 3	Selecting items from a list
	Completing sentences
	Answering questions

Speaking

Part 2	Describing a school/an achievement
Part 3	Discussing aspirations/opportunities

Writing

Task 2	Describing advantages and disadvantages

Other

Language focus	Conditionals 1
Vocabulary 1	Work
Vocabulary 2	Collocations

Speaking
IELTS Part 3

Page 92

Lead-in

Elicit what we mean by *training* and how it differs from *studying* so students understand the meaning of learning for a specific skill or trade. You might want to talk about the part that training plays in education in general and the more traditional concept of *apprenticeship, in-service training, work placement* or *internship*.

1   Ask the students to look at the photos and discuss what is happening in each one. Explain any unknown vocabulary that might arise.

Answers

1 learning how to sail
2 training at work
3 school education
4 learning how to play a musical instrument

2   Follow the instructions in the Coursebook, or put the students into groups to answer at least one question each. Give them five minutes and monitor, checking they have understood what the questions are asking. Let them choose one person from each group to give feedback to the whole class.

To help students you might want to talk about how to begin their answers as follows:

In the recent/distant past/One generation ago/ Several generations ago …

It is crucial/important, because …

First of all, they can …

Nowadays … but in the past …

In the recent past …

Also encourage students to develop their answers giving reasons, examples, results, etc. Remind them not to use personal examples. You may want to encourage them to give feedback, using the Speaking checklist on page 210.

Vocabulary 1: Work   Page 93

1   Students do the activity in pairs. Check answers as a whole class. These are commonly confused words and students may need time to assimilate the nuances of meaning in context here:

work: a general term to talk about employment as a whole
job: particular work you do in order to earn money
occupation: mainly found on official forms to mean your job
profession: a job needing special training
career: work undertaken as a life-time plan
qualifications: examinations passed in order to do a particular profession
livelihood: the way you earn money in order to live

If they're still having problems, refer them to a good learner's dictionary or thesaurus.

Answers

1 livelihood
2 work
3 job
4 job
5 profession
6 profession
7 job, career
8 job

2 Discuss the question as a whole class.

Answer

It is possible to use *occupation* in sentence 3.

3 Go over the words and phrases, making sure students understand what they mean, then let them discuss in groups, giving examples.

Reading

IELTS Reading Passage   Page 93

Remind students of the rules for skimming the questions and, if there is no heading, to look at the last question and then skim the passage, or skim the passage first. Discourage them from reading the text in detail at this stage. However, encourage them to read the text at the end to see how much they have been able to extract by skimming, scanning and using the questions.

Questions 1–5

Go through the 'How to go about it' advice. Ask students to put a box around the names of specific people in the text, using the capital letters of the names to find them quickly. Tell them to look at the statements and underline key words, and then scan the text to find synonyms.

Questions 6–12

Ask students to decide on the required part of speech and to predict the word or type of word.

Question 13

Encourage students to underline key words. They should be able to answer the question using the information they have collected about the reading passage.

Students should time themselves. Remind them after 15 minutes that they have five minutes left. Allow extra time if the students have not finished. Ask the students to put a mark against the question they reached at 20 minutes. Encourage them to write their answers on a piece of paper or on an answer sheet as they do the test. Point out that they should pay particular attention to spelling, especially singular and plural nouns.

Tell the students to go over the answers in pairs, marking any changes they make during their discussion with another colour. Check as a whole class. Let them mark on their reading grid any problem areas.

Answers

1	B
2	E
3	H
4	D
5	A
6	traditional exams
7	team
8	teamwork
9	practical work
10	opinion
11	stressful
12	verbal presentations
13	A

Reacting to the text

Students could discuss the questions in pairs or groups of four. Get whole class feedback. Tell them to add any new vocabulary to their vocabulary books.

Listening

IELTS Section 3   Page 96

1–2 Follow the instructions in the Coursebook.

Questions 21–30

Go over the 'Don't forget!' advice and let students read the questions. Play the recording once and let them check their answers with a partner. They should listen a second time using a different colour pen to mark any changes in their answers. Play the listening a third time, pausing at each answer to note where it is in the text and why it is the correct one. Ask them to transfer their answers to a sheet of paper or an answer sheet. Remind them that they should pay particular attention to spelling, especially singular and plural nouns.

Answers

21–25	B, D, E, F, H in any order
26	information
27	foolish
28	nerves
29	good
30	questionnaires

7 The world of work and training

 1.11

T = Tutor; J = Jack; O = Olivia

T: We've got some time left for a feedback tutorial on your joint presentation today, if you have time.

J: Yeah, we can do it now while it's fresh in our minds.

T: So, Olivia, how do you think it went?

O: Well, em … I was really happy with it actually, but I'm glad it's over. I think the main advantage of doing the presentation was that we both learnt quite a lot about training and skills development for the workplace and how they improve people's opportunities in life.

J: And we learnt a lot from delivering it as well.

O: Yeah that was important too. Mmm … as I said, I was pleased with it, but if I had to do it again, I'd change a few things.

T: Like what?

O: Well, mm <u>the first thing I'd do is improve the speed of the talk by making the delivery slower</u>. And I'd keep a clock in front of me so that I was aware of the speed and … and the next thing is mmm … the length of the talk … <u>I'd make the presentation time 20 minutes for each of us, because I think ten minutes was much too short</u>. If we had given ourselves more time, it would have flowed better.

J: Yes, I agree. I thought the timing was a bit tight. I'd say maybe even 30 minutes each.

T: Mmm … 30 minutes might have been a bit long for both you and the audience.

J: Maybe you're right; 20 minutes is probably better.

O: And the next thing is <u>connected with the order of the data</u>. I thought the sequence was bad – it could have been a lot better.

T: Yes. If I had to give some particular advice, I'd say you need to give yourselves a run through once or twice using the equipment, just to see what it's like. Doing it without preparation like that is not that easy.

O: No it isn't. We were a bit stupid there. And another thing for me is that <u>we forgot to</u>

<u>give out the handouts</u> with the copies of our slides on them for people to take notes. <u>I should have given them out before we started</u>. And one final thing is … is I'd check that everyone can see the screen properly as a few people were sitting in awkward places, so <u>I'd check the arrangement of the chairs in the room</u>.

T: And Jack. What about you? How did you feel about it all?

J: Well, mmm … I agree with Olivia. Yeah … in everything she said. It's very difficult to make the delivery smooth. If I do it again, I'll spend more time practising to make it run more smoothly.

....

T: But would you add anything to what Olivia said?

J: Er … perhaps <u>I'd try not to pack too much information into the time given</u>. Em … I thought at first it would be the opposite. Em … <u>I was afraid that we would end up looking foolish</u>. And also I think I'd spend less time on the information gathering phase because unless people devote time to practising, they won't give a good performance.

T: Yeah, I think I'd agree. Anything else?

J: Yeah. I get very nervous when I speak in front of people. Were I to do it again, I'd make sure I practised speaking. I think the key for me is learning to reduce my <u>nerves</u>.

O: But you were very calm!

J: Not inside I wasn't!

T: Well, it didn't show.

O: I think you need the nerves to keep you going, but maybe try to take your mind off it beforehand by exercising or something.

T: Is that everything?

J: Yeah.

T: OK. Well, you'll be pleased to know the feedback from the class questionnaires was <u>good</u> from everyone, so well done. I have to say that I agree with them.

O: Oh, thanks.

T: And after the tutorial I'll make a copy for both of you of the <u>questionnaires</u> from the class, if you want. And if you do give a talk again, you can keep them to refer to.

Language focus: Conditionals 1

Page 97

1 Ask the students to identify the tenses in the sentences. Make sure that they understand the relationship between the two parts of the sentences and that they can name the different types of conditionals. Review the conditionals, and refer the students to the Grammar reference on page 223.

Answers

(3) If we'd given ourselves more time, it would've flowed better.

(2) ... but if I had to do it again, I'd change a few things.

(1) If I do it again, I'll spend more time making the delivery smooth.

2 Let the students do this exercise individually and go over it together, answering any questions they may have about the structure. There may need to be some reference made to the passive and active voice here. Make sure the students are clear about the grammar before moving on to make sure they don't get confused as they move to the freer activities that follow.

Answers

1 are given
2 had been devoted
3 will find
4 had worked
5 will turn out to be
6 will decline
7 would succeed
8 had

3 Monitor the students to ensure they are giving explanations. This will help prepare them for structures they may need in Part 3 of the speaking module. You may want to ask the students to use words like *because*, *for example*, *so*, *but*, and *like* in their explanations.

4 Do this exercise as a written activity, checking carefully for accuracy and helping where necessary.

5 Follow the instructions in the Coursebook.

Answers

1 **Unless** the educational process ...
2 Had there **not** been ...
3 ... I **would** have been born ...
4 If people did**n't** have ...

5 **If** some adults had ...
6 Had universities **been** permitted ...

6 Ask the students to choose two of the questions to ask their partner. Get them to ask and answer the questions, swapping roles as they go on. Monitor and check the use of the structures and relevance to the questions. Ask one student to give his/her answer to question 1 to the whole class. Repeat the process with different students for the remaining questions.

As an alternative, you can ask the students to work in groups. Encourage them to use the conditional sentences as part of their explanations.

7 Students discuss the question in pairs.

Vocabulary 2: Collocations   Page 98

1 Follow the instructions in the Coursebook. Encourage the students to put the noun and their collocates into their vocabulary books. Note that the collocates may come immediately before or after the noun, or later in the sentence.

Once again, refer the students to a good learner's dictionary if they are having difficulties. Native speakers automatically 'feel' which one does not collocate, but your students may not be able to do this yet. Unfortunately, often there is not a logical explanation as to why one word collocates and another does not.

Answers

1 make
2 education
3 silver
4 large
5 get
6 enjoy
7 achieve
8 accrue
9 take up
10 possess

2 Students should do this in pairs so they can discuss the choices. Suggest they identify the main noun first and then look through the alternatives from exercise 1 to decide on the other choices. Go over the exercise with them when they have finished.

Answers

1 success, guaranteed
2 failure, long-term, prospects, damaged

3 deserves, chance

4 improvement, scope/room

5 disadvantage, considerable/huge advantage/ benefit

6 benefits, accrue

7 represents, achievement

8 once-in-a-lifetime opportunity, seized

3 You could start this with the opportunity they now have in studying for IELTS and the reasons that led them to do so. Explain *thrown away* if necessary.

Speaking
IELTS Part 2   Page 99

1 After explaining what the students have to do, time them as they make their notes within one minute. Monitor and check they have written no more than the ten words required by the instructions. You could give them an example on the board:

piano exam

14

read music

enjoy other instruments/singing

2 Get students to look at the words from the previous section and see which ones they could incorporate and where.

Put the students into pairs and ask them to practise timing each other (1–2 minutes). Students should give feedback using the checklist on page 210. As before, the students can choose one or more criteria they would like to be assessed on. Monitor the students and make notes on good phrases you hear and phrases to correct at the end.

Writing
IELTS Task 2   Page 99

Photocopiable writing exercise on page 138.

1 Get the students to read the task and questions 1–4 which follow. Elicit the answers as a whole class activity.

Answers

1 Yes.

2 You don't have to devote equal space to each side. See 3 below.

3 You can have two ideas on each side or two advantages and one disadvantage or vice versa. Try not to write a list of ideas.

4 You need to use connecting words, but try not to overuse them. That is just as bad as not having any.

2 Ask students to read the text and underline the words from the vocabulary exercise as they find them. They should check the answers with their partners.

Answers

achievement, considerable benefit, gained, distinct, obvious, disadvantage, opportunities, enjoy success, seize opportunity

3 Give the students five minutes to come up with the synonyms from the text and go over the answers with them. Explain any answers where there was a shade of meaning that was not quite right for the given context.

Answers

assessing/examining: testing/evaluating/checking knowledge

preferred: most popular

various means: various forms/a range of alternative methods

while: although

methods: approaches

enormous: vast

derived: gained

angle: point of view

on the other hand: conversely

be appropriate for: suit

use: manipulate

4 Explain the exercise to the students and give an example of the first one to assist them. Monitor carefully, making sure they are doing it right. If possible, put the text with the answers in a different colour onto a transparency and project it onto the board.

a result: ... *then* it is easier to check it on a written paper than in a group problem-solving exercise/ Switching to written tests could *then* be problematic.

a condition: *if* factual knowledge is being tested/*if* they were asked to take a more practical exam.

a contrast: *However*, the obvious disadvantage of written tests is that they do not suit everyone./

Conversely, students used only to written tests would be at a distinct disadvantage.

an example: *For example*, from an administrative point of view, the former are generally easier to *deal with./Take students in Italy where oral exams are used as a means of checking knowledge.*

5 Students complete this exercise in pairs. Ask them to write their answers on the board as they finish.

Answers

1 ... practical. Moreover, it ...
2 ... vogue. However, knowledge ...
3 ... acquired. Take texting for example. This ... , but it ...
4 ... experience. Furthermore, skills ...
5 ... learnt, then ...

6 Ask students to read the task before going through the 'Don't forget!' advice step by step. Tell them to brainstorm their ideas individually before comparing in pairs or groups. Ask them to mark their ideas with an A and a D and then select which ones to include in their answer.

Students can either do this as a timed essay in class or at home. Ask them to note where they are in the essay when the 40 minutes are up. Remind them to check for 'silly' errors within the time. Ask them to use the checklist on page 209.

Sample answer

These days a wide range of courses can be studied at schools and colleges to create skilled workers to feed the economy. Builders and plumbers find courses that suit their individual educational background and their vocational needs and the skills required. However, while this certainly help the economy, there are some disadvantages to just concentrate on skills that fit particular jobs and not providing a more wider education.

The benefit of focusing on skill to fit particular jobs is saving time and then money. A quick glance at the range of careers we realise that many do not require years of studying in classroom. So then there is no reason why training tailored to the exact needs of the trainee and the economy should be provided. It might even seem ludicrous to some to spend huge amounts of money reaching a point which can be hit by far less effort on the job rather than in the classroom. Take for example IT workers specially trained to deal with specific areas of work, so an all round education for them does not appear to be necessary according to this way of thinking. They can learn on the job.

There are a few drawbacks, however. If the emphasis is placed on skills at the expense of more general knowledge that they pick up from books and studying more widely, then pupils or students are missing out on knowledge they need to live and work in society in general. For example, they may not learn about the history or literature or about geography. And how the world works in general. This will lead to other problems for people. Their lives will not be fulfilled. So I think it is important for people to learn skills and more general knowledge.

Word count: 296

Possible score: 7

Examiner's comment:

This response makes some ambitious lexical and structural choices. The markers employed seem a little limited, resulting occasionally in uneven expression. However, the range of vocabulary and structures attempted give this response an individual voice, despite some imprecise grammar. On balance, communication is not seriously impeded.

Review 7 answers Pages 102 and 103

Vocabulary

1
1 e
2 b
3 h
4 c
5 d
6 f
7 g
8 a

2
1 What qualifications are needed for the job? (livelihood)
2 Work is good for you both mentally and physically. (job)
3 He earns his living by making very delicate carvings in wood. (profession)
4 Working as a farmer is a very noble profession. (qualification)
5 The job I'd like to do in the future will have to be connected with social work. (profession)
6 Having an occupation like teaching is very demanding, but also rewarding. (career)
7 I would like to have a career in engineering if possible. (work)

8 I'm interested in a career in finance, especially banking. (occupation)

3

Possible answers

1 huge
2 gained considerable
3 (an) enormous
4 improved
5 squandered/thrown away
6 (a) distinct
7 room
8 impressive

Conditionals 1

1

1 If, would have succeeded
2 If, will need
3 If, won't succeed
4 If, encouraged
5 otherwise, will be
6 would be
7 If, will cause

2

1 Had they followed the guidelines, they would have succeeded.
2 New technologies need to be embraced with open arms; otherwise, the country won't progress.
3 Unless more effort is put into the scheme, it won't succeed.
4 Were the government to encourage more people to take up training, it would benefit us all.
5 If more houses aren't built, there will be a crisis.
6 I'd be very surprised if we were ever to inhabit the moon./If we were ever to inhabit the moon, I'd be very surprised.
7 Written exams should never be removed from the education system; otherwise, it will cause enormous upset.

Proof reading

1

opportunities, dissatisfied, relaxed, quite, Moreover, environment

2

1	Correct	7	qualifications
2	achievement	8	flexibility
3	Correct	9	conversely
4	improvement	10	Correct
5	Correct	11	Correct
6	career	12	excessive

8 The history of geography

Content overview

Themes

This unit is concerned with maps, places and migration.

Exam-related activities

Reading

Topic	Cartography
Question type	Matching sentence beginnings and endings
	Completing a table
	Selecting items from a list

Listening

Topic	Human migration
Section 4	Completing notes

Speaking

Part 2	Describing a special place

Writing

Task 1	Describing maps

Other

Language focus	Referring in a text
Vocabulary 1	Nouns relating to places
Vocabulary 2	Verbs relating to changes in maps

Vocabulary 1: Nouns relating to places   Page 104

1   Ask the students to look at the maps and explain the origins of each one after they have looked at the similarities and differences.

Answers

1

1 Eurocentric map: shows the world from a Eurocentric perspective.
2 Ptolemy's map: shows the world as it was at that time.
3 satellite aerial map of South America: shows the features of South America from space.

2   Refer the students to a dictionary or thesaurus if they need help, but try to encourage them to see how much they can do first. Then ask them to explain the meanings of the words as far as they can. Do not expect them to be able to give the meaning of all of the words.

region: a large area of a country or the world

zone: an area that is different from others around it

district: a particular area of a city or country

neighbourhood: a small area where people live near each other

area: a part of a country/town, etc.

vicinity: the area around a place. The focus is on the place, not the people. Compare the word 'neighbourhood'.

location: a particular place or position

space: an area that is available to be used or an area that is empty

Answers

2

1 neighbourhood/area, area/neighbourhood
2 place, spot
3 district, zone
4 location, region
5 area, space
6 vicinity, neighbourhood
7 places, regions, spots
8 setting, region

3 Let the students try this in pairs without any help from you initially. Monitor and explain any specific words they may not know, e.g., *teeming*, *pounded by*, *crags*. Go over the exercise as a whole class, showing photos if possible. You might like to add that the noun *crag* can be used as an adjective *craggy*, and *covered with trees* can become *tree-covered*.

Answers

1 b
2 a/d
3 d
4 c
5 h
6 e
7 i
8 h/j
9 a/g/i
10 b/f

4 Ask the students to look at word order and establish which words the italicised ones are referring to first (e.g., where there are adjective and noun combinations) and if there's a complete clause. You may want to do a quick review of basic word order. When the students have completed the exercise, ask them to put their sentences on the board for peer correction and discussion of how the language flows.

Answers

1 overlooking a small garden, neighbourhood with old buildings, disturbed only by the sound of birds and the odd car
2 stretching for miles along the seashore, with plenty of opportunity for lots of boating and swimming, built two hundred years ago
3 surrounded by beautiful mountains, with its purple flowers
4 a waterfall falling from a great height surrounded by trees, covered with trees but with views looking out

Speaking
IELTS Parts 2   Page 106

1 Elicit the questions from the students and correct any errors of pronunciation, stress or intonation. Let them do the exercise in pairs. Monitor for accuracy and use of the new vocabulary.

2 Put students in new pairs, and repeat the activity. Monitor the students as they speak.

3 Drill the students using the example so they can hear where the stress patterns occur. Demonstrate where stress falls in a sentence by first isolating the stressed words:

went   nice   place   sea   yesterday

Ask the students if they can understand what the speaker wants to say. Then isolate the unstressed words:

we   to   a   by   the

Ask them if they can understand what the speaker means now.

Elicit that the stressed words are generally words like nouns, verbs, adverbs, adjectives, and that the unstressed words are generally 'functional' words (i.e. the glue that sticks the sentence together). Of course, there are instances in contrastive stress where this might not be the case.

Answers

```
          o         o  o        0        o
1 I was living in a small flat when I first came here,
          o
  but then I …
          o        0      o  o              o
2 We stayed in a nice hotel overlooking the sea,
          o
  because …
```

```
         o     0  o              o
3 The place is very special to me, because it …
       0        o         o
4 The place I'm going to describe for you is …
     o      o        0      o
5 I like the area very much, because it's …
```

4 Drill the sentences in exercise 3 with different students in the class.

5–6 Follow the instructions in the Coursebook. Let the students work in pairs and let them take control of this activity. Ask them to time their partners taking the notes and time them as they speak. Ask them to check their partner's notes when they finish to make sure they are as brief as possible. Encourage them to check the rhythm of their partner's description.

Listening

IELTS Section 4   Page 107

Lead-in

Elicit whether Section 4 is a monologue or a dialogue. Review the skills the students need to employ when listening to this type of test. Ask them to underline the words in the questions that will warn them that they are about to hear the answers. Make sure they look at the information after the gaps as the information in the test may be the other way round. Also remind them to look at two questions at a time if they can, in case the answers come close together or are switched slightly in the text. Remind them also not to worry about any big gaps which can sometimes occur between the answers.

1 Elicit that lectures are usually organized like a written text with an introduction, several points with examples and support, and a conclusion. Discuss with the students the linking devices and sequencers used to signal the stages of the talk. These will help them identify when one topic (main idea) is ending and another beginning:

If we look at the first slide …

If you look at this second slide …

Now in this map on the next slide …

Before we look at …

I'd like to look at …

If we look at the map of Africa here on this next slide …

The speaker will usually introduce the main topic at the beginning (*Well, today we are going to look at early human migration out of Africa to colonize the world.*), and often give an outline of what secondary topics are to be covered in the introduction.

When students have done the listening test, ask them to look at the Listening script on page 232. Ask them to mark any devices they think will help guide them through future listening tasks.

2 Elicit that the subject is a history of migration, and find out what the students know already about the subject generally. Ask them the reasons for early man migrating and the geological influences. Pre-teach *AD* (vs *BC*) if necessary and *steppes*. Elicit that there are three main sections to the talk and ask how they know this.

Answer
The migration of humans over time.

3 Let students work through each of the questions here in pairs and emphasize that this is good practice and should be done anytime they meet these task types.

For question 2, tell them to be careful not to put an *s* onto adjectives before plural nouns.

For question 5, ask 'How can seas be crossed?' Tell them that they can predict the answer, but that they will still have to listen as there are several possible answers.

Check answers as a whole class.

Answers
1 31 number
32 noun
33 number
34 noun (phrase)
35 noun (phrase)
36 number (fraction or percentage)
37 noun
38 noun (place)
39 noun (phrase)
40 noun (phrase)
2 35 and 39 are likely to have plural nouns
3 31 and 33 relate to time
4 37 relates to a reason for something
5 35
6 36

Questions 31–40

Play the listening through once and monitor to see how the students perform. Play again if necessary and go through it with the class. Remind the students that unlike Sections 1–3 in the Listening module, there is only a pause of about five seconds in the middle, so they have to look at all of the questions 31–40 together before they listen. For this you need to train them to skim the questions quickly, analyze what is required and underline words to 'scan' the information in the listening test. Ask the students to transfer their answers onto a piece of paper or an answer sheet.

Answers
31 100,000
32 temperature
33 45,000
34 land mass
35 (simple) boats
36 30/thirty percent/per cent/%
37 yam
38 Sudan
39 work fields
40 military advantage

8 The history of geography

 2.1

Well, today we are going to look at early human migration out of Africa to colonize the world.

Throughout history there've been waves of humans migrating as people have moved from one locality to another, sometimes quickly over very short distances … and sometimes slowly over very great stretches of land, mmm … in search of a new or different or better life. There now appears to be general agreement that the first movement of people of any real significance in any part of our planet originated in East Africa about <u>100,000 years ago</u>. If we look at the first slide here, we can see the route this first group of modern humans took as they made their way across the Red Sea here, which was then a dry bed. Then through Arabia and into what is now the Middle East. But these early pioneers soon died out.

<u>But at that time, just like today, the earth was subject to shifts in temperature. About 70,000 years ago the planet became warmer</u> and another group of modern humans migrated out of their homeland of Africa, following basically the same route, and then moving on to South Asia. If you look at this second slide, you will see here that by about 50,000 years ago modern

humans had colonized China, and about <u>45,000 years</u> ago they had reached Europe. These early humans settled in the wide open spaces of Siberia about 40,000 years ago. And this line here on the map shows that about 20,000 years ago modern humans reached Japan, which as you can see from the map on the slide, was connected to the main <u>land mass</u> at that time.

Now, on this map on the next slide you can see that there was no land connection between Australia here and South-east Asia here, so the first Australians who arrived around 50,000 years ago must have made the journey across the sea in <u>simple boats</u> to settle on the Australian continent, as evidence shows here, here and … here on the map.

This next map shows the route which modern humans took from Asia to North America, which as you can see was reached across what is now the Bering Strait through Alaska. This migration happened between 15 and 13,000 years ago. There is also some evidence to suggest that modern humans came across pack ice via the North Atlantic, but this theory has been discounted by some. Since that time, the American continent has been the destination of waves of human settlement.

....

Before we look at more modern examples of human movement, like the Anglo-Saxon migrations to Britain in the 5th century AD, the migration of Turks during the Middle Ages and the migration of the Irish to America in the mid-19th century, I'd like to look at a migration within the continent of Africa itself, that I'm personally very interested in.

If we look at the map of Africa here on this next slide, we can see some patterns that are common to other waves of human movement throughout history. The routes here show what is probably the most significant migration in Africa itself: that of the Bantu, who spread out from a small region in West Africa near the present day border of Nigeria and Cameroon, just around here on the map … to occupy roughly <u>30 per cent</u> of the continent by the year 1000 AD.

A trigger for this movement may have been the result of cultivation of the <u>yam</u>, a starchy root vegetable, which Bantu farmers started to grow as part of their staple diet. This cultivation began around 2750 BC, resulting in the expansion of the population. The Bantu people then spread out into the neighbouring territories, which were then sparsely populated.

As the land of the rainforest could not sustain the farmers and their families for longer than a few years, they moved on, felling trees and creating new clearances in the forest to cultivate yams. With the numbers of the Bantu on the increase between 2500 and 400 BC the people were constantly on the move, migrating south down through modern day Congo … here in central Africa, and reaching Zimbabwe here and modern-day South Africa by about 100 AD.

It was contact with <u>Sudan</u> in north Africa that introduced the Bantu to iron production, in which they excelled. Once they had exchanged knowledge of working in iron from Sudan, the quality of their work rivalled that produced by the Mediterranean people of the time. The Bantu now had better tools to fell trees, clear forests and <u>work fields</u>. And there is one other benefit iron gave the Bantu, and that was a <u>military advantage</u> over their neighbours.

I'd say that migration has transformed the world from early times, and we all reap the benefits of different peoples coming into contact with each other.

Language focus: Referring in a text
Page 108

1 Do this exercise as a class activity. Point out that the words in bold are synonyms which are used to refer back to a previous noun or noun phrase.

Answers
1 this first group of modern humans, they
2 the earth

2–4 Go through the explanations here carefully so that the students grasp the difference in use between *it* and *this*. Pronouns like *it* and *these* refer to the last nouns before they occur. The pronoun *it* has to have something specific to refer to, while *this* and *that* can focus on the last idea mentioned or a whole sequence of ideas up to a paragraph. Refer the students to the Grammar reference on page 223.

Answers
2
1 The neighbourhood
2 the region
3 The cost of farming has increased dramatically over the period.

3
The nouns would need to be in the latter part of the sentence or the whole sentence. They are too far away from *this* to refer to.

4
It is not really possible to work out what *it* refers to: *cost/farming/period/*the whole sentence or part of the sentence. If you keep the word *rise*, the phrase *This rise* refers to the latter part of the sentence from *increased* onwards. If you use *this* on its own, it can refer to the same part of the sentence or the whole sentence.

5 Let the students complete this individually and then compare in pairs.

Answers
1 It
2 That, it
3 This new development
4 it, it
5 This
6 they, This
7 those
8 these areas

6 Ask the students to do this in pairs, and then write their sentences on the board for peer correction and discussion.

Answers
1 The price of property in this region is increasing and **it/this** is set to continue.
2 The neighbourhood was poor once but **it** is rich now.
3 I like visiting the seaside when nobody is around. **It** is very relaxing.
4 If people make an effort to clean up after themselves when **they** visit parks, then **these places** will be much more inviting for the public in general.
5 He suggested I should go away for a couple of days. **This** is okay, but **it** is an expensive solution.
6 The government should pass laws to protect more areas of great natural beauty. **This** would benefit all of us.
7 Progress cannot be stopped. **It** is inevitable even if **it** is very slow and **it** stops altogether for a while. But **this** is unlikely to happen.

7 You could also do this as a whole class discussion. Use this exercise to generate ideas which may be useful in a Task 2 writing or a Part 3 speaking task. There is a similar discussion in Vocabulary 2 exercise 6 with useful phrases, so you might just like to do a quick brainstorming here rather than an in-depth discussion.

Reading

Page 108

Photocopiable reading exercise on page 139.

1 Follow the instructions in the Coursebook. You might like to give them a time limit, e.g., five minutes. Go over the exercise as a class.

Answers
1 complex
2 abstract
3 images
4 overtones
5 indigenous
6 posterity
7 secular
8 artefacts
9 profound
10 compile

2 In groups of four, students share the ideas they now have about the text.

Questions 1–13

Give the students 20 minutes to do the test. By this stage, students should be trying to skim the questions first and referring to the text, not reading the text from beginning to end first. You may want to let the weaker students skim the text first, although they will need to learn to move very fast if they are to get a good score so skimming the passage twice may be counterproductive.

For questions 1–5, go through the 'How to go about it' advice. Encourage the students to locate the items in the sentence beginnings in the text and put a box around them. Then ask them to focus on the endings A–G and underline words to scan in the boxes for information. For questions 6–11, check that the students are predicting word type for the gaps. Encourage them to write their answers on a piece of paper or an answer sheet as they do the test.

Go over the answers carefully at the end of the test.

Answers
1 C
2 E
3 F
4 G
5 D
6 time, space
7 bark
8 cosmos
9 plan
10 expeditions
11 clay tablets
12 and 13 B, E in any order

Reacting to the text

Discuss the question in small groups.

Vocabulary 2: Verbs relating to changes in maps   Page 111

1 Follow the instructions in the Coursebook and help the students with any unknown vocabulary. Check the answers and point out the use of the passive in six of the sentences.

Answers
1 g
2 b/c/d
3 a
4 b/c/d
5 b/c/d
6 e
7 a/f

2 Do the first one as an example and then let the students complete the exercise individually. Check answers around the class.

Answers
1 was extended
2 expanded
3 was constructed
4 completely changed/was completely changed
5 became
6 took place, altered
7 became
8 was developed/developed

3 Ask the whole class to feed back when they have completed this activity (they may have fun making up completely new non-existent words!).

Drill the pronunciation on these with the /ən/ endings.

Answers	
-ation:	alteration
-ition:	demolition
-sion:	extension, expansion, conversion
-tion:	construction
-ment:	development

4 Students continue working in pairs and then write the sentences on the board for peer correction and comment. If necessary, give an example of what to do: *1 There was an extension of the railway to the centre of town and three new stations were built.* Clear up any misunderstandings with word order and meaning here.

Answers

1 There was an extension of the railway to the centre of town and three new stations were built.

2 As the town expansion took place/happened/ occurred, all the open spaces were used up for housing.

3 The construction of an airport took place/ happened/occurred on a greenfield site on the edge of the town.

4 There was a complete change in the neighbourhood/A complete change in the neighbourhood occurred/took place/happened with the building of new apartments.

5 Not possible

6 A number of dramatic developments took place with the complete alteration of the character of the town.

7 Not possible

8 The development of the empty space near the university into a park took place/occurred.

5 Write the sentence with the alternatives on the board and let the students select the one they think is correct from the choices. Discuss why the alternatives are not appropriate. (Basically because they are the wrong register for an academic essay).

Answer

The area underwent a complete transformation over the period.

Writing
IELTS Task 1   Page 112

Lead-in

Elicit the points of the compass and show these on the board. Review adverbs of place with the students and list them. Remember that for some cultures it is natural to use the points of the compass to describe location, but for others, less so, and they might use prepositions of place instead.

Give students a map or use the one provided to make five sentences about buildings or places on the map but not stating which particular building they are referring to. Ask them to read the description to their partner who has to guess what each building/place is.

1–2 Follow the instructions in the Coursebook. Monitor for correct use of the target language and question forms.

Answers

1

1 A residential area is located <u>in the north-west</u> of the town.

2 <u>In the north and east</u> of the residential area, there are several derelict warehouses.

3 <u>South of the warehouses</u> in the north are located some offices./Some offices are located <u>south of</u> the warehouses in the north.

4 <u>West of the river and south of the</u> residential area <u>is situated</u> the Arts Centre./The Arts Centre is situated west of the river and south of the residential area.

5 The university is sited <u>in the north-east, west of</u> the woodland./<u>In the north-east, west of</u> the woodland is sited the university.

2

6 The shopping centre is situated in the south-west of the town.

7 There is a residential area in the south-east of the town.

8 The industrial complex is located in the centre, east of the river.

9 In the north-east (corner) of the town lies a woodland.

10 In the middle of the woodland in the north-east of the town there is a pond.

11 The school is located east of the river and west of the industrial complex.

3 Designate Student A and Student B in each pair. Do the pairwork as it is set up, checking that the students have the right information at each stage, because if they have made any errors it will have an impact on the subsequent step. Ensure students do not just look at each other's maps, but that they use the language as required.

Answers
1 Residential area
2 Shopping centre
3 School
4 Lake
5 Hotel
6 Railway station
7 Industrial zone
8 Park
9 Industrial wasteland
10 Entertainment area

4–5 Ask the students to complete the activities individually and then check their answers in pairs.

Answers
4
1 True
2 False
3 True
4 True
5 False
6 True
7 True
8 True
9 True
10 True
5
1 A hotel was built in place of the hospital in the west of the town./In the west of the town a hotel was built in place of the hospital.
2 The university gave way to a park.
3 An entertainment area was built on the site of the public gardens in the south-east of the town.
4 The school in the west of the town did not change.
5 The park was turned into an industrial wasteland.
6 The fields on the south-west border of the town were given over to an industrial zone.
7 The quarry just south of the centre of the town has become a lake.
8 The coach station in the centre of the town was reconstructed to become a railway station.

9 A shopping centre replaced part of the residential area/was built in the north of the town.

10 Overall, the town has undergone an urban transformation.

6 Go through the 'Don't forget!' advice for the writing task carefully. Do the exercise as a timed writing in class.

Ask the students to check their answers against the checklist on page 209. Ask them to peer correct if they do the writing in class.

Sample answer
The maps illustrate the changes that took place in Lakeside between 2000 and 2009.
It is clear that there was an almost complete transformation of the town of Lakeside with a significant decrease in the residential area by the end of the period. The residential neighbourhood in the southwest of the town were changed into a shopping centre and the industrial complex expanded to replace the residential are in the south east. While the woodland in the northeast of the town shrank and the lake became a small pond.
The old town and the derelict warehouse in the north were knocked down and a car park and offices were constructed. The arts centre was converted to a multiscreen cinema. In the west of the woodland a new university was built. The school was relocated to the centre of the town.
All in all, the maps show that Lakeside became more organized with less green area.
Word count: 161

Possible score: 6.5

Examiner's comment:

Some effective lexical choices and language structures are in evidence. The salient points are covered, although better sentence coordination might have helped this read less mechanically. Any grammatical and orthographical errors (e.g., subject-verb agreement in line 7, 'are' for 'area' in line 9) do not seriously impede communication.

Review 8 answers Pages 114 and 115
Vocabulary
1 place
2 Correct
3 region

4 zones

5 spaces

6 Correct

7 vicinity

8 district

Speaking

1

1d 2e 3a 4b 5c

2

And why it is this place so special for me? Well, I think it's because it is really peaceful over there. I can sit for hours without seeing anyone, just gazing into the distance space; it is so relaxing. There are no any noisy streets with the car radios and people, only a peaceful riverbank surrounded by trees and flowers with the only sounds be those of the birds and the river flowing down through the wood. I am often wonder how long it will stay like that.

3

      o o   o   O   o

1 The place I'd like to describe is a hillside covered ...

    o   o   o o   O

2 A place that's special for me is a mountain with ...

    o o   o o   O o

3 The place I like the best is a park stretching ...

    o   o   O   o

4 It has to be a forest teeming ...

    o   o o   O   o

5 I'd like to tell you about a valley surrounded ...

Referring in a text

1 It

2 they

3 This

4 this/it

5 It, this, It, These/This, it

6 This, This

Proof reading

1 illustrates (illustrate)

2 tranformation (transformation)

3 substituted (replaced)

4 chopped (knocked)

5 surrounding (surrounded)

6 change (changes)

7 (were) erected

8 turned (into) offices

9 territory (area)

10 increase (increased)

9 What is beauty?

Content overview

Themes

This unit is concerned with beauty, architecture and beautiful surroundings.

Exam-related activities

Reading

Topic	The architect, Giles Gilbert Scott
Question type	Completing sentences
	Classification
	Selecting items from a list

Listening

Topic	Discussion of a student project
Section 3	Multiple-choice questions
	Completing sentences

Speaking

Part 2	Describing your favourite building
Part 3	Discussing beautiful surroundings/ concepts of beauty

Writing

Task 2	Agreeing or disagreeing with a statement

Other

Language focus	Modal verbs for evaluating
Vocabulary	Beauty
Word building	Prefixes under- and over-

Vocabulary: Beauty   Page 116

1 In groups, students describe the buildings and decide which country they come from. Check their answers as a whole class activity.

Answers

1 I.M. Pei's Louvre Pyramid in Paris, France

2 Zaha Hadid's Innsbruck railway station, Austria

3 modern skyscraper

4 the tombs at Petra in Jordan

5 modern social housing

Students discuss the questions in the same groups as before. Encourage them to give their reactions to the buildings and discuss their feelings about them, giving opinions on beauty. Ask them to compare the buildings with buildings and monuments they are familiar with and like.

2 Ask students to rank the buildings individually and then compare similarities and differences with the others in their group. They should discuss and justify their choices.

3 Students complete the statements with their own ideas.

4 When they have successfully done this exercise, ask them to transfer the adjectives to their vocabulary books.

Answers

A tall, ancient, spacious, high, stone

B evocative, overawed, melancholic, thoughtful, dazzling, humbling, beautiful, magnificent, impressive, overwhelmed, emotional, ecstatic, overjoyed, nostalgic, majestic

5 Ask the students to do this activity individually and check their answers in pairs. Ensure they understand the vocabulary and the context the words are used in.

Answers

1 beautify

2 humble

3 emotion/awe

4 melancholy

5 evoke

6 think

6 Students work in groups of three and transform three chosen sentences. Re-group and have one student from each group share their transformed sentences. Alternatively, get each group to put their transformed sentences on an OHT or the board to share with the whole class. Where they chose the same sentences, ask the students to compare answers.

Answers

1 They tried to make the town centre beautiful by putting flowers …

2 … the Sphinx was very humbling/filled me with humility.

3 The sight of the Himalayas made me feel emotional./The sight of the Himalayas moved me …

4 … that I love sometimes makes me melancholic …

5 … my home country, they are evocative of so many memories …

6 … wandering through the ruins made me thoughtful about life …

7 Elicit what we mean by *national monuments* and give some examples from other countries, e.g., Arc de Triomphe in Paris, the Victory Monument in Bangkok. If you have a mono-lingual class, you can also select examples from countries other than theirs. Write the following

expressions on the board and encourage students to use them:

What makes/made/has made (the monument) important to people in my country is …

I chose this monument because …

(The monument) makes people feel …

Students share their ideas with a partner.

Listening
IELTS Section 3   Page 118

1 Explain the activity and, as ever, remind the students how important prediction is for successful listening.

Answer

The project is about the photographs he took of India.

2 Ask the students to work in groups and share their knowledge first before using a dictionary. You can clarify any doubts now or wait until after they have heard the words and phrases in context. If the students want to know the definitions, concept check by getting them to give you examples in sentences as a round-the-class activity. Drill all the words for pronunciation.

Answers

1 perception: way of looking at things

2 collage: arrangement/random collection of items

3 take in: understand/absorb

4 grandeur: magnificence

5 digital stills: digital images

6 narrow down: limit

7 access: get into

8 discipline: control

9 fade: weaken, become pale, disappear

10 click: select (on a computer)

Questions 21–30

Go through the 'Don't forget!' advice carefully. The students can work in the same groups or individually and you can give them any explanations they need or want.

Play the listening once all the way through. Ask the students to transfer their answers to an answer sheet and check spelling, especially as regards singular and plural and the apostrophe with the possessive. Go through a second time to check, pausing at the answers. Ask the students to count up and record their scores.

Answers	
21	A
22	C
23	A
24	B
25	C
26	time limit
27	attention span
28	department website
29	project('s) background
30	4/four

9 What is beauty?

 2.2

T = Tutor; M = Malcolm

T: Hi Malcolm. How are you?

M: Fine, thanks. And you?

T: Yes, I'm OK. You left a message when you booked this tutorial to say that you wanted to talk about your film project. Am I right?

M: Yeah.

T: So, how can I help you?

M: Well, I'm having difficulty getting started. I should have been about halfway through about now, but I haven't done anything at all really. I think I'm feeling a bit overwhelmed.

T: Overwhelmed? In what way?

M: Mmm … I don't know. I may have chosen something too abstract.

T: Which is? Remind me … ?

M: It's 'Perceptions of beauty in India'.

T: Yeah. That's a good subject; it's probably quite challenging, but very appealing.

M: I wanted to put together a moving digital photo collage of my travels around India last summer showing the beauty of the place. I was completely overawed.

T: How many did you take in all?

M: At least 600.

T: That is a lot. I'm sure it's a wonderful photographic record, but I think your problem lies there. Can you tell me? What did you take photographs of?

M: Buildings like palaces and official places like the government buildings in New Dehli by Lutyens – I think they're really underrated. People just think of the Taj Mahal and poverty, but India's not all like that. It's huge: it's got tradition, colour and beauty at every corner. I've also got some dazzling images of places like the Ganges at Varanasi; the grandeur and splendour of the images simply take your breath away.

T: OK, I have a suggestion.

M: Yeah?

T: What about going through your digital stills on the computer and selecting the ten images which appeal to you the most? And …

M: I don't know if I could narrow it down to that.

T: Well, you'll be surprised. Select the top hundred, and then narrow that down to 25. And then you could …

M: I've just thought of an idea.

T: Yes?

M: I could mmm … Yes that's it! I could select the top ten as you suggest, and then find various people's views on these … and then do a video collage with the pictures swirling around like a pop video. Why didn't I think of that before! That's it!

T: Problem solved?

M: Yes, but now I have to do all the work!

....

M: Can the film be longer than 15 minutes?

T: I wouldn't advise it. There might have been a few people on the course last year who made 20-minute, or even 25-minute films, but I have to say they were the least successful. I think you'll find that it's good discipline to try to work within a time limit.

M: Mmm …

T: And I'd say that ten minutes might be good …

M: Ten minutes! That's almost nothing.

T: You'll be very surprised. One minute per place fading out and in. It could be very effective. Remember the work we did on adverts and the short attention span of people generally, especially these days.

M: Yeah, I suppose you're right. I'm just thinking of all the materials – 600 plus stills down to ten, and then reduced to a ten-minute film. What about the format? How do I need to submit it?

T: Mmm … all the information is on the <u>department website</u>. You access it as per usual.

M: What's it under?

T: Go to 'Digital Photography'. Then 'Year One', and then click on 'Film Project', and everything is there. And don't forget you have to fill in a submission form detailing <u>the project's background</u>.

M: Yeah, I … I know all that. But can't I just email it to you when it's done?

T: You can. But we also want copies burned on DVD, … <u>four copies</u> are needed with the submission form.

M: OK, I can do that.

3 Students discuss the questions in pairs or small groups. This might lead on to a discussion about films like *Slumdog Millionaire* or other mainstream or art-house films about specific places and impressions.

Word building: Prefixes *under-* and *over-*   Page 119

Photocopiable word building exercise on page 139.

1 Elicit other examples from the students using *over-* and *under-* as prefixes. Explain that they sometimes, but not always, have a negative connotation. As the students do the activity, get them to identify the adjectives that are not negative (6, 9, 10). Ensure they understand the meanings before moving on. Get them to add the vocabulary to their vocabulary books.

Answers
1 underestimated
2 overrun
3 overrated
4 undervalued
5 overcome
6 overtook
7 underfunded
8 underrated
9 understated
10 overawed

2 Give students sufficient time to do this exercise and explain clearly, demonstrating with an example of your own and with reasons. Monitor to make sure the students are using the target vocabulary correctly.

Speaking
IELTS Part 2   Page 120

1 Get the students to look at the discourse markers and point out that these should be used in both writing and speaking. Using a variety of these markers effectively will enhance their cohesion in both these skills. Show how some of the markers can go at the beginning or in the middle of two clauses, but others generally do not go at the beginning.

Check that the students understand the phrases before getting them to write the sentences. Point out that they can use the negative words to emphasize the appeal something has to them by contrasting their positive attitude, feelings, etc. with something negative.

2 Get the students to read out their sentences to the class. Monitor for correct stress and structural accuracy and correct as necessary.

3 Follow the instructions, checking to see which sentences they decide to use. Monitor the groups for extended language, encouraging their use of the phrases. Make sure you encourage the students to use the **Useful expressions**.

4–5 Tell the students they should put their notes to the previous activities away before embarking on the actual test practice. Ask students to time each other strictly on the note-making and the actual task. Let them check their original notes when they finish. Ask the students to use the checklist on page 210 to give feedback on each other's work. Point out they do not have to give feedback on everything and that they should be constructive. Suggest extra practice for any students who are still not making concise notes and who are not keeping to time or extending their language use.

Speaking
IELTS Part 3   Page 121

Put the students into groups for this discussion at first, to pool ideas. Go through the 'Don't forget!' advice with the class. Ask half the class to discuss the questions on 'Beautiful surroundings' and the other half the questions on 'Concepts of beauty'. Then pair them up with one from each half and conduct the interview as in the exam with one as the 'examiner' and the other as the student.

Ask them to switch roles. This way they both get ideas for the two topics.

Reading

IELTS Reading Passage   Page 121

1–2 Ask the students to work in groups and follow the instructions in the Coursebook. Monitor the information they come up with and give input as necessary.

3 Give them no more than five minutes to scan for the antonyms.

Answers
1 fused
2 familiar
3 beloved
4 romanticized
5 obfuscating
6 showed youthful promise
7 ingenious

Questions 1–13

Look at the 'How to go about it' tip as a guide for questions 7–11 before completing the reading task. Give them a time check after 15 minutes. Remind students to write their answers on a sheet of paper or an answer sheet. Ask the students to go over the test in pairs first and then as a whole class, ensuring they all know where the correct answers are in the text.

Answers
1 industrial structures
2 architectural heritage
3 conservative
4 (very) advanced
5 green
6 (popular) success
7 B
8 C
9 A
10 A
11 B
12 and 13   A, D in any order

Reacting to the text

Complete the task with the discussion.

Language focus: Modal verbs for evaluating   Page 124

1 Explain this use of modals for assessing situations and ask them to provide examples in their own lives when they should or shouldn't have done something. Refer them to the Grammar reference on page 224.

2–3 Follow the instructions in the Coursebook. Students work in pairs. Go over the answers when they have finished. Ensure they understand the reasons for the choices which could be either structural or semantic.

Answers
2
1 should
2 could have
3 might have
4 might
5 must
6 could be
7 should be
8 ought to
9 must
3
1, 2, 4

4 Do this exercise as a class activity so they fully recognize the function of each of the modals in the context of the sentences.

Answers
a conclusion: 5, 9
a criticism: 1, 2, 4
a regret: 4
an expectation: 7
a suggestion: 8
a possibility/weak suggestion: 6

5 Put the students in groups and ask them to choose someone to take notes and someone to give feedback to the whole class. If you have a multi-national class, group the students according to country or make sure each group is from a different country. If you have a mono-national class, group them according to region. Alternatively, just get the students to discuss the town/city they are studying in if they have been there long enough to have obtained some local knowledge.

Give the students 15 minutes to discuss the task. Monitor and encourage them to use the modals and vocabulary previously studied. As the 'reporters' report back, encourage the other groups to notice where ideas are similar or different from their own so they can comment when it's their turn using terms like *We agree/We differ* ..., etc.

Writing
IELTS Task 2

Page 124

Lead-in

You might like to expand on this topic by using all the vocabulary from the start of the unit and discussing different architectural styles. You could bring in some photos of, e.g., Khmer, Chinese and Japanese styles of architecture, as well as more Western styles like Palladian, Art Deco, Gothic, etc. Remember to accommodate all your students' backgrounds if possible. You could ask each student to bring in a photo of a building to discuss in groups. When students have discussed their photos in their groups they can swap photos with other groups. You can ask them to vote on the three most popular buildings.

1 Do the first one together as an example. Some students may need time to decode the words; however, this is a very useful exercise for enhancing reading skills. They have to do four things here: separate the words, identify the linkers, and put the two sentences in order identifying cause and effect as they do so (either with or without signalling words).

Answers
1 Everything in the physical world around us makes an impression on us directly or indirectly, and so neighbourhoods in many cities where people live are being made more appealing.
2 People are able to see and appreciate different cities all around the world thanks to cheap travel and the Internet.
3 Some countries are now becoming richer than in the past, leading to pride in their national standing.
4 For example, a park was opened and trees were planted and then suddenly the health of the people in that district of the city improved.
5 The lack of space has saved many old buildings with planners turning to renovation rather than erecting new buildings.
6 As a result of turning old ruins into gardens, people are happier and are now more productive.

2 Follow the instructions in the Coursebook.

Answers
a 1 cause b, effect a
2 cause b, effect a
3 cause a, effect b
4 cause a, effect b
5 cause a, effect b
6 cause b, effect a
b Cause:
2 thanks to
Effect:
1 and so
3 leading to
4 and then
5 with
6 As a result of
c In sentence 2 the prepositional phrase *thanks to* indicates the cause without any linking device. In sentence 3 the gerund is used to show a result and in sentence 5 the effect is contained in the prepositional clause beginning with the preposition *with*. In 6 the prepositional phrase *as a result of* introduces the cause.
d In 4 the word *then* could be left out.

3 Point out that the boxes **A** and **B** are mixed so sometimes a word/phrase from box **A** might fill the first gap, and sometimes from **B**.

Answers
1 shouldn't have relaxed, As a result there are
2 should be attractive, thanks to,
3 Thanks to/With, now lighten up
4 has a positive effect, which in turn
5 With/Thanks to, are focusing on

4–5 Ask the students to discuss the topic in pairs. Get them to write the essay in 40 minutes, either in class or for homework. Remind them to use the checklist on page 209. Ask the students to look at the sample and discuss it as a whole class, using the writing checklist. At this stage in the course, they should be seeing an improvement and should have fewer areas for attention than in the beginning.

Sample answer

Enormous importance has been laid on making school children aware of the natural environment in recent years. Many people now feel that more time should be given to the part architecture plays in our lives. Children are sometimes overwhelmed by information about the nature and it is perhaps learning about the built world is a good counterbalance.

I think knowledge of the built environment is important for everyone, but especially school children. For example, if children learn to distinguish different types of buildings like those from before, it will help them learn about its part in the history and it will bring it into the life. Children can go visits to see buildings for themselves rather than learning about them from books. In this way both buildings and history will be brought to life.

The importance of old buildings where the children live or pass through on the way to school will be brought home to them. They are then less likely want to damage them by writing graffitti on the building or damaging them in some way. In this way, they will grow learning to respect the built environment in same way as the natural world.

Learning about the built environment can introduce children to areas of study that they might not otherwise be interested in. Studying buildings also involves the way that they are laid out and gives children the appreciation of the way towns and cities are designed, which may lead to an interest in infrastructure like town-planning or transport or designing open spaces or squares.

So learning about built environment will help in children's general education.

Word count: 270

Possible score: 7.5

Examiner's comment:

Ideas are logically organized and supported by appropriate examples. Despite some ungrammatical phrasing which impedes communication, overall a sophisticated level of grammatical expression is displayed with good paragraphing and transitions in evidence. The lexical choices are skilful, although the conclusion is somewhat abrupt.

Review 9 answers Pages 126 and 127

Vocabulary

1

1 a, e
2 d
3 c
4 b

2

1 Part 3. It is abstract.
2 Part 2. It is personal and describing something.
3 Part 1. It is personal.
4 Part 1. It is personal.

3

1 beautiful
2 thoughtful
3 evocative
4 nostalgia
5 humbling
6 melancholic
7 impression
8 ecstasy

4

2 … made me think.
3 The old town evoked a bygone age.
4 I was very nostalgic when I looked at the photographs.
5 … Angkor Wat filled me with humility.
6 The building filled me with melancholy at first …
7 The city of Tokyo was hugely impressive the first time I visited it.
8 … they have the power to make people feel ecstatic.

Word building

1

1 The last time I visited the **magnificent** city of Pompeii it left me cold. It was so **overrun** by tourists.
2 The photographs of my home town brought back lots of **memories**. I was really overcome by **emotion**.
3 The countryside around where I was brought up is very **bleak**, but I am still **overawed** by it each time I go home.
4 The vast open spaces of the Steppes are **beautiful**. Their beauty is so **underestimated**, perhaps because it is so difficult to get there.
5 The architecture of the railway station is not **understated**; it is just **plain** and subtle. That is why it is appealing.

6 The preservation of the architecture of former times reflects the traditions and values of a nation. When such precious national items are **undervalued** by people generally, it unfortunately leads to them being **underfunded** or not supported financially at all.

7 If tourist attractions are **overpriced** it puts people off visiting them. So the main way to attract tourists and increase revenue is to make the cost of travel to and from the attractions **cheaper** and reduce the entrance fees.

2 Students' own answers

Modal verbs for evaluating

1
should be
shouldn't have been demolished
ought to have been preserved
could have erected
should now make
might have started

2
1 A criticism: shouldn't have been demolished; ought to have been preserved; might have started
2 An expectation: should now make
3 A weak suggestion: could have erected
4 A recommendation: should be (sensitive)

IELTS Academic Writing Module
Task 1
Describing a graph
Describing a bar chart
Describing a table
Describing a process
Describing a map
Task 2
Common question types

Introduction   Page 128

Optional lead-in

Before the students open their books, read out the statements below and ask the students to say whether they refer to:

1 Task 1
2 Task 2
N Neither
B Both

1 You should start writing the essay as soon as you get the paper.

2 No specialist knowledge is required.

3 It is usually a description of a chart, graph or table.

4 You should plan for 3–4 minutes, and leave 2–3 minutes for checking.

5 You should summarize and include significant information.

6 Notes may be made on the test paper.

7 You may be required to give your opinion.

8 Answers in note form are acceptable.

Answers
1 N
2 B
3 1
4 2
5 1
6 B
7 2
8 N

Read through the introduction with the class. Answer any questions they may have regarding both tasks.

Task 1 Page 128

Elicit the strategies to be employed in Task 1 and the time needed for preparation before writing, and for checking. Elicit the 'trend' or descriptive vocabulary they need to use, and link them to the different chart types, e.g., a (line) graph, bar chart, pie chart, table, process, diagram or map.

Describing a graph   Page 128

1–2 Follow the instructions in the Coursebook.

Answers

1
All except 5 and 18.
2
generally speaking
a gradual fall
the dramatic decrease
contrasted with the steady recovery
latter part of the period
an upward trend
peak at
proportion

3 Students do the activity in pairs and then work with another pair to compare their answers before whole class feedback.

Answers

1 A better overview would be:
Generally speaking, there was a variation in the trends for the four groups (downwards for children of 0–4 and 15–19 years; and upwards for those aged 5–9 and 10–14) with the decline in the birth rate, which was evident in the 0–4 group, being the most striking feature.

The structure with *despite* does not work, as there is no real contrast between the decline in the birth rate and the contrasting trends.

2 Yes. *In the youngest age group, there was an increase during the first two years from just below 26% in 1990 to about 26.6% in 1992 followed by a gradual fall to 23.5%, the lowest percentage in 2001./Looking at the former group, the percentage peaked at approximately 26.4% in 1997 but the final proportion (about 25.4%) remained greater than the initial (nearly 24.6%).*

3 The student summarizes the information. See the overview and the second sentence in 2 as examples.

4 Yes. *Regarding the 15–19 age group, By contrast, Looking at the former group, As regards the latter*

5 *despite the two contrasting trends, the most striking point, In the youngest age group, the lowest percentage, can be contrasted with/the latter part, By contrast/the former group, greater than, the latter, the greatest*

6 There are more nouns: *an increase, a gradual fall, the dramatic decrease, the steady recovery.* It makes it easier to summarize and to compare and contrast.

7 *peaked at, increased*

8 *children of 0–4 and 15–19 years, those aged 5–9 and 10–14, the youngest age group, the 15–19 age group, children aged 5–9 and 10–14, the former group, the latter, the children in this category*

4 Do the writing task as a timed activity in class and peer correct.

Describing a bar chart   Page 130

1 Get the students to write their sentences on the board for this. Compare and choose the best ones as a whole class.

Answer

The chart provides a breakdown by gender and occupation of employment information in the United Kingdom ranging from managerial to basic posts in 2007.

2 Follow the instructions in the Coursebook. Ensure students give valid reasons for their choice.

Answer

Overview 2, because it contrasts both males and females and the types of jobs.

3 Students work in small groups as suggested. Discuss answers as a whole class.

Answer

Managerial and senior officials: 2, 3, 6, 7, 8, 9, 10, 13
Professional: 2, 5, 6, 7, 8, 13
Associate professional and technical: 2, 6, 7, 8, 13
Administrative and secretarial: 2, 3, 4, 6, 7, 8, 13
Skilled trades: 2, 3, 6, 7, 8, 10, 11, 13
Personal service: 2, 3, 6, 7, 8, 13

Sales and customer service: 2, 3, 6, 7, 8, 13

Process, plant and machine operatives: 2, 3, 4, 6, 7, 8, 10, 13

Elementary: 1, 2, 5, 6, 7, 8, 13

4 Do the writing task as a timed activity in class and peer correct.

Sample answer

The bar chart gives approximate percentages of a Labour Force Survey in the United Kingdom by gender and occupation (9 different categories) in 2007. The research reveals striking variations between both sexes according to the post.

The most obvious differential was in administrative and secretarial posts in which the proportion of women was four times higher than men, just above 20% (by far the highest figure in the table) and just under 5% respectively. By contrast, the proportion of men (nearly 19%) was 9 folds bigger than women (approximately 2%) in skilled trades.

Managers and senior officials showed more men with 19% than women at 11%. There was only a 2% difference between men and women in professional employment where men accounted for 19% of the workforce compared to women at 17%. Meanwhile, women (21%) occupied more associate professional and technical jobs than men (13%).

In conclusion, all employment varied according to sex and occupation with men being employed in professional jobs with women being in more clerical posts.

Word count: 167

Possible score: 7.0

Examiner's comment:

Not all the data from the table is mentioned and the analytical focus is skewed towards male employment, but overall the answer is reasonably effective and coherent. Language structures are confidently handled. Markers are employed appositely. The range of vocabulary is flexible and, on the whole, accurate.

Describing a table   Page 131

1 Ask students to do this individually and then compare answers in pairs.

Answers

Asia, Africa, Population density

2–3 Students complete the exercises in their pairs. Tell students that the words and phrases in exercise 3 are not in the order in which they appear in the text. Get whole class feedback.

Answers

2

compares, features (not figures), show, life expectancy, as regards, Turning to North America, stood

3

1 standing at

2 among those studied

3 despite having

4 turning to

5 was second

6 exceeded

7 with a higher total fertility rate of

---

4 Put the students in groups and get them to write the overview on a large sheet of paper, or an OHT if possible. Peer correct, and discuss the different overviews as a whole class.

Describing a process   Page 132

1 Let students work through the exercise and discuss the answers as a whole class.

Answers

1 At either point.

2 The sun's rays.

3 It is pumped around. See the Controller on the diagram.

4 It warms up. The colour changes.

5 It controls the flow of water around the system.

6 It flows down into the pipes/into the tank.

7 Yes.

8 They are two separate systems.

9 No

10 Yes

2–5 Put the students into groups, and get them to write their answers, one question per group, on the board to share and discuss.

Answers

Possible answers

2

heat up, warm (up), cool, pump, push, flow (down/through/out of), rise (up), come out of, repeat, go round

3

first(ly), first of all, second(ly), then, next, after that, afterwards, subsequently, following that, when, where, and so, as a result, consequently, finally

4

The diagram shows how hot water is produced in the home using solar energy.

5

The process involves a series of steps from feeding cold water into the tank to producing hot water for domestic use, including heating.

6   This can be a timed writing in class, or if you're short of time, a self-study activity.

Sample answer

The diagram shows how the solar energy can be used to heat water in the domestic field.

To heat the water, two separate immersion loops are fitted in the tank; the top one is connected to the boiler while the one at the bottom is a part of the 'Solar Heating System' (SHS). Both are heated up by the flowing hot water inside them which in turn heats the tank water indirectly.

The pump circulates the water in the SHS with the flow rate according to the received signals from the controller. As the cold water is piped up to the solar collector, thermal energy is captured from sun's rays and transferred to the pipe. Subsequently, the heated water is directed down to the bottom immersion loop for heating the tank water to provide hot water through the taps and for heating. The cooled water then returns to the pump and the cycle repeats itself.

The incoming cold feed fills the tank up as the hot water is taken out via hot water taps. This way the steady flow of hot water to the taps is assured.

Word count: 187

Possible score: 8.5

Examiner's comment:

Well organized with very confident use of sentence structure. Very broad vocabulary range and good language resource overall. Both active and passive verb forms are used fluently and to good effect. Relevant markers are introduced appropriately.

Describing a map   Page 134

1   Students look at the verbs and identify the tenses; look at the nouns and elicit the verb forms.

2   Students can do this as an individual activity and compare their answers in pairs.

Answers

1 changes
2 took place
3 became
4 turned into
5 had been replaced
6 development
7 relocation
8 urbanization/changes
9 were demolished
10 construction
11 conversion
12 expansion

3   Students do this activity as a timed writing exercise, either in class or for self-study. Refer them to the checklist and the model text.

Task 2   Page 136

Elicit the strategies employed in analyzing the title and in making a plan. Discuss the timings for this task and emphasize the importance of checking for 'silly mistakes'.

1   The students decide on the key words and the focus of the essay.

2   Divide the board into two sections and get the students to come up and put the ideas under the appropriate heading on the board: *local* or *(inter) national*.

Answers

Local: can see the results, charity begins at home, help needed in own country, poverty relative, money often badly spent, want to help specific areas/'pet projects', see value

(Inter)national: people more needy elsewhere,

international administration costs

(Inter)national and local: difficulty tracking expenditure, people weary of appeals, depends on the charity, people's aims, makes them feel good

3 Divide the class into groups, giving two groups the same question. The students brainstorm in their groups, following the instructions in the Coursebook, and then pool their ideas with the other group with the same question. Divide the board into three. Students put their ideas on the board to share with the class.

4 Follow the instructions in the Coursebook. If possible, put a template on an OHT for them to mark the punctuation on when they have finished.

Answers

Nowadays there are demands on both parents to work and look after their children at the same **time**. **For** this reason I think that children should be sent to school early, **but** during the first years priority should be given to play rather than to formal **study**.

Play is **crucial because** it develops **children's coordination, communication** and social interaction **skills. For example**, if children are throwing a ball to each other the physical and mental skills required are sophisticated as eye to hand coordination is involved. **Furthermore,** children develop a sense of communication and socialize with each **other. The** mental and physical development brought about by these games must also be taken into **account. And** what is **more, while** playing children compete with each other and learn to **lose, which** is as essential as learning to succeed in **life. Children** fully engaged in play activities from an early age under their **parents' supervision** gain various skills that they will need in their **adulthood**.

5 Do the exercise orally as a whole class. Discuss the difference in focus of the two questions.

Answers

Essay question 1

6 Check as a whole class when they have written the numbers next to the text.

Answers

1 The writer's opinion: *For this reason I think that children should be sent to school early but during the first years priority should be given to play rather than to formal study.*

2 Reasons: *... because it develops children's coordination, communication and social interaction skills./Furthermore, children develop a sense of communication and socialize with each other.*

3 A complex sentence with a condition and example: *For example, if children are throwing a ball to each other the physical and mental skills required are sophisticated as eye to hand coordination is involved.*

4 Additional information: *which is as essential as learning to succeed in life ... /Furthermore, children develop a sense of communication and socialize with each other./And what is more, while playing children compete with each other and learn to lose*

5 A contrast: *However, in modern society both parents need to work ...*

6 A purpose: *... in order to afford the increasing cost of living and to ensure a bright future for their families.*

7 Recommendations: *schools should focus more on play to compensate for the lack of play experience they may miss at home. Teachers in nursery and reception classes and even in the first years of primary school should take ...*

7 Do this as a timed writing exercise in class, if possible. Tell the students you will be focusing on the reasons for their ideas and complex sentences when you mark their answers. Refer them to the checklist and the sample answer.

Sample answer

Health is very important for people. In some countries there are two main types of health care systems, the state and the independent. Some people have argued about the private health care sectors, but both providers have one great purpose, which is to keep public healthy. In my opinion, the state and the private health care systems have many benefits and some disadvantages.

Firstly, it is essential that all children have free health care, because all countries have to have healthy next generation. Secondly, there are some dangerous transmitted infectious diseases like VD, which have to treat by the state. Thirdly, in the modern world many patients are suffering by blood cancer for instance, this is worldwide problem. In this case no doubt about, free treatment.

The private health care is paid for separately, usually through the insurance. This sector is

---

expensive and do not easy accessible to everybody, but provides faster and better quality services than state system. For example, in England patients are waiting for their operations a few months, while in the private hospital the same treatments waiting time is about 4–5 days. Moreover, in some cases people are purchasing one-off treatments because of the government financial deficits. In addition, a fast diagnostic system and relatively treatment at the early stage of some diseases could be is much more effective. These services always do not offer the free clinics, because they are crowded.

To sum up, people always worry about their health problems .To address this public concerns, patients should have high standard the state or private health care services, which provide the effective treatments for all their patients.

Word count: 272

Possible score: 6.0

Examiner's comment:

Ideas are presented quite coherently and logically with some flexibility and precision of vocabulary in evidence. The question focus is on private care, but this response compares and contrasts the two systems, concluding rather unconvincingly. Good use of markers, but ungrammatical phrasing in paragraphs three and four causes strain on the reader.

10 Is it art?

Content overview

Themes

This unit is concerned with the arts, graffiti, describing a work of art, and involvement in the arts.

Exam-related activities

Reading

Topic	Graffiti
Question type	Summary with wordlist
	Classification

Listening

Topic	A news report
Section 2	Answering a question
	Selecting items from a list
	Multiple-choice questions
	Completing sentences

Speaking

Part 2	Describing your favourite work of art
Part 3	Discussing the arts and funding

Writing

Task 2	Agreeing or disagreeing with a statement

Other

Language focus	Defining and non-defining clauses
Vocabulary	Art

Speaking
IELTS Part 3 Page 140

1 Before looking at the photos, brainstorm different art forms and types of artists to build up some background vocabulary. Don't give any input yourself at this stage as this comes up in more detail in the Vocabulary section. Look at the photos and see which ones the students have already thought of, and discuss the ones they haven't. Ask the students about famous local, national and international artists from the past and present.

Answers
1 painting
2 architecture
3 cinema
4 dance
5 theatre

Extension

Ask students to name their favourite artists, and then to vote on the best one.

2 Divide the class into groups and allocate a question to each group. Give help with ideas and vocabulary as necessary.

3 Regroup the students so there is at least one from each of the previous groups in the new groups, if possible. Follow the instructions in the Coursebook. Monitor and check if the assessments are accurate. When you have finished, give whole class feedback.

Further practice

Set one of the questions from exercise 2 as a writing exercise for homework at a later date.

Page 141

1 Elicit vocabulary concerning art exhibitions, especially regarding the types of exhibits. Note that the second question concerns the 'kind' of opinions people in general might have, not just the opinions of the students themselves. Point out that they are looking at the opinions in the abstract.

2 Ask the students to scan the questions and underline words that will help them identify the answer as they listen. Point out that, as a general rule, they should look at information after gaps as the detail on the recording may be in a slightly different order.

Questions 11–20

Play the listening through once. Ask the students to check their answers in pairs and then check the answers with the whole class. Now play the recording straight through a second time, or pause at the answers for them to check and understand. Answer any questions that come up about vocabulary.

Answers
11 a sensation
12–14 A, D and F, in any order
15 A
16 A
17 B
18 reporters
19 test
20 department store

10 Is it art?

 2.3

Welcome on this lazy Saturday morning to Radio Hope here in Australia. This is Davy Chester, your host on your favourite show *Your Chance*, and boy do we have a lot for you on the show this week. There's the new Street Art exhibition; a new exhibition, which opened last weekend at the Horn Gallery in George Street, and which has caused <u>a sensation</u> judging by our email survey. And then we have the decision by the government to make all museums and art galleries free of charge from next January. And for families and kids there's the new theme park, which has opened just outside the town.

But first to the Street Art exhibition. We've had many people saying how brilliant the exhibition is, and others saying what a load of rubbish it is, and <u>that public money was being misspent</u>. Apart from the criticism regarding the waste of money, some people complained that the exhibition would <u>encourage graffiti and vandalism</u> all over town. I put this point to Mrs Cook, the director of the art gallery, which, incidentally, I visited myself on Thursday evening, and she said that graffiti was already appearing without the Street Art exhibition. Some people who emailed in said that <u>instead of promoting graffiti, the gallery could have used the opportunity to support local artists</u>, who get no help from the council. And Mrs Cook did point out that when there were attempts to remove the huge mural based on Aboriginal art at the end of Coin Street there was a huge public outcry – thousands of people turned out to stop the authorities removing the mural, and there was a vigil with volunteers for three weeks until the local council reversed their decision.

While I was at the exhibition, I asked Mrs Cook what she thought about the decision to make all museums and art galleries free of charge. She said that there had been a fierce debate about this over the past year or so, because <u>people were deterred from visiting places of a cultural nature like the Horn Gallery because of the cost</u>. And while children were able to get in free, they rarely came with their parents, and this was a bad thing. So, basically, she was for the change. <u>From the email survey we've had on the show website, I think about 70 per cent said that they would agree with Mrs Cook</u>, only ten per cent were very definitely against and 20 per cent said they didn't know, which I think reflects the national consensus, give or take a few points.

Now, er … <u>when I spoke to Mrs Cook she said that there was one thing she and other people working in the gallery world were worried about and that is the level of government funding</u>. They have always had subsidies from the government to run the galleries, but this was always topped up by entrance fees. They're waiting to see if this will be reflected in the government's arts funding for next year.

....

Now, as you all know, we have been wanting to do a walk-about on the show for a long time, and this week for the first time we will have <u>two reporters</u> on the street. We have one reporter, Angie Hunter, standing by outside the Horn Gallery with Mrs Cook to <u>test</u> opinions on the Street Art exhibition itself. And we'll see what people really think about their art galleries being free or not. To make sure we get as wide a spectrum of people as possible we have another reporter, Alex Grey, who's standing outside the <u>department store</u> in White's shopping precinct in the pedestrian area. So, if you are listening and want to make your views known, pop down to the precinct or the gallery. We'll be starting the walk-about in 15 minutes at 12.45, after we have got through the other items today, so …

Vocabulary: Art   Page 142

1   Ask the students to do this exercise in pairs and check with another pair to see how many people they can come up with. Put the types of art forms across the top of the board and get the students to write up the people associated with each one underneath. Fill in any they missed. Check pronunciation, especially *sculptor/sculpture*, *percussionist*, *choreographer*, *distributor* and *contributor*, checking the last two in particular for correct stress. Ask the students about any local or national art forms that are not mentioned here. For example, is the word *symphony* familiar to them? Are there dance forms other than *ballet*?

Further practice
You could extend this into a discussion about outside influences or local/national influences at an international level.

Answers
Possible answers
1   play: actor, actress, lead (role), playwright, director, producer, costume designer, set designer
2   orchestra: conductor, musician, pianist, violinist, percussionist

3   novel: novelist, writer, author, reader, editor
4   book: novelist, writer, author, reader, editor
5   newspaper: journalist, columnist, editor, printer, contributor, reader
6   sculpture: sculptor, artist
7   song: singer, songwriter
8   symphony: composer, musician, conductor
9   ballet: dancer, choreographer, composer, musician
10   film: actor, actress, director, star, starlet, producer, distributor, scriptwriter

2   When the students have completed the matching task, suggest they transfer any unfamiliar words to their vocabulary books.

Answers
1   draw, illustrate, artist, sketch
2   stories, fiction, novels
3   musician, symphony, compose, conduct

3   Students should do this exercise individually and then check in pairs. You might need to explain *props*, *high-/lowbrow*, *serialized*, but elicit possible explanations from the students first.

Answers
1   drama, scenery, produced, play, highbrow
2   work, drew, Abstract, classical, allusions
3   modern, appreciate, critical
4   novels, masterpieces, tales, tell, popular, soap operas

4   Check the word forms as well as choice here.

Answers
1   exhibition
2   sculptures
3   criticism
4   collection
5   critics
6   scenery
7   visual

5   Encourage the students to use the vocabulary they have just collected and monitor for correct usage. They might like to discuss some popular art forms from their own cultures that have not been mentioned, e.g., shadow puppetry, traditional dance and artwork. Ask them to discuss their preferences.

Language focus: Defining and non-defining clauses   Page 144

Photocopiable language focus exercise on page 140.

Go over the grammar points carefully and refer the students to the Grammar reference on page 224 for further explanations. This is an area which can cause some confusion for students, not necessarily in comprehension as the context can clarify this, but in the use of the relative pronouns. Because of this, students will use longer, simpler grammatical expressions to avoid using defining and non-defining clauses. It also has an effect on students' ability to use and recognize complex sentences in all four main skills.

While discussing the sentences in this section, indicate how much more interesting for the reader/speaker/listener they are, because they can be used to add information and aid fluency. When monitoring students' spoken practice or marking their written work, point out any places where they missed the chance to use them.

Extension

Ask students to explain how relative clauses are translated into their own languages. Write a sentence with a defining clause on the board and then write a literal translation underneath. If you have a multi-lingual class, write up several examples. This can lead to a lively discussion and make students aware of the languages of their peers. It can also make them more tolerant of each other's mistakes and questions. In addition, it can give you insight into the mistakes the students make and why they make them. This type of activity can also be used for other grammar areas.

1   Do the first pair of sentences with the whole class as an example. Then ask the students to complete the exercise in pairs. You might need to explain *anthem* in 2b. Check the answers carefully. Ensure the students are clear about the differences before moving on.

Answers

Possible answers

1 a a play about which additional information is being given regarding age

   b defining clause needed to identify a particular play

2 a additional information not necessary for identification

   b defining clause needed to identify which anthem

3 a defining clause is needed to distinguish the man/woman from others

   b there is only one and he/she has just left

4 a defining clause is needed to distinguish between exhibitions

   b extra information given which is not needed

5 a defining clause to point out which architect it was

   b additional information

6 a defining clause to point out which singer it is

   b the singer is not being identified

2   Ask the students to do this exercise in pairs as suggested and check as a class. When checking the answers, point out that *whom* in 8 is quite formal and more commonly found in reading. Add that *that* or *nothing* are more common usage.

Answers

1 – , that/which are also possible

2 whose

3 which

4 which

5 – , that/which are also possible

6 who

7 – , that/which are also possible

8 – , that/who/whom are also possible

3   Students do this individually and check in pairs. Ensure the punctuation is correct here when you go over this.

Answers

1 c My uncle's flat, which overlooks the opera house, is empty for the next two weeks, so I'm staying there.

2 d The friend whose father is the film director got me into the film preview.

3 b One of my sculptures, which I made when I started the art course, has just won an art prize.

4 f The film, which has some breathtaking locations, starts in a few minutes.

5 g I like literature that is not dumbed down or simplified in any way.

6 a Is that the folk concert that you were praising last night because of the quality of the singer?

7 e The culture tour, which was incredibly expensive for the length of the trip, was dazzling.

4 Follow the instructions in the Coursebook and monitor the class carefully for correct usage. Share good examples with the whole class. Tell them you'll be looking for use of these in their writing and speaking practice. When you set an essay in future, you may want to insist that it contains at least one defining or non-defining relative clause, but also point out that they should not overuse them.

Further practice

Write some examples of good practice with a reason and example up on the board to show how students are able to write complex sentences.

Writing
IELTS Task 2   Page 145

1 Remind the students that as they discuss the task they can recycle some of the vocabulary they used in the previous unit on the feelings architecture induces and indeed other units in the coursebook, e.g., cause and effect, *-ing* and *-ed* adjectives. Get them to write some of their ideas on the board under 'positive' and 'negative' headings.

2 Get them to complete the gaps individually. Ask them to check their answers in pairs before going over it with the whole class.

Answers
1 arts
2 artistic
3 galleries
4 participating
5 Take
6 physical
7 coordination
8 Likewise
9 exhibition
10 gallery

3 Ask the students to do this activity individually, underlining the appropriate sections of the text. Then ask them to compare the answers in pairs. If possible, put the complete text on an OHT and project it onto the board to check and see the text in its entirety.

Answers
1 but it does not mean that we should not be involved in some kind of artistic activity even if

it only means visiting art galleries or attending lectures on the arts.

2 ... , which benefit the individual and the nation as a whole, ... ; Dance, which requires a lot of movement, ... ; ... coordination, which is a skill that is missing in a lot of education today as children focus on learning through computers.

3 There are no defining clauses. However, you could remove the commas from the following and make it into a defining clause: *Dance which requires a lot of movement is ...* . This would mean only dance that requires a lot of movement, not dance that requires gentle movement.

4 to gain more knowledge

5 Take dancing, for example.

4 Ask students to write the paragraph together or in pairs. Encourage them to (or insist that they) write at least one relative clause.

Reading
IELTS Reading Passage   Page 146

1 Ask the students to work in groups and discuss the statements. Set a time limit, but allow them to continue for longer if the discussion is going well. Ask groups to volunteer a member to give feedback to the whole class. Make sure you give enough time for each group to have a chance to feed back.

2 Ask the students to keep in the same groups and decide on the answers. If they do not know an answer, tell them to ask other students. Have dictionaries available if they want to check meanings.

Answers
1 Correct
2 Correct
3 Correct
4 Correct
5 Incorrect: means 'group'
6 Incorrect: means 'go/run quickly to'
7 Incorrect: means 'backward-looking'
8 Correct
9 Incorrect: means 'honest'
10 Correct

3 Ask the students to work in the same groups, scanning for the words from exercise 2 in the text and deciding on the meaning. You can turn this into a competition between groups. Check the answers at the end. When you have checked the answers, ask the students what they can tell you about the text and list the information on the board. They will probably be very surprised by how much they have picked up even when they have not been focusing on the content. Use this to reassure the students about not having to read every word and as evidence for the effectiveness of skimming and scanning.

Questions 1–13

Ask the student to look at the questions for the reading passage and at the picture. Set a strict time limit of 20 minutes. Give the students a five-minute warning after 15 minutes and ask them to note which question they are doing but to continue for a few more minutes. Tell the students to write their answers on a sheet of paper or on an answer sheet. Ask them to check their answers in pairs, paying attention to spelling. Remind the students that the answers that they choose for the summary need to reflect the meaning in the text and not just fit grammatically. Elicit whether they think the summary covers part or the whole of the passage and why.

Watch the students while they are reading and give feedback on technique: reading rather than skimming/scanning; underlining too much; spending too much time on one question; not leaving a question and coming back to it at the end. You may want to focus on one or more of these areas.

Answers
1 D
2 G
3 L
4 P
5 I
6 H
7 J
8 F
9 Q
10 F
11 E
12 A
13 B

Reacting to the text

Students discuss the questions in small groups.

Speaking
IELTS Part 2   Page 149

1–2 Ask the students to look at the task card in exercise 1. Ask them to write the numbers next to the relevant part of the text.

Answers
1 I'm going to describe a piece of art, which I think is a work of great craftsmanship and the most beautiful object in the world for me. It is *David* by Michelangelo, who is a great Italian sculptor.
2 The first time I saw it was when I went from Rome to Florence to see my aunt … . One day she took me there to visit the statue *David*. I didn't want to go as I hated art galleries and museums. … I thought they were boring and old-fashioned … . But I was completely overawed, because it is such a breathtaking sculpture … .
3 As for its appearance, it is very tall and it is made of marble. The statue is looking off into the distance as if he is looking into the future … .
4 Because *David* changed the way I looked at art galleries, I shall always be very fond of it.

3 When the students have isolated the words, ask them to compare and justify the words and phrases that they have chosen. If the students have chosen too many, write the list on the board and ask them to remove words until there are only a maximum of ten.

Answers
David, Florence, aunt, hated galleries, boring, overawed, tall, changed (view)

4 Keep the students in pairs and get them to add phrases and sentences to the text to make it longer. The number of words will depend on the student. You could ask them to read the text naturally and time each other with a stopwatch. Is it more than 200 words in two minutes?

Answers
Sample phrases (to be added in the order of the gaps in the text):
, who was working there at the time.
And up until then I had always avoided visiting them.
, because I did not think they offered anything for young people.
and I had never seen anything like it before.
and you want to see where he is looking.

5 Start this activity as a whole class exercise. Show students how to do it without breathing and with breathing at the appropriate places. Point out that the breaths are shallow breaths that are barely noticeable. Get them to practise the first sentence as an example.

6–7 Ask students to follow the procedure as before for Part 2, using the checklist for feedback. Remind them about their breathing as they speak.

Review 10 answers Pages 150 and 151

Vocabulary

1

1 (soap) operas
2 composed (the symphony)
3 (great) novelist
4 (many) plays
5 (an) artist
6 (great) sculptor
7 (actors and) actresses
8 (some of the) dancers

2

1 drama, stages, scenery, Drama, produce, plays, highbrow
2 abstract, classical, allusions, art
3 appreciate, favourable

3

a 3
b 2
c 1

Defining and non-defining clauses

1

1 I saw the film which/that/– you recommended to me last week.
2 That is the house which/that/– I bought last year.
3 Literature, which is compulsory in the school curriculum, is popular in my country.
4 The gallery, which is at the end of the street, had its main piece of art stolen./The gallery that/which is at the end of the street had its main piece of art stolen./The gallery that/which had its main piece of art stolen is at the end of the street./The gallery, which had its main piece of art stolen, is at the end of the street.
5 Some children, whose parents take them to museums, are very advanced at school.
6 The film, which was four hours long, was attacked by the critics.

The film that/which was four hours long was attacked by the critics.

7 Many books that/which do not sell many copies are published each year in the UK.
8 My favourite work of art, which is not a huge tourist attraction, is a building in Ireland.
9 Some types of music that/which are very popular in my country are not well known elsewhere.
10 The man that/who is wearing a red hat is the director of the film.

2

1 who
2 which
3 that/–
4 which
5 whose
6 which
7 that/–
8 that/which

Proof reading

1 exhibitions
2 sculptures
3 relaxing, than
4 environment
5 Literature which is more than 100 years old is not really relevant to the modern world.
6 boundaries
7 visual

Psychology and sociology

Content overview

Themes

This unit is concerned with psychology and sociology, family and kinship.

Exam-related activities

Reading

Topic	Growing up in an African village
Question type	Matching statements to paragraphs
	Completing sentences
	Selecting items from a list

Listening

Topic	A school trip
Section 1	Completing notes

Speaking

Part 2	Describing a person/period of your life

Writing

Task 2	Agreeing or disagreeing with a statement

Other

Language focus	Conditionals 2
Vocabulary	The family
Word building	Suffixes -*hood* and -*ship*

Vocabulary: The family   Page 152

Lead-in

Ask the students what they think the title of the unit means. Then ask about family relationships in their countries, what is traditional and what (if anything) has changed in recent years. Get the students to talk about family sizes and the concept of nuclear and extended families.

1   Look at the photos and get the students to answer the questions in pairs.

Answers
1 village community
2 nuclear family
3 large extended family
4 grandparent and child

2   This can be done as a whole class quiz with the students in groups, or it can be done first as a matching exercise in groups. Put the questions on one set of cards and the answers on another (different colour card for questions and answers), one set for each group. Then, if you want to exploit it further, you can play *pelmanism* (mixing the cards face down and turning over one question and one answer card, remembering

where the matches are). You can also do the pelmanism as a whole class exercise, asking groups to identify the matches. The group with the most matches wins.

Note that for 12, *dwelling* isn't necessarily a house; it is a unit of accommodation in which one or more individuals live.

Answers
1 parents
2 grandparents
3 siblings
4 family tree
5 someone whose husband has died
6 someone whose wife has died
7 someone who guarantees to support and give religious education to a child at the time of baptism; male – godfather; female – godmother
8 relatives
9 ancestor
10 niece/nephew
11 family
12 household
13 offspring
14 orphan

3   Ask the students to work in pairs and match the two parts of the sentences. If you think your students need consolidation, ask them to write out the complete sentences.

Answers
1 b
2 e
3 f
4 a
5 c
6 d
7 g

4   This exercise is an extension of exercise 3 and the lead-in discussion incorporating the new vocabulary. Monitor the students for correct usage. You might like to explain first the difference between *home*, relating to place, and *household*, relating to the people in that place.

Word building: Suffixes -*hood* and -*ship*
Page 153

Lead-in

Explain that suffixes are used to make abstract

nouns (nouns used to express a concept, a state of being or a quality rather than an object) and that they are used in combination with other nouns; *-hood* often for family terms, and *-ship* often for status.

Write the five categories on the board, and ask students to add words of their own.

1 Ask the students to do the exercise in pairs and check as a whole class.

Answers

1 He faced a period of great **hardship** in his early life, so it is inspiring to see him being so successful now.

2 When the former colony finally achieved **nationhood**, there was widespread celebration.

3 He had **leadership** qualities, and therefore he received enormous backing from the public.

4 The **relationship** problems between the two countries were quickly overcome.

5 I have such happy memories of my **childhood** in New Zealand.

6 **Parenthood** does not suit some people at all.

7 Various businesses set up a **sponsorship** scheme to enable young people to visit other countries.

8 **Motherhood** demands a lot of skill and hard work from women.

9 The aim of the organization is to encourage **friendship** between nations.

Further practice

You could do the following activity if it's practical to set up. Put *-hood* on a card on one side of the classroom, *-ship* on the other and *neither* on the back wall. Read out some common nouns and ask the students to walk to the part of the classroom that fits.

2 Students do this in the same pairs and write their answers on the board when they have finished.

Answers

1 cultivated, friendship
2 withdrew sponsorship
3 facing, hardship
4 spent, childhood
5 Nationhood, reached
6 showed, leadership
7 maintain(ed), relationship

3 Remind the class or elicit what *collocate* means. You may want to allow the students to use dictionaries or allow them to consult other pairs. Get whole class feedback. If the students make errors, point out why the word they chose either does not collocate or is the wrong form.

Answers

1 special
2 professional
3 lasting
4 close
5 Family
6 parent-child
7 build
8 fragile
9 problems
10 network

4 Concept-check the rubric after the students have read it and let them speak in pairs, monitoring for appropriacy and language use.

Reading
IELTS Reading Passage   Page 154

1 Students do the prediction activity and discuss their ideas.

2 Ask them to underline the key words in each paragraph individually and follow up with whole class feedback.

Answers

Possible answers

Paragraph A: socialize, child, community, relatives, kinship, familial and kinship relations, network of relatives, upbringing

Paragraph B: adolescence, society, initiation ceremonies, mark the transition from childhood, adulthood, conduct and behaviour, duties and responsibilities, interests of the entire community

Paragraph C: Kinship and family, individual interests, Young people, process, initiation from childhood to adulthood, the society, good and bad times, bond, members, same age-grade, taught the historical information, cultural group, rituals, marry

Paragraph D: Seniority, age, respected and admired, wisdom, respect, counsel, crisis, certain responsibilities, elder, unemotional, arbiter, above partisan differences, synonymous with honour (etc.), ability, manifest these qualities in old age, elevated status in society

Paragraph E: good care of senior citizens, good example, respect, good treatment in old age, procreation, somebody, old age, Children brought up well, asset, children see that their grandparents are treated well, learn by example

Paragraph F: elder is the pillar, nuclear, extended family, link between the living and ancestors, unite the family, reinforces kinship ideology, helps to socialize, provide guidance, pass the baton, all members of the society take socialization seriously

Questions 1–13

Review the strategies for matching sentences to paragraphs, sentence completion and selecting ideas. Give the students 20 minutes to complete the questions. Make sure they write their answers on a piece of paper or an answer sheet as they do the test. Remind them to be careful about spelling and that they put the answers against the correct number.

Put the students into groups of four to discuss their answers. Stipulate that where there are differences in answers, they must go back to the text and examine it carefully again. Check as a whole class.

Answers
1 C
2 A
3 E
4 E
5 B
6 F
7 Western society
8 interests
9 responsibilities
10 (elevated) status
11–13   C, E, G, in any order

Reacting to the text

Put students into groups and ask them to choose someone to write down ideas and someone to report back. Discuss both parts of the activity. As a follow-up you might like to ask students to write an answer to the second set of questions.

Speaking
IELTS Part 2
Page 157

1–2 Give the students time to read the topics and choose one only. When they have done that,

tell them to imagine the person or situation as they make their notes. Monitor them to ensure they write no more than 10 words. Give them one minute exactly, then ask them to talk about the topic.

Put the students into pairs, ensuring that they have chosen different topics, and follow the procedure in the Coursebook. Monitor and get one or two students to model their answers.

3 Students compare their notes.

4 Ask the class to read the extract and match the topic. They should underline the parts that address the bullet points.

Answers
Topic Card A:
who the friendship was with: *It was with my best friend at the time.*
when you first met your friend: *whom I met when I first went to secondary school.*
what you did together: *... and we would sit next to each other, play the same games together ...*
and *explain why this friendship was important to you: Firstly, because we gave each other support at a time when we were both nervous about being in a new place. And secondly, where I grew up we didn't face any hardship, but I didn't have any siblings, so it was nice to have the companionship of someone at school ... And I suppose I felt that I was leaving childhood behind, and it was the first friendship of my adolescence.*

5 If possible, ask students in their groups to write their answer on an OHT for easy comparison and assessment.

Answers
Two possible additions at the gaps:
We used to go for long walks together or go swimming in the local river and of course chat a lot. When we could, we would go with both our families on holiday as our parents were also close, but sometimes these were only day trips.
We helped each other with our work in class and homework and would always try to be in the same teams if we played sport. Sometimes, however, we would be on opposing teams, which we didn't like.

6 Follow the instructions in the Coursebook. This is a particularly useful comparison for those who chose this topic.

friendship, teens, secondary, same class/
games, support, first friendship, adolescence

7 Students discuss two more topics in pairs.
Monitor and time as before. When they finish,
let them analyze their own performance on both
topics and see if there was any improvement
from the first time to the second.

Listening
IELTS Section 1   Page 158

1 Without looking at the questions, ask students
to think of things a school secretary and a parent
might discuss. If they find this concept a bit
alien, put a mixture of topics on the board and let
them suggest which ones might be appropriate
and which ones not. If you are teaching students
who were not exposed in their schooling to such
trips, you might like to do a small brainstorming
exercise on what they think such trips include
and their purpose.

Answers

Possible answers

cost, time, deposit, accommodation, numbers,
teachers, registration, clothes

Go over the 'Don't forget!' advice. This should be
automatic for them by this stage in the course.
Monitor those who may still not be doing this
effectively.

Questions 1–10
Play the listening through once. Give the
students a chance to transfer their answers to
an answer sheet or a piece of paper. If necessary,
play the recording again and check as usual,
pausing at the answers.

Answers

1   Peru
2   in pairs
3   15
4   spending money
5   holidays
6   29th September
7   interview
8   20/twenty
9   2/two
10 100/one hundred

---

11 Psychology and sociology

   2.4

S = school administrator; P = parent

S: Headmaster's office, Damian speaking.
How may I help you?

P: Yes, hi. It's Margaret Williams here.

S: Oh. Hi there.

P: My daughter Helen is in the fifth year and
…

S: Ah yes, I know her…

P: Mmm … well, I understand that the
International Friendship Club is planning
a trip this year and just wanted to know
more about it.

S: Yes, well, we normally print a factsheet
for pupils to take to their parents, but that
won't be done for another … month I don't
think, but I can still help you with some
details from the information I have.

P: OK.

S: Well, let's see … Now, mm … school trips
2000 and … ah, here it is. It hasn't been
entered into the computer yet. But what
exactly would you like to know?

P: Em … well, first of all, where's the trip to,
how much is it and when is it?

S: The trip in the current school year will
be to … South America, … to Peru
specifically.

P: To Peru, wow! That sounds thrilling. That
never happened in my childhood.

S: Nor mine either! Mmm … it says here
the group will be staying with families
connected with a school just outside the
capital, Lima, and then will be making
trips to the surrounding areas.

P: OK. Will each of them be on their own with
the family?

S: No, there'll be no students on their own;
students will all be in pairs.

P: I see. What about the cost?

S: It's surprisingly cheap actually. At the
moment it's … £495 for the 15 days all
inclusive, but obviously not including gifts
for the host families and spending money.

P: Mmm … , it's still a lot as I'm a single
parent.

S: Well, there are some bursaries, and it may be that the price comes down; this is only the initial price. Last year, if it were not for the school fund, it would have been a lot more. Last year, it came down by about £120 per student, so it depends on how much is available in the school hardship fund.

P: Oh, I see. And when is the trip?

S: Em … it takes place during the spring <u>holidays</u>.

....

P: OK. Can I ask you … how Helen goes about applying?

S: Applying? Well, the application is quite simple. There will be a deadline to get the application in ten days after the date of the advert, which will come out on the <u>29th of September</u>.

P: OK.

S: And then when the applications are received, each student will have to have <u>an interview</u> to assess whether they are suitable or not.

P: How many places are there?

S: <u>20</u> with a minimum age of 16, so it's restricted to the upper years.

P: And are any teachers going?

S: Oh yes. There'll be places for six adults, four of whom will be teachers, and <u>two</u> parents, who will go free.

P: Right. Do they apply as well?

S: Yes. You interested?

P: Yes! And when it comes to paying, provided Helen's application is successful, can we pay by instalments? Say, £50 a month?

S: Oh yes, that's not a problem provided you make a deposit of <u>£100</u>, and then pay the rest by instalments with the final balance due three weeks before the departure date. Students will only be allowed to go on the trip if all the money is paid in advance – I'm afraid we've had problems in the past with money not being paid, so we are very strict about it now.

P: I see. That's totally understandable.

2 Ask the students to discuss the questions in pairs.

Language focus: Conditionals 2
Page 159

Photocopiable language focus exercise on page 140.

1 Ask the students to look at the examples and answer the questions. Refer them to the Grammar reference on page 224. You may also want to go through examples of the conditionals and refer them back to page 223.

Answers

Example 1: Second conditional *were not, would*
Example 2: Present simple
In the second example, the following is also possible with no change of meaning: *That will not be a problem, …*

2 Look at the sentences and get them to underline the conditional marker in each one. Explain that **b** is meant to be a paraphrase of **a**, and elicit the meaning.

Answers

1 Paraphrase
2 … if there aren't any free places. Remove *even* and the comma before it.
3 There's a possibility there will be a change in society if the government addresses social issues like crime and poverty.
4 If future generations are even more highly trained than they are now, will their lives be better?
5 Unless/(If) people are psychologically well adapted to …
6 Paraphrase
7 Paraphrase
8 I didn't study psychotherapy and I now regret it.

3–4 Follow the instructions in the Coursebook and check as a whole class at the end.

Answers

3
1 Unless
2 If only
3 Even if
4 Provided
5 If
6 Supposing

4
2, 5

5 Go through the example. Ask the students to do the exercise in pairs and check as a whole class.

Answers

1 Families can help to make society a better place, provided the government gives them support.

2 If the government funded more community centres, this would provide a place for people to meet.

3 If globalization hadn't occurred, there would now be fewer social and cultural problems around the world.

4 If it were not for volunteer workers helping people deal with the psychological aspect of change, the situation would have been worse.

5 Even though social interaction between different cultures is increasing, still more contact is necessary.

6 Supposing social intelligence were taught in schools, would it be beneficial?

6 Write the following expressions on the board and encourage students to use them in their discussions:

If I hadn't ... , I'd ...

If only I'd ... , I'd ...

If it weren't for ... , I'd ...

Provided I ... , I'll ...

Unless I ... , I'll ...

Monitor the pairs for correct structure and usage.

Writing

IELTS Task 2   Page 160

1 Go over the rubric and ensure the students understand what is required. You might like to allot a topic to each group so that all are covered.

The lists could be put onto A3-sized sheets, one for each group. When the groups have finished, they circulate the sheets to look at the other groups' ideas and add any of their own to the list.

Answers

Possible ideas

1

First view:

world smaller

some countries richer than others

one humanity

have responsibility

unethical not to help

Second view:

charity begins at home

why go abroad when problems closer to home?

responsibility for own people first

can't help everybody

2

For:

gives people: passport/independence/freedom/chance for development

Against:

not the only way

social help

financial help

basic necessities

depends on situation and individual

3

For:

parents' responsibility

their children

early years with parents

Against:

children spend time at school

parents at work need help

financial/social support needed

parenting skills

opinion: share the responsibility – 'three parties'

2–4 Students decide which essay each extract comes from and underline the text for replacement, and the irrelevant piece of information. Discuss the reasons as a whole class.

Answers

2

Extract 1: 1

Extract 2: 2

3

Extract 1:

It is a natural human instinct for people to help each other, so this characteristic should be harnessed for the betterment of mankind.

Extract 2:

Let's say someone is well educated but has not made even one or two friends in their life. Their life would be affected.

4

Extract 1:
Shopping is a good example here of people helping the elderly.

Extract 2:
Learning a skill like pottery can help make people's lives relevant and help them relax.

5 Let students do the task for homework, and stress the need for them to be strict about the 40-minute time limit. Tell them that as you mark their work, you will be looking for examples of the vocabulary and conditional sentences practised in the unit. Alternatively, you could do this as a class test. Ask the students to look at the sample answer.

Sample answer

From the beginning of the last century women fight hardly to take a position in work place either in private sector or in government offices. Since that time they have always proved their ability to perform just like any male colleague. For a woman to take any leading position she need to work harder than a men because of the fact that most of the people in management and leading positions are men. Until now the salary for women is less than the salary of a men having the same job in a developed country like U.K. Therefore it is not easy for a women to have a leading position.

The reasons why many people opposing women's rights in work that they think the natural place for women is the home and their responsibility in leading the family is much more import than any other job. Others say women have so much to do in their home and if they take managerial jobs at work, they will not be able to perform efficiently.

In spite of all these obstacles women through the history proved their ability in taking responsibility of leadership and we have many examples of women who have led their countries and their people in a successful way and achieve a lot in developing their country like queen Victoria in the UK. Her reign as a queen lasted 63 years, and the Victorian era was a time of industrial, political, scientific and military progress within the UK.

I think women have all the elements of successes as a leader and as a manager and home responsibility should be shard between men and women. Women all over the world should have the same rights as

men and they should have the same opportunity in leading position.

Word count: 298

Possible score: 6.0

Examiner's comment:

Although the argumentation in this response is quite well structured, it is replete with grammatical errors which impose some strain on the reader (e.g., the conclusion) and so diminish its overall impact. Paragraphing is quite well handled with some varied sentence patterns in evidence.

Review 11 answers Pages 162 and 163

Vocabulary
1 family tree
2 ancestors
3 widow
4 relative/descendant
5 siblings
6 relatives
7 generation

Word building: Suffixes *-hood* and *-ship*

1
1 c ii
2 d iii
3 a viii
4 b i / h vii
5 h vii / b i
6 g vi
7 f v
8 e iv

3
1 relationships
2 households
3 relationships
4 generational
5 hardship
6 leadership
7 friendship
8 childhood

Speaking

A I have maintained a number of strong **D** relationships with people who were my childhood friends, but the friendship I **E** would like to describe is one that began only early last year with a friend from the **C** restaurant where I work

H part-time. We first met when we were working on an evening shift. It was very busy, **G** but we still managed to help each other out. Since that day we have developed **B** a very deep friendship. I think **I** the main reason why we get on is because **F** we have very similar interests. So I think what really makes the friendship work **K** is that both of us like reading and **J** doing the same sports, and we rarely disagree on anything.

Question: Describe a friendship that is important to you.

Conditionals 2

1 Even if it costs a lot, I shall try to keep the whole family together.
2 Unless the seminar on culture and the family has spaces, I'll attend the seminar on kinship.
3 Families depend on the community centre to meet up; otherwise, they would have nowhere else to go.
4 They kept the family together and so they are in such a strong position now.

Proof reading

others think
raising children
the parents
social skills
schools as agencies
teach children to form
warm relationships with
peers
knowledge and information
adults
skills

Content overview

Themes

This unit is concerned with travelling around the world, journeys, and places of interest.

Exam-related activities

Reading

Topic	The Great Barrier Reef
Question type	Summary without a wordlist
	TRUE/FALSE/NOT GIVEN
	Short answers

Listening

Topic	Talk on travelling advice
Section 2	Multiple-choice questions
	Completing a summary

Speaking

Part 1	Discussing transport
Part 2	Describing a memorable journey

Writing

Task 2	Discussing two views and giving your own opinion

Other

Language focus	Articles
Vocabulary	Adjectives with multiple meanings
Word building	Words related to memory

Listening
IELTS Section 2   Page 164

1 Ask the students what place they would most like to visit and why. Then ask them to look at the photographs and see if anything there is similar to their choice.

Go through all the pre-listening questions with the students in pairs. You might like to check their understanding of *exotic*. Elicit their checklists and write the items on the board.

Answers

1 a secluded beach
2 a city
3 ancient ruins

2 In pairs students make a list of preparations for going on a trip. Get whole class feedback.

Questions 11–20

Students look at all the listening questions and underline key words. Remind them to predict word type for questions 16–20, and also to pay attention to singular and plural nouns. Play the recording and check answers as usual.

12 Travelling around the world

 2.5

Now that the main summer holiday season is almost upon us, we are devoting this week's Health Spot in our programme to all of you young people who are setting off on backpacking holidays to sunny shores. We hope you have the time of your life, but to help that dream come true we've got a few tips for you before you head off.

The first thing to do is to make yourself a checklist of all the things you need to do and take with you, especially if you, like me, <u>are very forgetful</u>. Apart from the usual things like checking you have your tickets and passport and the necessary visas, there are practical things that you need to do. I'm going to pick a few things at random from the checklist we've made here, but <u>you can get</u> extra information from our <u>website</u>, where you can download the details. Or, if you would rather have someone to listen to, you can download the podcast for free with all the information from the website.

So, the first item that I think is important is sun protection, especially if you are fair-skinned. To protect yourself you can buy sun creams and special clothing and a hat – a wide-brimmed hat – and sunglasses. Provided you are well protected, you'll be OK. But the best form of protection against ultraviolet rays is to <u>stay out of the sun</u>. Stick to the shade; especially between 11 and 4 pm, as this is the most dangerous time. You can also buy special clothing that has built-in protection like sun cream.

Mmm, now … ah, OK, another tip here about clothing, em … is … besides a hat and so on, one item on the checklist that is indispensible is a good pair of walking shoes. Good walking shoes do not come cheap, but it is money well-spent, because if you're walking around a lot <u>your feet will need some support</u>. Some sandals are OK for walking, but you may be better off with shoes.

Customs? Ah yes … make yourself familiar with the customs of the country you are going to, so that you don't <u>cause problems</u>. It's easy to assume that people everywhere behave like ourselves. You cannot know everything, but you can find out about the main types of behaviour like what to wear and where to wear it.

....

Now, a very important point. When you are away, it's easy, if you're enjoying yourself, to lose contact with your family at home. But try and prevent this from happening so your family don't experience any <u>anxiety</u> unnecessarily and mmm, er … possibly waste <u>resources</u>. One good tip here is to remember to have a particular time to make contact. You can use a mobile phone to text your family. In these days of the Internet there is no excuse for at least not sending a quick message or a quick text on the mobile.

Let's see … Some kind of waterproof cover: something that is light but effective … And yes another good tip here – an essential for your backpack is a simple first aid kit with <u>plasters</u> in case you cut yourself, or tread on something sharp – and if you do, some antiseptic <u>wipes</u> would be very handy too, so you can clean the skin to prevent infection and so on …

And yes, this is a good piece of advice. Remember to keep valuables like <u>cameras</u> safe at all times. As tourists you can't be careful enough, and don't let your guard down for a second.

Remember to enjoy yourselves. Look out for novel experiences, and open your minds to the strange and the new!

3 Students discuss the questions. Remember that for many cultures, the idea of staying out in the sun is very strange, and so your students might feel the discussion personally redundant. Refer them to tourists who come to their countries and their behaviour in the sun.

Vocabulary: Adjectives with multiple meanings Page 166

1 Do the sample question and explain that because of the breadth of the English language, many words have similar meanings.

Answers
It means 'original'/'new'/'different'. It can also mean a 'work of fiction'.

2 In pairs, students work through the activity. If there are any unfamiliar words, encourage the class to look them up in a learner's dictionary, and then record the words in their vocabulary books.

Answers
1 relevant
2 apathetic
3 film
4 treasured
5 different
6 new
7 odd
8 extra
9 similar
10 uncomfortable

3 Students complete the consolidation activity.

Answers
1 novel, novelty
2 different, difference
3 strange, strangeness
4 unique, uniqueness
5 curious, curiosity
6 foreign, foreignness
7 odd, oddity/oddness
8 new, newness

9 fresh, freshness
10 alien, alienation

4 Write the following expressions on the board and encourage students to use them:

A _____ thing happened to me when I was …

What happened was …

It was really …

It changed my life.

I have never seen/experienced anything like it.

Drill for pronunciation (linking and weak forms). Put students in groups of three to describe their new experiences with the adjectives and nouns from this section.

Alternative procedure

Give the pairs of students a set of the nouns and adjectives on cards. They each pick two or three randomly from the cards, which have been placed upside-down, and use these choices to describe their new experience.

 **Reading**
IELTS·Reading Passage   Page 167

1 Students discuss the statements in pairs, and then as a whole class. If you have Internet access in the classroom, let the students check any they're not sure of. If not, give them the information yourself.

Answers
1 True
2 True
3 False – Australia
4 False – Mexico in Central America
5 False – Athens in Greece
6 False – East Africa
7 True
8 True
9 False – St Petersburg
10 False – Iran

2 Elicit and discuss three facts about the Great Barrier Reef, e.g., it's off Queensland, Australia, it's a coral reef, it's a conservation area, etc. See further suggestions below.

Answers

Possible answers

perhaps where it is in Australia; it is in the Ocean; it is large; internationally important from the environmental point of view

3–4 Ask the students to predict the possible meanings used in the passage and then underline the words as they scan the passage to check which meaning is actually used. Don't check this as an exercise until after they have read the passage.

Answers

1 shelf: ledge
2 maturity: fully-developed
3 system: organism
4 range: variety
5 list: catalogue
6 vulnerable: in danger
7 breed: reproduce
8 colony: collection
9 historic: ancient
10 sanctuary: place of safety

Questions 1–13

Remind students about summary skills, TRUE/FALSE/NOT GIVEN questions, and comprehension questions. Give them a 20-minute time limit. Monitor to make sure the first thing they do is to look at the questions, underline key words, and skim the text effectively. Make a note of those who are still not employing these strategies and suggest alternative practice after the class. Make sure they don't study the whole text in detail. Ask them to write their answers on a sheet of paper or an answer sheet. Remind them to be careful with the spelling and singular and plural nouns.

Let them go over the answers in groups, again making sure that any differences in answers are fully discussed and the text examined in detail. Then do a whole class feedback, sorting out any problems.

Answers

The answers are all in the first two paragraphs:
1 continental shelf
2 protected areas
3 diversity
4 ecosystem
5 coral(-)reef
6 biological

7 FALSE. Paragraph 4: *Contrary to popular belief, the Great Barrier Reef is not a continuous barrier, ...*
8 NOT GIVEN. Paragraph 6: *More than 4,000 mollusc species and over 1,500 species of sponges have been identified.* The molluscs and species are mentioned, but there is no information given about a comparison with other sites in the world.
9 TRUE. Paragraph 9: *The reef contains nesting grounds of world significance for the endangered loggerhead turtle.*
10 NOT GIVEN. Paragraph 11: *There are over 30 historic shipwrecks in the area, ...* The shipwrecks are mentioned, but no mention is made of whether there are plans to raise them or not.
11 No-take zones. Paragraph 14: *The proportion of the Marine Park protected by no-take zones was increased from less than five per cent to over 33 per cent, and now ... the entire Marine Park.*
12 (the) regulatory framework. Paragraph 15: *... the regulatory framework significantly enhances the resilience of the Great Barrier Reef.*
13 overall management. Paragraph 16: *... the Australian Government agency responsible for overall management, and the Queensland Government, ...*

Reacting to the text

In the same groups as before, students discuss the questions using any new vocabulary they have come across in the unit so far.

Word building: Words related to memory   Page 170

1 Elicit the word *memento* from the students, using dictionaries if necessary. Ask them to talk about any mementoes they may have brought back from a holiday. Compare with *souvenir* and *keepsake*.

Answers

souvenir or memento
Words with the route *mem-*:
memento, memo/memorandum, memoir, memoirs, memorable, memorial, memorabilia, memorize, memory

2 Ensure all pairs have at least one good monolingual dictionary to use and let them do the activity. Make a spidergram on the board with *memory* in the middle. When students have finished, get them to add all the other related words. They can then transfer this to their vocabulary books.

Answers

1 memories
2 remember
3 memoirs
4 memorabilia
5 memorize
6 memorable
7 memorials
8 memo/memorandum
9 memento
10 memory

3 Do this exercise as a whole class. Concept-check by giving a few definitions and asking the students to give the word or vice versa. Encourage the students to add any words they don't know to their vocabulary lists.

Answers

1 memories
2 memorabilia
3 mementos
4 memoirs
5 memorial ·
6 memorable
7 remember
8 memorize

4 Write the following language on the board:

Do you find it easy to memorize … ?

Are you the sort of person who collects … memorabilia?

What is your (most treasured/fond/vivid) memory?

What details do you remember about … ?

What was your most memorable … ?

Give one or two examples to highlight structure (e.g., 'to' infinitive; *who* + third person verb) and meaning. Monitor for correct form and appropriate use of target vocabulary as they make the questions. Model one or two good ones to the whole class.

Speaking

IELTS Part 1   Page 171

1–3 Elicit the appropriate answer beginnings and explain why the structure of the other two are inaccurate, if necessary. Monitor the answers students give for form and variety of response and ask two or three to model examples. You

might like to put up some of their ideas on the board for reference.

Answers

1
More and more people use …
Most travellers …

2
(Possible beginnings to answers)

1 I think most people either use …/Some people use … and others …
2 The main difficulties/(ones/problems/hitches) are … /One (difficulty) is … another is …
3 They stop me …/They don't really cause me any difficulties, because …
4 First of all, I'd improve … What I'd do first is …

Speaking

IELTS Part 2   Page 171

1 Go over the points in the Part 2 questions. In pairs, students answer questions 1–6 to prepare for the task. Provide them with extra vocabulary as necessary, or let them refer to their dictionaries. They should make a page entitled 'Journeys' in their vocabulary books to record this.

Students often get confused with words like *tour, excursion, expedition, outing, trip, journey, voyage* and *travel* so you might like to give them some examples to contextualize these words:

tour: travelling from one place to another with the purpose of visiting various places and in the end coming back to where you started

excursion: a day trip made for pleasure, usually by a group of people

expedition: a journey undertaken by a group of people (organized) with a definite objective

outing: a short pleasure trip usually lasting no more than a day

trip: a journey for some purpose, usually including the return

journey: a trip of considerable length or daily routine, mainly by land, for business or pleasure, a return is not necessarily indicated. It may indicate a long distance or a short one travelled regularly (daily journey to work, for example).

voyage: a journey by sea

travel: the act of travelling, e.g., *air travel*, or in its plural form *travels*, it means *time spent travelling*, e.g., *When are you off on your travels?* More usually used as a verb, *to travel*.

Answers

Possible answers

1 tour, excursion, expedition, outing, trip, voyage, travel

2 luggage, suitcase, plane, train, car, tickets, hotel, boat

3 pleasant, exciting, long, tiring, excruciating, memorable, fantastic, comfortable, uncomfortable

4 travel, fly, stay, stop, stop over, journey, sail

5 hotel, seaside, mountains, beaches, city centre, ski resort

6 for a holiday, for work, to visit friends, to study

2 Follow the instructions in the Coursebook.

3 Give the students a moment to choose two of the criteria to give their partner. Time them as they make notes. As they speak, monitor for use of target vocabulary, with partners checking the time and giving feedback. Give individual feedback if necessary before whole class feedback.

Language focus: Articles   Page 172

Photocopiable language focus exercise on page 141.

Students often have a problem with articles as they do not occur in many languages, or are used differently. In listening, they are usually unstressed so may easily be missed by learners. Articles give signals to what is being said, and so this failure to recognize them or use them can cause miscommunication. For this reason, focus students' attention on articles and their usage. If there are persistent problems with them, advise extra practice from the various grammar books that are available.

1 Elicit what we mean by the three kinds of articles and give the students a few minutes to find them in the extract. Refer them to the Grammar reference on page 225.

Answers

1 the definite article: *the Great Barrier Reef, the mainland*

2 the zero article: *popular belief, 2,900 individual reefs, fringing reefs, islands*

3 the indefinite article: *a continuous barrier, a broken maze*

2 Follow the instructions in the Coursebook or do this activity with the whole class. From this activity, you can focus on the various uses of the articles.

Answers

1 The sun

2 Stars, the moon, the planets, the Milky Way

3 A star

4 We can call it a star when we look at it in the galaxy or when we look at it as an astronomical object.

5 Yes

6 Mount Everest

7 The Himalayas

8 Tokyo

9 The capital. There is only one capital not several.

10 Yes. The Atlantic Ocean, the Pacific Ocean, the Indian Ocean, the Arctic Ocean, the Southern Ocean.

3–4 Follow the instructions in the Coursebook. Monitor and assist the students as they complete the exercises, stopping them if there are consistent misunderstandings, to clarify to the whole class.

Answers

3

1 b The. The phrase *I visited were old* makes the monuments specific, not just any or all 'old monuments'.

2 b the. The Himalayas are a particular group of mountains, not just mountains in general.

3 a the. The sun in the sky/our solar system.

4 b the. The Nile is a specific river.

5 a The. The phrase *of Mexico* makes the word capital specific. Mexico City does not need an article as there is only one Mexico City.

6 a The. The United Kingdom is used to distinguish the kingdom from other kingdoms.

7 a The. The definite article can be used if it refers to a particular country. Sentence b is about prime ministers in general.

8 a The. There is only one heart in the body, not various hearts.

4 (extra articles listed)

the Brazil

the sisters

the Rio de Janeiro

the beaches

the fun

a sightseeing

the living

the holidays

Further practice

As a consolidation activity, you can do 'right/wrong' for a list of sentences, with the students going to one side of the class if the sentence is correct, and the other side if it's incorrect.

Writing
IELTS Task 2   Page 173

1 Ask the students to look at the task and discuss ideas 1–7 in pairs. Put any additional ideas on the board and discuss as a whole class.

Answers

1
1, 2, 3, 7
Other possible ideas
View 1:
- gives people new ideas and experiences, languages
- helps develop international relations
- provides education
- removes prejudice
- helps people appreciate other cultures

View 2:
- makes people more prejudiced/less tolerant
- confirms prejudices
- makes people more insular

2 Follow the instructions in the Coursebook. When the students have finished, they can write their replacement sentences on the board. Discuss and give suggestions.

Answers

Possible answers

2 Trains go in and out of fashion in all countries, as they often depend on the support of politicians. At the moment, for example, more people are travelling by coach rather than by railway.

3 Tourism can have a negative impact on the local culture, so tourists should be careful about how they behave when they visit other cultures.

5 Older people find it more difficult to rough it while on holiday compared to the younger generation. This is surely because they need to have more comfortable surroundings because of their age.

3 When the groups have discussed their ideas, divide the board into the number of groups and get them to put up their ideas about view 1 and view 2.

4 If the students do the writing for homework, then you will have to do this the next time you meet. Ask the students to check their own work first as part of the 40 minutes as good practice. Then they can re-check it as an exercise after their partner has done so.

You might find that in their error-correction checklist proposed at the beginning of the course, the students will have already noted if articles are a problem. Hopefully, this section will have been of help and they can notice a marked improvement.

Sample answer

Although it might appear so obvious that roving around the world is probably the best and most direct way of learning about life in other places, there are some who claim that it would only reinforces the biased ideas some people have about outsiders.

Fortunately the various modes of transport have developed hugely over recent years so that almost everybody can afford the time and cost of travelling and at least glance around and if interested in observing and studying other cultures more closely there are various means of transport to fit individual's needs and plans. What makes it more convenient is not only the speed but budget price tickets offered by airlines such as 'easyjet' which provides an excellent opportunity for people from different walks of life to travel and experience a new set of life.

What could be more real and true than those immediate impressions that people get directly through seeing directly and personally and not relying on the narratives which at times could be biased and reflect only few views, especially if they are broadcasted on TV and funded by a particular group. Why not experience it first-hand.

I do not tend to think that travelling would provoke misunderstandings, quite conversely it will dispel any prejudices, albeit assuming "the observer" needs to be fair and reasonable. The worst that could happen is realising all those horrid rumours about that particular part of the world have been true, which is still an achievement. At least those so-called hatred or disaprobations will find a firm base in reality.

Personally I do believe that travelling can only clarify our judgments, helping us to unify and integrate more and more. this unification seems one the best approaches to address our global concerns; a vital step to achieve peace on earth.

Word count: 302

Possible score: 6.5

Examiner's comment:

There are some relevant ideas supported by valid examples here. However, the response demonstrates uneven grammar and sharp shifts in style which impose some strain on the reader. Surprising lexical choices indicate a potentially accomplished writer, although these are somewhat undercut by inaccuracies in sentence structure throughout the answer.

Review 12 answers Pages 174 and 175

Vocabulary
1 foreign
2 fresh
3 novel
4 new
5 curious
6 differences
7 different
8 strange

Word building

1
Possible answers:
remember, memoirs, memorabilia, memorize, memorable, memorial, memo/memorandum, memento

2
1 d
2 f
3 a
4 g
5 b
6 e
7 c

3
1 memorable
2 memorabilia
3 memorize
4 Memoirs
5 remember
6 memory

Articles

1
1 the monument, a temple, the north
2 Correct
3 the trip
4 the mind, the education some people ... , the opposite
5 Correct
6 The information on the website
7 The quality of hotels

2
the human activities
The Significant regional differences
The reefs of the Southeast Asia
including the approximately 60,000 square kilometres
where the reefs cover
the higher risk is greater in the former

3
Yes. The first sentence is an overview and the text is a few words short of 150 words.
Possible introduction:
The chart provides information about the area of coral reef endangered by human beings.

4
Information about the Indian Ocean is missing.

Ready for Speaking

<table>
<tr><td colspan="2">IELTS Speaking Module</td></tr>
<tr><td>Part 1</td><td>Introduction and interview</td></tr>
<tr><td>Part 2</td><td>Individual long turn</td></tr>
<tr><td>Part 3</td><td>Two-way discussion</td></tr>
</table>

Introduction   Page 176

Optional lead-in

Before the students open the Coursebook, read out the following sentences about the Speaking test, and ask students to decide whether they are true or false:

1   The Speaking test has to be done on the same day as the Listening, Reading and Writing tests.

2   In Part 2 of the Speaking test you have to ask some questions.

3   The total Speaking test time is 11–14 minutes.

4   If you make any grammar errors you will not pass the Speaking test.

5   If you are not good at speaking, the interview only takes 10 minutes.

<table>
<tr><td>Answers</td></tr>
<tr><td>

1 False

2 False

3 True

4 False

5 False
</td></tr>
</table>

Elicit the criteria against which they will be marked in the Speaking test. Students then open their books and go through the introduction. Reassure them that the recording is for standardization purposes only and is not used outside the IELTS arena. In some countries, recording is a sensitive issue, so make the necessity for the recording clear. If possible, practise recording your students.

Part 1 Page 176

1–2 Ask the students to brainstorm their ideas in pairs. They then ask each other the questions. When students have done exercise 2, ask them to give different beginnings for Set B. Point out that there is more than one possible answer and that the beginning and indeed the whole answer must fit the question.

<table>
<tr><td>Answer</td></tr>
<tr><td>

2

1 The question asks the candidate to state a preference about doing something, e.g., I prefer going out with a (large/small) group of people/ friends/people I know.
</td></tr>
</table>

3   Remind students that stress and intonation are generally more critical to intelligibility than individual phoneme sounds so practising these is very important.

<table>
<tr><td>Answer</td></tr>
<tr><td>

Stressed words in sentence 4: many reasons, perhaps, most important
</td></tr>
</table>

4–6   Monitor as they do these exercises and help them where necessary. Have good examples of each one modelled for the whole class. Beware of over-exaggeration.

<table>
<tr><td>Answers</td></tr>
<tr><td>

4

Stressed words in set A:

prefer, go out, one friend, group, friends, Why do you go out

think, important, keep, contact, friends, make, work, courses, Why/Why not?

people, stay friends, long time

Stressed words in set B:

favourite form, art (painting, sculpture, music, drama)

think art, important, our lives, Why

Tell, traditional, form, art, your country

think art, popular, future, Why/Why not?

5

Possible beginnings for Set B:

I like/love/sculpture/painting best …/My favourite form of art is sculpture/painting…

Yes, I think it's crucial/essential/very important, because …

A very common art form where I come from is …

Oh yes. I think it will be much more central to our lives than now, because …

Words to stress:

like, sculpture best/favourite form, art, sculpture

Yes, think, crucial/essential/very important, (because)

very common art form, come, is…

Oh yes. think, much more central, lives now (because)
</td></tr>
</table>

6 Students repeat exercise 1, this time swapping sets with their partner.

Part 2 Page 178

Go through the advice with the students about taking notes.

1 Students do this matching exercise in pairs. You could put the words on pieces of card, too, so they can physically match them. Ask them to make a note of these ideas in the speaking section of their notebooks.

It's a good idea to paste the topics onto separate cards and laminate or cover them in plastic. This way you can have a bank of topic cards, which can be recycled and exchanged throughout the course for speaking practice. Make your own cards modelled on the topics given here and elsewhere in the Coursebook.

Answers
1 d
2 f
3 e
4 c
5 b
6 a

2–3 Follow the instructions in the Coursebook.

Answers
2
The words match the following parts of the topics:
Topic 1
café:
where this place is: near college
when you first visited this place: a month ago
what this place is like: cheerful, relaxing, friendly
and explain why you enjoy studying there: great view
Topic 2
Oxfam:
how you first became aware of this organization: television appeals
what this organization does: relieves poverty, sickness, famine
where this organization operates: everywhere
and explain why you admire the work of this charitable organization: saves lives

3
soon: in the coming year
annoying: irritating
privately: one-to-one tuition
relaxing: soothing
healthy: good for your health
helps concentration/work: improves their ability to focus

4 Students practise in pairs, timing each other and assessing notes and performance. Monitor as they do this and take note of any general errors for feedback.

Part 3 Page 180

Elicit information about this part of the exam. Ask the students what makes Part 3 different from Parts 1 and 2.

1 Let them brainstorm their ideas and then put them on the board for the whole class to look at and compare.

2 Students do this in groups of three as in the Coursebook. Go through the 'Don't forget!' advice with them. Make sure they know how to interpret the criteria for feedback. Monitor their performance and help them as they do this.

3 Play the recording through once and ask the class to give an overall assessment of the student.

Ready for Speaking Part 2 and 3

 2.6

E = Examiner; C = Candidate

E: Now, I'm going to give you a card with a topic to look at. You have one minute to make notes and then I'm going to ask you to talk about the topic.

E: Can you talk about the topic?

C: The skill that I'd like to talk about is playing a musical instrument, mmm … like the piano, and I'd like to learn it in the near future. I know it's possible to go to a class to learn to play the piano, but mmm … I know I'd find that very annoying. I think learning to play the piano's one of those skills that'd be better to learn … to acquire by paying for individual tuition. I realize that it might be expensive, but it'd be mmm … very rewarding in other ways.

Why I'd like to be able to take up the piano is because … it's mmm … very soothing to play and to listen to. It's a wonderful feeling to lose yourself in the music as you're playing. I've got several friends who are mad about music, and I've listened to them many times. They've played both classical and pop music to me, and they've found it thrilling to play for someone. And to me it is a very peaceful experience just sitting there and listening. As well as helping to calm people down, playing an instrument like the piano's er … very good for the brain as it keeps it active. One of my friends, who plays the guitar and the piano, says that he plays for about … half an hour before he does any homework, and it helps him to focus on his work and concentrate more. And it's healthy, because it helps take away part of the stress of modern lifestyle. Friends've also told me that it improves their ability to focus, and so they play before they study or do any work, which I think would mm … benefit me too.

E: OK. Thank you. Which type of music would you like to learn to play?

C: Er … I'd like to start with classical, but I'd like to learn jazz music later on and maybe some pop music.

E: Do you think it's important to keep acquiring new skills throughout one's life?

C: Yes, I think it is.

E: Why do you think so?

C: Well, mmm, at the moment life is changing so fast with the advances that have been made in technology, and also through em … globalization in the past few decades, so it's important for people of all ages to keep up-to-date with skills of all kinds.

E: How essential do you think it'll be for workforces in the future to be proficient technologically?

C: Mmm, I'd say it is vital, because more and more of the work that is done nowadays requires a lot of input using one form of technology or another, so that in the near future it will be almost impossible to find work, even basic work, without practical computing skills. Take car design, for example. It seems that technical drawing done by hand is less important now than knowing how to create new products on the screen. Soon designers'll be

creating holograms of cars not just three-dimensional computer images. And the same applies to architecture and teaching too.

E: In what way do you think learning only computing skills can be a disadvantage in life?

C: Em … first of all, people are already becoming over-reliant on computers for virtually everything. In the current knowledge-based society, where information is available literally at people's fingertips, there's a danger that people's knowledge'll decrease and accessing information'll become just like switching on the light without necessarily understanding what's happening. And people're in danger of losing their ability to do basic things.

E: Mmm, er, should preparation of children and young people for work focus on computing skills at the expense of practical skills?

C: Mmm … I think it's a matter of balance, because we need the people to build computers and so on, and the people to learn to be able to use them for their work. Also, if any machines break down, we need people to be able to fix them. And so if education concentrates on training people to use machines to access knowledge at the expense of training technicians etc., then there'll be a major problem.

E: Do you think people will have to work longer in the future?

C: At one time it was thought that people would have more leisure time in the future, but it seems that the opposite is true. As people are living longer worldwide, they're also being asked to work longer with the result that the age at which people will be drawing a pension, if they have one, will be later than it is now. And in fact it's already starting to happen in many countries like the UK and France.

E: How can people ensure that work does not control their lives?

C: It's not easy, but not impossible either. One way is to ensure that one has interests outside work, and that these interests are not connected with work in any way. For example, if people are involved in working in computers all day, they could find something that requires manual skills like pottery.

Part 2

 2.7

E = Examiner; C = Candidate

E: Now, I'm going to give you a card with a topic to look at. You have one minute to make notes and then I'm going to ask you to talk about the topic.

E: Can you talk about the topic?

C: The skill that I'd like to talk about is playing a musical instrument, mmm … like the piano, and I'd like to learn it in the near future. I know it's possible to go to a class to learn to play the piano, but mmm … I know I'd find that very annoying. I think learning to play the piano's one of those skills that'd be better to learn … to acquire by paying for individual tuition. I realize that it might be expensive, but it'd be mmm … very rewarding in other ways.

Why I'd like to be able to take up the piano is because … it's mmm … very soothing to play and to listen to. It's a wonderful feeling to lose yourself in the music as you're playing. I've got several friends who are mad about music, and I've listened to them many times. They've played both classical and pop music to me, and they've found it thrilling to play for someone. And to me it is a very peaceful experience just sitting there and listening. As well as helping to calm people down, playing an instrument like the piano's er … very good for the brain as it keeps it active. One of my friends, who plays the guitar and the piano, says that he plays for about … half an hour before he does any homework, and it helps him to focus on his work and concentrate more. And it's healthy, because it helps take away part of the stress of modern lifestyle. Friends've also told me that it improves their ability to focus, and so they play before they study or do any work, which I think would mm … benefit me too.

E: OK. Thank you. Which type of music would you like to learn to play?

C: Er … I'd like to start with classical, but I'd like to learn jazz music later on and maybe some pop music.

Part 3

 2.8

E = Examiner; C = Candidate

E: Do you think it's important to keep acquiring new skills throughout one's life?

C: Yes, I think it is.

E: Why do you think so?

C: Well, mmm, at the moment life is changing so fast with the advances that have been made in technology, and also through em … globalization in the past few decades, so it's important for people of all ages to keep up-to-date with skills of all kinds.

E: How essential do you think it'll be for workforces in the future to be proficient technologically?

C: Mmm, I'd say it is vital, because more and more of the work that is done nowadays requires a lot of input using one form of technology or another, so that in the near future it will be almost impossible to find work, even basic work, without practical computing skills. Take car design, for example. It seems that technical drawing done by hand is less important now than knowing how to create new products on the screen. Soon designers'll be creating holograms of cars not just three-dimensional computer images. And the same applies to architecture and teaching too.

E: In what way do you think learning only computing skills can be a disadvantage in life?

C: Em … first of all, people are already becoming over-reliant on computers for virtually everything. In the current knowledge-based society, where information is available literally at people's fingertips, there's a danger that people's knowledge'll decrease and accessing information'll become just like switching on the light without necessarily understanding what's happening. And people're in danger of losing their ability to do basic things.

E: Mmm, er, should preparation of children and young people for work focus on computing skills at the expense of practical skills?

C: Mmm … I think it's a matter of balance, because we need the people to build computers and so on, and the people to learn to be able to use them for their work. Also, if any machines break down, we need people to be able to fix them. And so if education concentrates on training people to use machines to access knowledge at the expense of training technicians etc, then there'll be a major problem.

E: Do you think people will have to work longer in the future?

C: At one time it was thought that people would have more leisure time in the future, but it seems that the opposite is true. As people are living longer worldwide, they're also being asked to work longer with the result that the age at which people will be drawing a pension, if they have one, will be later than it is now. And in fact it's already starting to happen in many countries like the UK and France.

E: How can people ensure that work does not control their lives?

C: It's not easy, but not impossible either. One way is to ensure that one has interests outside work, and that these interests are not connected with work in any way. For example, if people are involved in working in computers all day, they could find something that requires manual skills like pottery.

One of my friends, who plays the guitar and the piano, says that he plays for about … half an hour before he does any homework, and it helps him to focus on his work and concentrate more.

5

2 Do you think it's important to keep acquiring new skills throughout one's life?

1 How essential do you think it will be for workforces in the future to be proficient technologically?

6 In what way do you think learning only computing skills can be a disadvantage in life?

3 Should preparation of children and young people for work focus on computing skills at the expense of practical skills?

4 Do you think people will have to work longer in the future?

5 How can people ensure that work does not control their lives?

4–6 Follow the instructions in the Coursebook. Troubleshoot any problems the students may have with the Speaking test.

Answers

4

Differences

in the near future – in the coming year

annoying – irritating

individual – one-to-one

Why – The reason

mad about – keen on

healthy – good for your health

benefit me – help me

Additional information:

They've played both classical and pop music to me, and they've found it thrilling to play for someone. And to me it is a very peaceful experience just sitting there and listening.

Content Overview

Themes

This unit is concerned with systems and infrastructure.

Exam-related activities

Reading

Topic	Road tolls
Question type	Matching statements to paragraphs
	YES/NO/NOT GIVEN
	Multiple choice

Listening

Topic	A research project
Section 3	Multiple choice
	Matching items
	Selecting items from a list

Speaking

Part 2	Talking about a memorable journey

Writing

Task 1	Describing a table

Other

Language focus	Concession
Vocabulary	Nouns related to systems
Word building	Modal verbs to adjectives

Vocabulary: Nouns related to systems   Page 182

1 Check that students know the meaning of *infrastructure* and what the main elements of an *urban infrastructure* are. Discuss which of these elements they have in their own cities. Then look at the photos and see which are represented there. Discuss the advantages and disadvantages of the various types of infrastructure.

Answers

1 road/motorway network with flyovers
2 tunnel for a train or even water supply
3 train station as part of railway network
4 motorways/highways

2/3 Look at the questionnaire on page 208 and check the students understand the items mentioned, like *GPS = Global Positioning System*. Ask them to give an example of each type. Elicit the question they'll need to ask: *Have you used … today?* Get the students to tick for themselves and then make sure they get out of their seats to ask two other students in the class (not just their neighbours!).

Answers

Possible answers
1 buses
2 a roundabout
3 water from the tap
4 for shaving/toothbrush
5 the Internet
6 mobile use
7 BBC World Service
8 TV
9 email
10 cars

4 Put the students in groups when they have finished. Ask them to collate the answers, first in their groups, and then as a whole class. Put their findings on the board as a class survey.

5 Ask the students to look at the lists of words associated with the nouns on the left. They should decide which general service or natural resource they might be connected with, before looking at the list below to check. Answer any questions about vocabulary they may have (e.g., *slick*, *viaduct*, *host access*, *appliance*) and tell them to start a page in their vocabulary books under the heading *infrastructure*.

Answers

1 oil
2 railway
3 telephone
4 satellite
5 Internet
6 water
7 electricity
8 gas

6 Check their understanding of the remaining vocabulary by identifying what part of the whole system each word conveys.

7 Students do the exercise in pairs, and then check their answers with other students. Encourage them to discuss any discrepancies before you give whole class feedback.

Answers

1 Electricity, grid
2 gas, pipelines, fields
3 water supply, purification
4 oil, wells, refineries

5 satellite, weather
6 infrastructure, lines
7 access, web, connection

8 In pairs, students discuss a recent example from their lives when a machine or system has malfunctioned or been faulty, e.g., a power cut, and their reactions to it.

Reading

IELTS Reading Passage   Page 184

1 Elicit the meaning of *toll roads* from the whole class and discuss the questions.

Answer

Roads which you have to pay to use.

2 Follow the instructions in the Coursebook. Check as a whole class.

Answers

highways, Interstate, lanes, Interstate, artery, thoroughfare

Questions 1–13

Give students 20 minutes to do the test. Ask them to write their answers on a sheet of paper or an answer sheet. They should check and discuss answers in groups and follow this with whole class discussion. Clear up any misunderstandings.

Answers

1 F
2 B
3 J: the text says: *There, cameras take pictures of every license plate, video recognition software reads the numbers and the owner is charged.*
4 C
5 I
6 YES. Paragraph A: *Electronic toll collection is increasingly the obvious answer.*
7 NOT GIVEN. Paragraph C: *Cash transactions are costly, though, because highway agencies must pay toll-takers, maintain plazas and safely transfer the cash to banks.* There is no mention of the cost of cash tolls being expensive to administer because of the expense of security guards at toll plazas.
8 NO. Paragraph D: *... tolling agencies are introducing a variety of technologies to streamline the process and increase profits.*

9 NOT GIVEN. Paragraph F: *businessmen do not need to save fistfuls of receipts for their expense reports.* However there is no comparison between business people and other users.

Questions 10–13

10 D. Paragraph G: *And because they are part of the car, they will be harder to steal.*
11 A. Paragraph H: *A study by an economist at M.I.T., Amy Finkelstein, found that drivers who pay their tolls electronically are less aware of the rates they pay.*
12 A. Paragraph J: *... more than 71 percent of transactions at the Port Authority's tunnels and bridges include an E-ZPass – up from 52 percent in 2000 ...*
13 C. Paragraph J: *Mr. Lamba said that drivers are increasingly comfortable with electronic tolling.*

Reacting to the text

Students discuss the questions in groups.

Word building: Modal verbs to adjectives   Page 186

Lead-in

Review the concepts of possibility, probability and obligation, and elicit the modals and adjectives we commonly use. Some examples:

Possible: *prospective, at some time in the future, possible in the near future*

Probable: *expected, eventually, likely, in the course of time, it is probable that, expected*

Definite: *imminent, inevitable, approaching, impending, certain*

1 Look at the example above using *likely* and ask the students to work in pairs through the activity. Go over the exercise with the whole class, clearing up any difficulties.

Answers

1 possible
2 unwilling
3 unnecessary
4 expected
5 probable
6 able
7 compulsory
8 certain
9 essential

2 Ask the students to do this exercise in groups. If possible, give each group an OHT to write their reworded paragraph on. Project the answers and compare them, correcting as necessary. Point out that this is a link to Part 3 of the Speaking test and as such is good exam practice. Encourage the students to use language of speculation in conjunction with the phrases they have just been working with. Give them a few minutes to think of their answer, helping with language where necessary. In their pairs, they can explain their situation and then share their ideas with other students and the whole class.

Answers

Examiner: <u>Is it possible for</u> communications systems like broadband to have an impact on people's lives?

Candidate: I think <u>it is possible for</u> the development of faster communication systems than exist now to have an impact on local as well as national economies, as <u>the expected outcome</u> is that it will enable people to do business faster. Obviously, <u>it is not possible for them/they aren't able</u> to solve every problem, but <u>it is at least possible for them</u> to help. For a while governments <u>were unwilling to invest</u> in fibre optics, but now the cables are being installed everywhere. For example, in my home country they provide jobs for local people …

3 Discuss the questions in small groups.

Listening
IELTS Section 3   Page 187

1 Ask students in pairs to discuss different types of research and any they might have conducted themselves. Look at the list and, as a class, decide which ones are connected to research and what they refer to in the process. Put them in the correct order.

Answers

1, 3, 4, 5 and 7 are directly related. 2 and 6 may be indirectly related.

1 aims and objectives: what the research intends to do/show, etc.

3 research question: the question the researcher is seeking to answer

4 research findings: the results/conclusions of the research

5 data analysis: the examination of the data/ information collected

7 literature review: a review or analysis of the books/journals/articles related to the research

2 Discuss the question as a whole class.

Questions 21–30

Play the listening through once and follow the usual procedure for transferring answers and checking answers. In this particular test, all of the answers are letters of the alphabet so students must be careful about transferring the answers correctly. Ask them to check their answers in pairs and then play the recording again, pausing for them to mark their answers. Clarify any misunderstandings.

Answers

21 B
22 A
23 B
24 B
25 G
26 F
27 A
28 E
29–30 A, E, in any order

---

13 The importance of infrastructure

 2.9

J = Janice; A = Ahmed

J: Hi Ahmed. How is the research project going?

A: I've just started, and it's giving me a headache already. I didn't really think it would be like this at all really, but then …

J: The beginning is always the worst part. I always hate getting started.

A: Yeah, it's always a real problem.

J: <u>So … you're doing something … on the relationship between the public and systems like roads and transport in cities?</u>

A: Yes, that's it. And you are doing … ?

J: Cityscapes and their impact on people's moods.

A: Ah, yes.

J: It has given me lots of headaches too. What's your problem?

A: Oh, everything basically. I am just trying to get my head around everything and don't know where to start.

J: Mmm … I'm in the middle of looking at data analysis, and <u>I am having a bit of a struggle</u> myself at the moment.

A: You're at the data stage. Oh right. You're quite far on then.

J: Yeah. I am …

A: Could you tell me what your experiences have been as you are further along than me? It might make me feel a bit better.

J: Yeah sure. <u>Looking back I don't know how I got to this stage, but mm … I found it really difficult to get going. I thought I was never going to get started</u>, but then it all came together.

A: That's good to hear. I thought I was the only one. But can you tell me about your experience say of em … doing the research question?

J: <u>I thought I would have difficulty turning my ideas into a research question, but it wasn't as bad as I thought. In fact, I found it extremely easy.</u>

A: OK … I might ask for your help on that then. What about the literature review?

J: <u>The literature review? That I found really took up a lot of time.</u> Although it can eat into the time, I actually like digging into things and getting to the bottom of problems.

A: Yes, I agree it can be fun. I'm reading a lot to try and get myself to frame my research question, and I'm really getting into the literature.

J: <u>Well, the thing I was very glad to get out of the way was writing the research proposal. I was exhausted after that,</u> because it's important to make sure the research proposal is really clear on the focus of your research. It's not easy summarizing everything and bringing it together.

A: <u>And designing the methods?</u>

J: <u>That was quite easy to do</u> – I enjoy analyzing systems and putting them together, so I think I sorted the methods design out really quickly. <u>But what I found really agonizing was writing the aims and objectives. That was probably the most difficult thing of all.</u>

A: Yeah … they aren't easy.

....

J: Is all of this any help Ahmed?

A: Oh yes. One of the problems is that it's OK to see things written on paper but it's the thinking behind it.

J: Yes, of course. It is.

A: Yeah. I appreciate it. My spoken English is not a problem, I think, but I've not done much writing and I'm going to find that bit difficult.

J: Well, you can get help you know.

A: Yeah? Mm, do you think I need a private tutor?

J: Oh no, that's not necessary, I'm sure. <u>I know there's language support in the university if you are not a full-time student; you just need to contact the Language Centre.</u>

A: OK, thanks for that.

J: <u>And you can get help through the main library.</u> It's not just for lending books you know.

A: Really? I never thought of that.

J: It's so easy to get isolated and not know everything that's available.

Language focus: Concession   Page 188

1 Elicit what is meant by *concession* and look at the example. This is a very common 'softening' device when giving opinions or disagreeing with another's opinions. Explain this is necessary in English to avoid sounding too strident, which can happen with students, and thus cause misunderstanding. You might also like to mention that intonation also plays a large part in moderating disagreement. Refer students to the Grammar reference on page 225.

Answers

California, Pennsylvania, Texas and Virginia **may** be quite different in many ways when it comes to the presidential primaries, but they do have one thing in common …

Although California, Pennsylvania, Texas and Virginia **may** be quite different in many ways when it comes to the presidential primaries, they do have one thing in common …

2 Ask the students to do the exercise in pairs and point out the tip regarding punctuation. Alternatively, divide the class into two – half of the pairs doing 1–4, and the other 5–8. When they have finished, get them to write their sentences on the large sheets of paper for the whole class to look at and peer-correct, if necessary.

Answers

1 Although increasing the capacity of the network may be a good solution to the problem, it is not the only one.

2 This may be a sound argument, but I think I'd want to see more funds made available for new carriages as well.

3 While inner city conditions may be cramped, the facilities available are endless.

4 I don't like the idea of computers controlling systems like transport. Nevertheless, they perform a vital function.

5 Much as I agree with the creation of high-speed communication systems, I can't help thinking that they will lead to more demands on workers and hence more stress.

6 Extensive metro systems may exist in many major cities, but they are expensive to maintain and upgrade.

7 I partly agree with the opinion expressed here, but I think it is naive to suggest that increasing the fares will in the end lead to a better transport service.

8 It's clear the quality of public services is improving. Nonetheless, more needs to be done.

3 Do this as a class activity, linking the developments to the sentences on the board.

Answers

a 7

b 2

c 4

d 1

e 5

4 Ask the students to work in pairs and think of further ideas to develop the other three sentences, and report them to the class as a whole.

5–6 Students should be regularly following current events by now to build up their background knowledge and so should have little problem finding issues to discuss here. Give them time to make some notes first and then let them discuss the points in pairs. Monitor here for the use of the language of concession. Ask a pair to work with another pair to expand the discussion. Give feedback on their performance and usage of the target language.

Extension

Choose a controversial subject and divide the class into two to prepare arguments 'for' and 'against'. Work with both groups and help the students decide on three or four main points which support their arguments. Let them come up with supporting ideas. Ask them to nominate a 'speaker' to represent the group on each point (i.e. 3 or 4 'speakers'). You can then set up the discussion for the whole class. Some possible topics are: euthanasia, capital punishment, international money loans, censorship, etc. However, be mindful of the reaction to more sensitive issues.

Speaking
IELTS Part 2   Page 189

1 First get the students to skim the text and decide on the topic. Then they write the corrected version in their notebooks. Ask them to compare their answers with their partner and a version you have put on the board, OHP, or electronic whiteboard. Go through each of the errors and indicate what the exact problem is so that they can try to avoid them themselves.

Answers

– What I would like to describe is a journey that I made to see a friend in France last winter.

– The trip was a short five-day break to a small village in the Loire valley, which is full of the most wonderful castles.

– I took the train to Paris and then to Tours, which is the largest city near the village I was visiting.

– The journey was exciting because it was my first visit to France.

– I was able to catch the train which goes through the Channel Tunnel to Paris and take another train to Tours.

– The journey was very smooth, because the train network in France runs exceptionally well and the Eurostar train is well integrated with the French system.

– What made the journey special for me was the fact the trip marked my first journey to France, and my first time in the tunnel under the English Channel.

– But what made it magical, not just special or thrilling, was the snow.

– As we passed through the countryside the snow fell on the fairytale castles along the Loire. It was a truly enchanting time.

2 Students choose the correct topic.

Answer

Topic 1

3–4 Monitor the students' notes and keep a close eye on their timing. Let them speak in their pairs. The 'examiner' in each pair should look out for any of the errors in the previous activity.

Writing
IELTS Task 1

Page 190

Photocopiable writing exercise on page 141.

1 Students look at the table and answer the questions below it in pairs. Monitor that they are circling and marking significant data on the table. Go over the answers as a class.

Answers

1 four
2 upward but mixed
3 it reflects the last two years
4 All visits
5 upward
6 2003 and 2005

2 Study the example and grammatical alternatives with the students as a class. Emphasize the importance of using a variety of structures such as these in their own essays.

Answers

1 and 3

3 Let them do the exercise in pairs and write the sentences up on the board for whole class discussion.

Answers

1 There was a rise in expenditure on holidays over the period with spending increasing from £1,053 million to £1,230 million.

2 The general trend for miscellaneous expenditure was clearly upward, rising from £318 million to £557 million, a near 60% increase.

3 Spending on business trips also went up with a climb from £859 million to £1,108 million.

4 Climbing from £539 million in 2002, expenditure on visiting friends or relatives rose only slightly to £585 million, with most of the growth taking place between 2005 and 2006.

5 The overall money spent went up from £2,780 million in 2002 to £3,390 million in 2006 (a 20.1% increase), miscellaneous expenditure clearly accounting for the bulk of the rise.

4–5 Ask the students to discuss the task and write their own answer as a timed task in class or for homework. When they check their writing, ask them to focus particularly on the structures practised in the previous activity.

Sample answer

The table depicts the reasons why people from Europe came to UK and the money they spent from 2002 to 2006.

Overall, it is clear that the money Europeans spend for different reasons in the UK increased over the period. For example, the most significant expenditure was on Holidays which rose from £1640 million to £2655 million over the period. Business and Visiting friends or relatives had almost the same level of increase from 2002 to 2006 from £1833 million to £2614 million and £1061 million to £1830 million respectively. As for the miscellaneous, although the expenditure on this category was the lowest, there was also a steady rise from £1001 million to £1454 million over the period.

In contrast, the expenditure on all visits showed a different picture. Here the increase at the beginning of the period was much lower than the latter period, from £5549 million to £5888 million in 2002-2003 compared to almost 1 million pound increase every year till the end of the period.

Word count: 167

Possible score: 7.5

Examiner's comment:

The response is well introduced. Generally, skilful lexical choices and language structures are displayed and the main points are covered. However, some content in the last paragraph is actually inaccurate and therefore slightly confusing. On the whole, however, this is an effective answer.

Review 13 answers Pages 192 and 193

Vocabulary

1

1 bridges
2 cables
3 the Internet
4 a satellite
5 oil and gas
6 electricity
7 gas
8 water
9 national grid
10 road network

2

Possible answers

2 Cables can be laid underground to carry optic fibres.
3 The Internet can be accessed from a computer to get information.
4 Information is beamed to earth from space by satellites.
5 Oil and gas can be found in fields.
6 Electricity is carried on tall towers or on cables under the ground.
7 Gas is sometimes burned as fuel to cook food in an oven.
8 Water is filtered, treated and purified before being supplied to houses.
9 Each house is connected to the national grid that supplies electricity.
10 A series of interconnecting roads is called a road network.

3

crucial, infrastructure, network, different services, electricity, granted, appreciate, service industries, supply, national grid, reconnect

The candidate was answering question 2.

Reading

grappling, cash lanes, streamline, arteries, upkeep, cash transactions, manned (booths), windshield, licence/se plates

Word building

1

1 g 2 a 3 c 4 b 5 d 6 e 7 f

2

1 necessary/essential
2 necessary/essential
3 unwilling
4 possible
5 essential
6 certain

Concession

1 … but **unfortunately** there are places in the world where it is rare.
2 … to every home looks **impossible**, it is a worthy aim.
3 … the rail network is **as** chaotic as it used to be.
4 … , I **don't** feel safe while doing so.
5 He **may** say he's an expert …
6 … as people say, I will **not** go near it.

125

Money and happiness

Content overview

Themes

This unit is concerned with money, happiness, and satisfaction with work and living standards.

Exam-related activities

Reading

Topic	Money and happiness
Question type	Matching statements to paragraphs
	TRUE/FALSE/NOT GIVEN
	Completing sentences
	Global multiple choice

Listening

Topic	Happiness in the workplace
Section 4	Multiple-choice questions
	Completing sentences

Speaking

Part 3	Discussing money and happiness/the influence of money

Writing

Task 1	Describing a pie chart and a table

Other

Language focus	Substitution and ellipsis
Vocabulary	Money matters
Word building	Values and beliefs

Vocabulary: Money matters   Page 194

Photocopiable vocabulary exercise on page 142.

Optional lead-in

Put two or three of the following proverbs on the board and ask the students to decide what they mean:

A fool and his money are soon parted.

All that glistens is not gold.

Money is the root of all evil.

When poverty comes in at the door, love flies out of the window.

One law for the rich and another for the poor.

A full cup must be carried steadily.

If you don't speculate, you can't accumulate.

It's better to be born lucky than rich.

Money talks.

The best things in life are free.

Elicit some from their own languages – you may find that some are the same in different languages. Add the other proverbs to the list on the board or dictate them. Ask the students to discuss the proverbs in groups, identifying any that are similar in their own languages.

1 Elicit the double meaning of the title of the Vocabulary section, *Money matters* ('topics to do with money' and 'money is important'). Ask the students to describe each of the photos.

Answers

1 bank notes and coins
2 bartering
3 cowry shell money

Coins are thought to have been first used in China and the Lydian kingdom in modern day Turkey in the eighth and seventh centuries BC.

2 Ask each group to put their lists of words that they associate with money on the board. You might like to remind them that the word *money* is an uncountable noun, but *coins* and *notes* are countable.

Answers

Possible answers

coins, banks, currency, spend, notes, dollars, dinars, pesos

3 Look at the collocations and elicit why the word order is important in compound nouns. The first noun acts as a modifying noun where there are two nouns, e.g., *money bag* – a bag for money. Sometimes compound nouns made up of two nouns are hyphenated, sometimes two words, sometimes one word. This can be confusing for the learner, but two alternatives will often be acceptable. Explain that as the language develops, new words are made, first from two words hyphenated and later combined together to make a new word. Point out the importance of this for completing gaps in the reading test. Remind the students that they must always follow what is in each individual text.

Answers

No in both cases.
1 money management
2 money market
3 taxpayers' money
4 money laundering

5 paper money

6 sponsorship money

7 counterfeit money

8 public money

4 Let students practise with the words in pairs and then put them on the board to see the sense of them when combined with *money*. Ask them to start a page in their vocabulary books under compound nouns with a sub-heading, 'money'.

Answers

1 *finance*	director/minister/department
2 company/government/state/family/household *finances*	
3 *cash*	reserves/flow/payment/settlement/ limit/crisis/crop
4 *currency*	conversion/markets/speculation/ fluctuation/reserves/crisis
5 *credit*	agreement/arrangement/facilities/ terms/limit/transfer
6 *debt*	collection/collector/burden/ mountain
7 *savings*	account/plan/bank
8 consumer/government/public/welfare/education *spending*	
9 *spending*	programme/target/cut/limit/money/ power/spree
10 consumer/government/public/welfare/education *expenditure*	
11 *price*	war/range/increase/cut/tag
12 capital/investment/household/family *income*	

5 Students do this activity individually and then check answers in pairs.

Answers

1 cash crop, cash flow, cash crisis

2 Paper money

3 Education expenditure, expenditure level

4 Family finances, finance minister

5 Money management

6 currency reserves, currency crisis

7 debt burden

8 spending money, spending spree

Further practice

You can consolidate this by putting the nouns on cards and get students to match them in a game of pelmanism.

6 Give the students two minutes to list three ways that their lives have been affected by money in the past week. They should describe their experiences in groups. Encourage other members of the group to ask pertinent questions. Point out the link to Part 2 Speaking.

Listening
IELTS Section 4   Page 196

1 Ask students to skim the questions to find the topic of the talk. Don't worry if they are not exact about the detail as long as they get the main topic.

Reinforce the importance of underlining key words and phrases (the students should know all of these and should have practised them many times by now). Check they have underlined the relevant key words.

Answers

a company training scheme

2 Students discuss the questions in pairs.

Questions 31–40

Play the recording once only. Ask the students to transfer their answers onto an answer sheet or a sheet of paper. Remind them to be careful about singular and plural nouns and also spelling. Ask them to discuss their answers in pairs and look at differences. Play the recording again, pausing at the answers to check the context with the students.

Answers

31 B

32 A

33 B

34 B

35 fulfilment/fulfillment

36 2/two hours

37 give training

38 (Staff) absences

39 15/fifteen %/percent/per cent

40 recruitment costs

14 Money and happiness

 2.10

Good afternoon to you all. My name's Diana Simpson, and I'm from the City Business Forum. I'm managing director of a firm of accountants which employs over 2,000 people here and abroad. I'd like to thank you for coming today, and I'd like to thank Professor Beacon for inviting me here to talk to you today about an example of a training scheme to create a happy workforce, which we are trying to promote as a model of good practice.

Before I say something about our training scheme I'd like to tell you a little bit about business values and the values of our company. When people think of business they often mistakenly think of money and profits, and at times businessmen and women have a negative press. However, business is not all bad; not just about making profits, though there is no denying that this is important. It is about creating something, often out of nothing, building it up from scratch. And an obvious plus is that business is about providing new employment opportunities that in turn enrich people's lives. It is also about bringing people together and making links and contributing to the economy of the country. But in doing so our accountancy firm adheres to a strict ethical code. We have set ourselves high standards, and we seek to improve the communities we work within by returning some of the profits back into those communities.

The training scheme I'd like to talk about is one we have been developing within our company for the past seven years. At the beginning of the training scheme, before I actually became managing director of the company we had, like many companies, staff meetings and training sessions, which were conducted by staff in-house on financial matters.

But the training scheme has evolved almost naturally to its present state using minimal resources. Initially we allocated a certain number of hours per year for staff to follow their own training by company trainers paid for by the company. This was delivered in-house once a fortnight during office hours at different times of the day including early morning and late evening. This development worked very well with courses being offered on languages, stress-busting, arts and crafts and physical exercise. Vouchers or discounts were also offered to staff to go to local gyms, and some

staff members formed their own running and swimming clubs.

As the scheme has further evolved, we have actively encouraged staff in our company to aim for personal fulfilment and not just to focus on their professional development.

About 18 months ago we decided to devote more time to training by giving each full-time worker two hours a week for training, and a proportionate amount for part-time workers. A further development has been that some of the more experienced staff decided to use the time they were allocated to give training free of charge to various organizations who need professional help.

....

And the results of the company's move from professional development on work-related matters to a focus on staff happiness? Well, quite frankly, they are startling. Staff absences? Well the number of staff absences from sickness have been reduced substantially – a 25 per cent decline as you can see from the bar chart here. The fact that working hours have been reduced has not affected productivity; actually, it is the reverse. Company profits have increased with a rise of 15 per cent. So the company profits are in a healthy state now. But the most important impact on the company as a whole has been the drop in staff turnover. All companies, large or small, have some staff turnover, but we have managed to reduce ours by a whopping 90 per cent. The knock-on effect has been reduced recruitment costs and the expense on training new staff with a further impact on profitability. We are looking at other ways of developing this further and promoting the model as a means of good practice.

3 In groups of four, students discuss the topic and decide which viewpoint they agree with and why. Open the discussion up to the whole class to see where the opinions of most of the class lie.

Word building: Values and beliefs
Page 197

1 Elicit what the students think is the difference between *ethics* and *morals*, as a whole class. Put their ideas on the board.

Answers

Moral code is possible, but codes for organizations are generally related to *ethics*. *Ethics* relates to the principles or the philosophy on which people's morals are based.

2 Before the lesson starts, make sets of words and meanings on card and cut them up. Divide the class into groups and get them to match the words and their meanings. This should generate some discussion as the distinctions are fine for some items. When the students have finished, they can check their definitions of morals and ethics from the previous activity.

Answers
1 f
2 e
3 g
4 c
5 a
6 b
7 d

3 Encourage the students to think of as many words as they can themselves before resorting to the dictionary. Any new words need to be recorded in their vocabulary books. Ask them to note any words that have useful affixes, e.g., *valueless*. Note that *invaluable* means the opposite of what it appears to mean and can thus confuse students.

Answers
invaluable, value, valuable, valuation, valuer, valueless

4–6 Ask the students to do these activities individually and get them to check them in pairs after each exercise. Sort out any difficulties as you monitor and focus on any that the whole class are finding problematic.

Answers
4
Values, value, Valuables, invaluable, valueless
5
principles, principled, unprincipled, principles
6
idealistic, ideals, morals, ethical

7 Follow the instructions in the Coursebook. Make sure students look at both the advantages and the disadvantages so that when you sub-divide them, both sides have something to work

on. (Religion may play a part for some students in the question of values, so make them aware that their arguments should be objective not subjective).

Language focus: Substitution and ellipsis   Page 198

1 Discuss the example and illustrate that these devices are useful in providing fluency and cohesion in our writing. Warn the students of the dangers of overuse, as they need to be clear about the words they are substituting. For example, they need to be aware of what their readers are already aware of so that any reference to it is clear. Students may have a tendency to provide too much information, thus having the opposite effect to that intended.

Show students how to write less without losing any of the message. You can do this by highlighting in texts where ellipsis and substitution successfully occur (use some of the reading texts from their books). You can draw their attention to substitution and ellipsis by asking what information is missing and what certain words or phrases refer to. This way the students will gradually recognize substitution devices and have more confidence in using them in their own writing and speaking.

Refer the students to the Grammar reference on page 226 and study the substitution devices there.

Answers
1 The word *so* replaces *about bringing people together and making links and contributing to the economy of the country.*
2 Repeating the words means that there is no real connection between the sentences.
3 Overuse of substitution can make writing or speaking difficult to understand.
4 *I think so.*

2–3 Ask the students to match the halves in pairs. They should underline the word or phrase that is being substituted, and the substitution device that is employed.

Answers
2
1 h
2 a
3 g
4 f

5 e

6 b

7 c

8 d

3

1 ... by putting back some of the profits they have made from the local people./Such philanthropic behaviour

2 ... told us how to behave .../to do so ...

3 ... the traditions and ways of the society they belong to .../... such customs ...

4 ... introduce philosophy into the school curriculum./... doing so ...

5 I left home when I was 18 to go to university./ I did so ...

6 Detailed analysis ... on what makes people happy,/... such research ...

7 ... adhered to the traditions of the community we came from .../... do so ...

8 moral standards on television ... should therefore be raised/... in doing so ...

4 Let them do this activity individually and then check in pairs before writing the new sentences up on the board. Discuss any difficulties with the whole class.

Answers

1 Although the government wanted to stop funding the railway venture, they weren't able to.

2 The banks didn't want the policy on extending loans to small businesses to change, but the government did.

3 Some people don't believe that there is a clear link between happiness and money, while others do.

4 The fact that health, wealth and happiness are often linked together when people talk must mean they are.

5 The college was praised for student behaviour and success as it hoped it would be.

6 The university didn't invest as much in delivering subjects like philosophy as it could have.

7 My father laid down the law with us when we were children, but my mother didn't.

Speaking
IELTS Part 3   Page 199

1 Ask the students to work in groups, and match the ideas with the questions. Some may be used for more than one question.

Answers

Possible answers

Do you think people associate money with happiness? Why?

– technological gadgets, reduces anxiety

Do you think it's possible to lead a happy life without money? How?

– life can be difficult without

What advantages does money bring to people's lives?

– brings freedom, reduces anxiety, allows people to do things they want, indulge in buying consumer goods, having more time

What other factors do you think are necessary to lead a happy life?

– money not everything, other factors, health/work/ friends

Do people attach too much importance to money nowadays? Why?

– overemphasize/overrate money

How can money sometimes control people's lives?

– it controls, restricts, governs every aspect of people's lives

In what ways can money be used for the good of humanity?

– redistribution of wealth, richer nations helping poor nations/people

2 Students choose two or three of the questions and discuss them, noting down any ideas they come up with for future reference for speaking or for a Task 2 writing.

For exam practice, put them into pairs to practise a timed Part 3 speaking, using the checklist on page 210, and noting anything specific they want their partner to focus on.

Reading

IELTS Reading Passage   Page 199

1 Give the students a time limit to scan for the synonyms of the words listed.

Answers

1 tackle (paragraph A)

2 contentment (paragraph A)/well-being (paragraph D, E, F, G)

3 abject (paragraph B/E)

4 endless (paragraph D)

5 penury (paragraph E)

6 rung (paragraph E)

7 budge (paragraph F)

8 civic (paragraph G)

2 If you think students are choosing the same paragraph, allot each pair of students a paragraph to make sure all the paragraphs are covered by the class. Ask them to skim their paragraph and make brief notes about the main content of the paragraph. They then compare their ideas with another pair.

Questions 1–13

Give students 20 minutes to complete the reading questions, pointing out that they have already skimmed the text and made notes, so the answers for questions 1–5 should be easier to identify now. Monitor to make sure they are underlining key words and using whatever strategies they can. When the time is up, put them into groups to discuss their answers and then go over them as a whole class.

Answers

1 Paragraph G: *If a nation wants to increase its population's sense of well-being, says Veenhoven, it should make 'less investment in economic growth and more in policies that promote good governance, liberties, democracy, trust and public safety.'*

2 Paragraph E: *But before you assume that money does buy happiness after all ... one economic rung above the homeless – rate themselves at 4.6.*

3 Paragraph G: *... and are more frequently due to factors such as social relationships and enjoyment at work.' Other researchers add fulfilment, a sense that life has meaning, belonging to civic and other groups, and living in a democracy that respects individual rights and the rule of law.*

4 Paragraph A: See the whole paragraph.

5 Paragraph F: See the whole paragraph.

6 TRUE. Paragraph B: *... and they have generally concluded that wealth increases human happiness when it lifts people out of abject poverty and into the middle class but that it does little to increase happiness thereafter.*

7 FALSE. Paragraph D: *Studies show that people like selecting from among maybe half a dozen kinds of pasta at the grocery store but find 27 choices overwhelming, leaving them chronically on edge that they could have chosen a better one than they did.*

8 NOT GIVEN. In paragraph E where multimillionaires are mentioned, but there is no mention of expectations about their numbers.

9 NOT GIVEN. In paragraph F. There is no mention of money's influence on people's happiness before the Second World War.

10 shortcomings (paragraph F)

11 life satisfaction (paragraph F)

12 social relationships (paragraph G)

13 B

Reacting to the text

Students discuss the follow-up question in small groups.

Writing

IELTS Task 1   Page 202

1 Ask the students to look at the graph and pie chart in pairs. Check comprehension of lexis, and get them to highlight significant points on the charts. Elicit the tenses they will use and the kinds of trend/descriptive phrases they can use.

2–3 Students look at the sample answer individually and identify the errors. Ask them to compare their answers with their partner when they have both finished and feed back to the whole class.

Answers

2

1 Regarding the dissatisfaction (not 'As regarding')

2 age group were slightly less content (not 'content less slightly')

3 dissatisfaction (not 'disatisfaction')

4 with the pie chart indicating (not 'with pie chart')

5 with 83 per cent being happy (not 'be very happy')

3

1 b (shows how happy various age groups were about)

2 a indicated that they were very content with

3 a For example, the positive rating for those 60 and over

4 b the greater part

5 a fewer people

4 Ask the students to do this as timed writing in class or for homework. Ensure they self-check before handing it in to you to be marked. Ask them to use the writing checklist to check their answers.

Sample answer

The bar chart provides the outcome of a survey carried out about the Daily Happiness-Stress Index in the USA during 3 months from Jan 1st to May 25th in 2008.

On the whole, the proportion of happiness and stress changed significantly over the weekends with happiness increasing and stress decreasing. It is seen that the DHSI remained almost flat the weekdays especially from Monday to Thursday standing at about 43% of 'With a lot of enjoyment' and around 10% of 'With a lot of stress'. During these days there was over four times as many happiness as worry.

By contrast, on Fridays minor changes occurred with the percentage of enjoyment climbing slightly at approximately 46% while that of worry went down to just below 10%. The most variation was experienced over the weekends when the proportion of happiness reached about 57% compared to the fall of stress which fell to about 7%.

Overall, the percentage of happiness was greater than that of stress over all the period and the gap between them widened from Fridays to Sundays.

Word count: 177

Possible score: 7

Examiner's comment:

The key points are presented logically with cohesive devices being used throughout. However, the effectiveness of the response is somewhat reduced by occasional errors in grammar and editing, although these do not seriously impede communication. Sentence coordination might have been improved in places by more judicious punctuation.

Review 14 answers Pages 204 and 205

Vocabulary

1

1	i	6	f
2	g	7	g/h
3	c	8	d
4	e/j	9	e
5	b	10	a/j

2

1 family income
2 debt mountain
3 cash crop
4 savings bank
5 currency reserves
6 paper money
7 Consumer spending
8 price war
9 credit limit
10 State finance

Word building

1

beliefs, principles, moralistic, ethics, standards

2

realistic, idealistic, ideals, moral

Examiner's question: Do you think young people today are too idealistic?

Substitution and ellipsis

1

1 The television presenter claimed that work was a very important factor in making people happy, *but the audience didn't.*

2 Some people don't believe in the need to save money for the future, *while others do.*

3 Many people don't want to do volunteer work to help others, *but fortunately there are many who do.*

4 Politicians often think the opinions of ordinary people are not important when they are in power, *but clearly they are.*

5 Just as I have had the chance to have a free education, *I think everyone else should.*

2

1 they want to
2 Such
3 do so
4 hasn't

Photocopiable activities

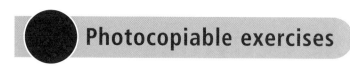

Unit 1

Writing Page 15

1 Look *quickly* at the graphs a–d below and decide what the overall trend is for all the data in each graph.

a   Student applications

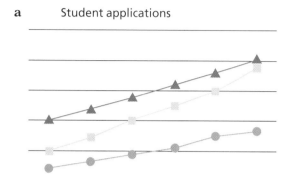

b   Percentage of hits on the site

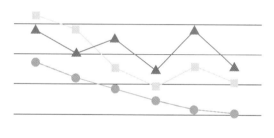

c   Profits

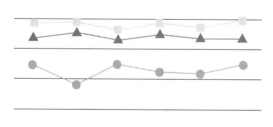

d   Drop-outs

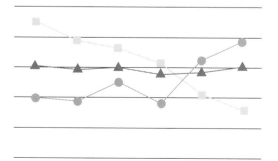

2 Match the overviews below to charts a–d in exercise 1.

1 There is a clear upward trend in numbers over the period. ☐

2 There is a downward trend in volumes. ☐

3 Numbers clearly rose during the period. ☐

4 Volumes fell. ☐

5 Numbers varied. ☐

6 Numbers rose. ☐

7 There is no clear overall trend in numbers. ☐

8 Numbers remained steady. ☐

9 There is an upward trend in numbers. ☐

10 The overall trend is fairly flat. ☐

3 Write out each sentence from exercise 2 using a relevant noun in each case, and making any changes that are necessary.

4 Which of the following phrases can you add to a sentence to indicate that it is an overview: *Moreover, It is clear, On top of that, Generally speaking, Overall, All in all?*

5 Reorder and expand the words below to create sentences, making any changes necessary.

1 book sales/overall/rise/period

_____

2 trend/attendances/clear/upward

_____

3 increase/numbers/over year

_____

4 percentages/fall/overall/past decade

_____

5 upward trend/cost/train journeys/generally speaking

_____

6 trend/prices/flat/overall

_____

7 last year/distance covered/shoppers/decline slowly/it is clear

_____

8 price grain/steady rise/recent years/generally

_____

9 flights abroad/clear/downward trend

_____

10 no trend/overall/last few years/visitor numbers/various museums

_____

Unit 1

Language focus 1   Page 10

1 In pairs, make questions with the words in brackets to develop the statement.

1 My family always wanted me to study English at university. (Why did …? Do they still …?)

_____

_____

2 I always rely on friends to help when things go wrong. (When did …?)

_____

_____

3 My friends are all planning to follow different careers from me. (What are …?)

_____

_____

4 As a child I daydreamed a lot. (What did …?/Do you …?)

_____

_____

5 My parents don't like travelling at all. (Why don't …?)

_____

_____

6 I still have friends that I first met when I was a child. (Do you …?/When was …?)

_____

_____

7 I am studying English. (Why …?/Do you …?)

_____

_____

8 My friends and I frequently go to parties. (What do you …?/When was …?)

_____

_____

9 I think I get on with people quite well. (Why do …?/Do you ever not …?)

_____

_____

2 Choose at least three sentences from exercise 1 which relate to you. Work in pairs using the questions to ask each other about the statements you chose.

Unit 2

Word building Page 24

1 Work in pairs and make questions with the following words.

Example: you think necessary learn languages?

Do you think it is necessary to learn languages?

1 opinion practical skills your future career?

_____

2 television play significant role your life?

_____

3 computers invaluable tools your opinion?

_____

4 career film industry appealing/unappealing you?

_____

5 you think work studying exciting?

_____

6 you think have good career is crucial life?

_____

7 you feel using technology beneficial detrimental for young people?

_____

2 Change partners and ask each other the questions. Give reasons and examples in your answers.

Unit 3

Word building Page 33

1 Complete the sentences below using the adjective in brackets in an *-ing* or *-ed* form.

1 Do you find any sporting activity _____ or are you never _____ by sport? (thrill)

2 Are you _____ in languages generally or are they not that _____ to you? (interest)

3 Do you get _____ doing grammar exercises or do you never find them _____? (bore)

4 Has using any form of technology like wi-fi ever made you feel _____? Or is this kind of technology not _____ for you? (exhilarate)

5 What is the most _____ thing you have done recently in class? Or don't you feel _____ by anything? (challenge)

6 Do you get _____ by travelling or is it no longer _____ for you? (excite)

7 Are you the kind of person who is not easily _____ or do you find other people _____? (motivate)

8 Have you ever been to a concert or play that has been _____? Or are you the sort of person who is rarely excited enough by anything to feel _____? (electrify)

9 How can learning be made _____ for children? Do you remember feeling _____ by your early education? (stimulate)

10 Do you get _____ easily when things don't go well or are you the sort of person who is easygoing and finds nothing _____? (irritate)

2 Work with a partner. Choose three or more statements for your partner to ask you. When you reply, try to use either a noun or a verb made from the adjective in the question and an adjective form at least once.

136

Unit 4

Language focus 1 Page 51

Identify the six sentences below that are wrong and correct each one by moving two words in each sentence. Note you are not allowed to change anything else in the sentences. Different answers are possible.

1 Heavy luggage is very inconvenient when travelling so the secret is to buy suitcases that have wheels.

2 Tables made by hand is more expensive than furniture that are machine made.

3 If people ate fruit that is grown locally rather than buying apples and oranges produced in other countries, it would save the environment.

4 When people are encouraged to keep streets free of waste like bottles, then litter are less likely to cause problems.

5 As more and more people use electronic cards to pay for small items instead of coins, are cash going to become obsolete?

6 Information on virtually every subject is at people's fingertips when they want to check specific details on the Internet.

7 Dwellings in cities such as flats and maisonettes doesn't always occupy less space than accommodation like houses do.

8 Advice, for example, with suggestions rather than orders is given in leaflets to patients.

9 Clothing worn at school are one form of uniforms that always attracts controversy.

10 Music, whether they are wind, percussion or string, are a source of pleasure for people all over the world who are interested in instruments.

Unit 5

Writing Page 68

Look at the chart below and use the phrases a–h to fill the gaps 1–8.

Historic and projected carbon emissions by sector 1990–2020 (by source)

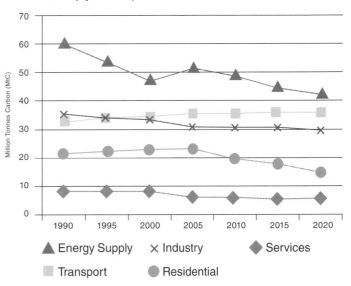

The graph provides **1** _____ carbon emissions in millions of tonnes in various sectors up to 2020.

It is clear that emissions are forecast to decline **2** _____ during the decade from 2010 to 2020 in all sectors **3** _____ transport. **4** _____ is expected to be in energy supply, from 60 million tonnes of carbon in 1990 to just over 40 million in 2020, **5** _____ of around 20 per cent. It is also estimated that emissions from industry and services **6** _____ 35 to 30 million tonnes and from approximately 9 to 7 million, respectively. **7** _____ , while emissions peaked at about 24 million tonnes in 2005 following a rise from just over 20 million in 1990, they are set to fall to about 15 million tonnes by the end of the period.

By contrast, **8** _____ is projected to be seen in the transport sector where emissions will rise slightly from around 34 to 35 million tonnes.

a As regards the residential sector

b the exception to the general decline

c a breakdown of past and projected

d will decrease from around

e The greatest fall

f a projected drop

g by varying degrees

h apart from

PHOTOCOPIABLE

Unit 6

Writing Page 80

1 Complete the first part of the model text below about the life of a mobile phone, using phrases from list **A** or **B**. You may use each item only once.

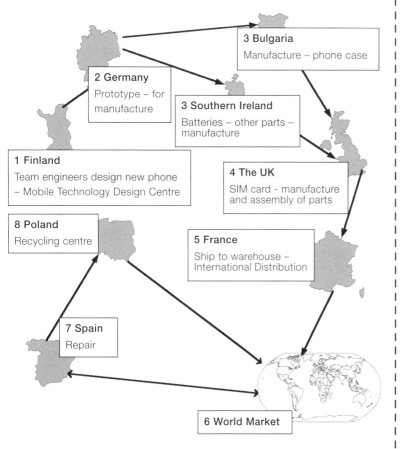

3 Bulgaria
Manufacture – phone case

2 Germany
Prototype – for manufacture

3 Southern Ireland
Batteries – other parts – manufacture

1 Finland
Team engineers design new phone – Mobile Technology Design Centre

4 The UK
SIM card - manufacture and assembly of parts

8 Poland
Recycling centre

5 France
Ship to warehouse – International Distribution

7 Spain
Repair

6 World Market

A constructed, is developed, are put together, is also produced, are manufactured, is created

B following the prototype stage, at the same time, secondly, first of all, after that

The diagram shows the various stages in the life of a new mobile phone from design to sale and then recycling. **1** _____ , the design for the new mobile **2** _____ by a team of engineers at the Mobile Technology Centre in Finland. **3** _____ , the design is sent to Germany where a prototype **4** _____ . **5** _____ , the batteries and various other parts **6** _____ in Southern Ireland and **7** _____ the phone case **8** _____ in Bulgaria. **9** _____ , the parts are sent to the UK where they **10** _____ . The SIM card is also **11** _____ at this stage.

2 Complete the description of the diagram in your own words.

Unit 7

Writing Page 99

Decide whether the sentences are A (Advantages) or D (Disadvantages) relating to skills.

1 Traditional learning skills are disappearing as people concentrate on using technology only. ☐

2 Using only technology stops children thinking for themselves which is very dangerous for their development. ☐

3 Reading books is a pleasurable activity which also helps to expand one's horizons. ☐

4 A focus on practical skills like using the computer hinders the development of analytical skills and creates an over-reliance on technology. ☐

5 Just learning factual knowledge holds young people back when it comes to applying for work as they don't have the practical skills modern jobs demand. ☐

6 Being flexible and being able to work in any setting with a range of skills rather than being weighed down by facts is obviously beneficial. ☐

7 It helps to make people more ready for the workplace where more and more practical knowledge than factual knowledge is now required. ☐

8 The concentration on practical skills prevents children learning information about the world around them. ☐

9 Learning practical skills like using technology allows people to access knowledge rather than just learning facts all the time. ☐

10 It improves the efficiency of the workforce enormously. ☐

Unit 8

Reading Page 108

Find words or phrases in the reading passage which can replace the underlined words below.

1 An analysis of cartography reveals <u>the impact of maps on</u> the history of mankind.

   _____

2 Generally speaking, cartography as a formal activity <u>is the result of</u> the evolution of highly developed societies.

   _____

3 People have <u>not much reason</u> to use landlines these days as mobile phones become more common.

   _____

4 The artefacts from this period can <u>generally be recognized</u> by zig-zag lines.

   _____

5 The music had <u>hints</u> of South American music, especially Brazilian.

   _____

6 Each species of animal has distinct <u>features</u>.

   _____

7 The books contain an important record of events for <u>future generations</u>.

   _____

8 Over a period of time, the companies were <u>combined</u> into one.

   _____

9 Teachers need to have <u>detailed information</u> about every subject, but a familiarity with general history, geography and literature helps.

   _____

10 The information was <u>accumulated</u> over a long period of time from various reliable sources.

   _____

Unit 9

Word building Page 119

The verbs in italics below are made up of the prefixes *over-* or *under-* and a verb. All of the italicized verbs are wrong. Change either the prefix or the verb to make the sentences correct.

Example:

The company *overstated* its profits. They were much higher. *Answer: understated*.

The company *underpriced* its profits. They were much higher. *Answer: underestimated*.

1 The play was completely *overestimated*. It was cheap, but the acting was terrible. _____

2 The contribution of employees to the success of a company is often *overvalued*, leading to their views not being taken into consideration.

   _____

3 The arts are consistently *underpriced*, yet more money could come from the government and sponsorship. _____

4 The town was *overtaken* by tourists visiting the sights during the holiday season. _____

5 I was completely *undercome* with emotion when I visited my home town again after 20 years. _____

6 It is important not to *overestimate* the power of the Internet in influencing people's decisions. It is a very potent force indeed. _____

7 Celebrities like sportsmen and women and TV stars are often *overrated* when it comes to providing role models in society. Their achievements should surely be highlighted more. _____

8 The latest electronic gadgets are always *overestimated* when they first come on the market. Then gradually the cost comes down.

   _____

Unit 10

Language focus   Page 144

Making any changes or additions necessary, add the words in italics to the sentences below using relative clauses. Where possible, omit the relative pronoun and be careful with the punctuation.

Example:

E-books are becoming more popular. *(be relatively recent development)*

E-books, which are a relatively recent development, are becoming more popular.

1 The car has broken down. *(I buy last year)*

2 My car is apparently worth a lot of money. *(incidentally just break down)*

3 Lorries should not be allowed on the roads and their drivers should be fined if they drive them. *(pollute environment)*

4 When I first arrived in this country, I lived in a village. *(be very pleasant experience)*

5 I live in a house. *(have very large garden at back)*

6 The mobile phone can now be found everywhere. *(introduce not that long ago)*

7 My father taught me how to play the piano as a child. *(be very good musician)*

8 I'd like to talk about a house. *(I live in when I be child)*

9 In my opinion, office blocks are better situated outside the centre of towns and cities. *(lie empty at weekend)*

10 Knowing the names of famous people is essential. *(shape history one's own country)*

Unit 11

Language focus   Page 159

Underline the correct alternative in italics in the sentences below. In some cases both alternatives are correct.

1 Even if the expansion of the railway system costs a lot of money, *the government will pay for it/it was paid for by the government.*

2 *If only I had started learning/Had I start learning* English when I was younger, I'd be a lot better now.

3 If it were not for the huge investment in community projects, young people *will have more/would have fewer* facilities at their disposal.

4 Data relating to individuals *needs to be more secure; otherwise,/would be more secure unless* people's personal details could be accessed by anyone.

5 *Unless something unexpected happens/If only something unexpected will happen*, the whole area will be transformed for the better.

6 Provided people's traditions and customs *would be/are* respected, they are more likely to respect other cultures themselves.

7 *If so much money hadn't been/Unless so much money were* spent on space research, there would be more schools and hospitals.

8 *Supposing/If* large companies gave more money to charity, it would help them put money back into society.

9 *Provided medicine would/If medicine should* find a way of prolonging life by decades, not everyone would want to live that long.

10 *If people begin/Provided people began* to live in colonies in outer space in the future, the societies they form may be very different from what we are used to now.

Unit 12

Language focus   Page 172

Move an article *a/an/the* from one sentence to an appropriate place in the other in each pair to make both sentences correct.

1

a Most important means of transport in the future will be flying cars.

b The transport will be transformed beyond the recognition in the coming decades.

2

a Bees have provided a people with honey for centuries.

b Bees are responsible for the growth of large number of flowers and crops.

3

a Countryside around my home town has some of the most beautiful scenery in the world.

b To appreciate the culture of the Bolivia, it is essential to visit small towns and not just cities.

4

a There are museums and art galleries of the international importance within the European community that must be seen.

b The responsibility for keeping towns and cities attractive for their inhabitants and tourists lies with government.

5

a I'd like to describe memorable occasion when I climbed the Alps with a group of students from my university.

b The advertising world has been undergoing a radical change in the methods that are used to target the public.

6

a You can find an advice about a good telescope to use to be able to see the features of the moon clearly on cloudless nights on the Internet.

b The flooding caused damage over area the size of London.

7

a United Arab Emirates is worth a visit to see all the developments taking place there.

b The liver is an organ that is responsible for filtering the blood to remove the impurities, so it is important that it functions well.

8

a I visited several well-known sights in Mexico that I had only read about in the books.

b It is crucial for people to show respect to culture that they are visiting and not give offence.

Unit 13

Writing   Page 190

Look at the model text for the table in exercise 1. Find the *ten* extra words in the text.

The table provides an information by purpose of visit of how much American visitors to the UK spent between 2002 and 2006.

While the overall expenditure has went up from £2,780 million in 2002 to £3,390 million in 2008 (a 20.1% increase), it is clear that in the years 2005 and 2006 miscellaneous expenditure was accounted for the bulk of the rise.

It is clear that the growth in expenditure increased as steadily with the biggest rise occurring between 2005 and 2006. Moreover, in the last two years of the period it is of evident that miscellaneous and business expenditure accounted for the nearly three-quarters of the growth in spending (45.9% and 23.6% respectively). As to regards expenditure on holidays, there was a rise over the period with money spending increasing from £1,053 million to £1,230 million. By contrast, miscellaneous spending experienced a larger increase, rising from £318 million to £557 million, a near 60% increase. Compared to expenditure on the holidays, spending on business trips also went up at a faster rate, from £859 million to £1,108 million.

The slowest growth was seen in visiting friends or relatives which rose only slightly to £585 million from £539 million in 2002 with most of the growth (12.1%) taking place in between 2005 and 2006 year.

Unit 14

Vocabulary   Page 194

1   Complete the sentences below related to the word *spend* using the following words:

public, cuts, curb, R&D, spending, spendthrift, spree, government, spendaholic.

1   A person who cannot stop themselves spending is called a _____.

2   A _____ is someone who squanders their money.

3   After all the bills are paid households are left with little _____ money.

4   Total _____ spending was boosted substantially in the early years of the new government.

5   The amount of _____ spending by companies has fallen slightly in recent years.

6   _____ spending rose as a proportion of Gross Domestic Product (GDP).

7   Spending _____ were introduced as a result of crisis after years of overspending.

8   He went on a spending _____ that lasted three days.

9   There are frequent calls for governments to _____ their spending, but at times spending limits need to be relaxed.

2   Work in pairs and decide whether each verb in italics collocates with the nouns in each sentence. If it doesn't, try to correct it. Ask other students or use a dictionary if necessary. As a last resort, look at the words in the box at the end of the exercise.

1   He *collected* a lot of money as he had a well-paid job, but he also *squandered* considerable sums on useless investments.

2   He *hoarded* money rather than *depositing* it in the bank, so he lost considerable sums of interest.

3   The charity dinner *lifted* cash for the local hospital.

4   The currency was *devalued* after the euro rose in value.

5   Trying to *repair* their debt is a serious burden for many poor countries.

6   It is pointless people trying to *build* wealth if it doesn't make them happy.

7   I am *living on* my savings from the work I did last summer, but I think they will soon *dry up*.

8   When banks *borrow* money to customers they charge interest on the amount borrowed.

9   The promotion will *boost* my finances, but I doubt if the extra work will do me any good.

10   I find it very difficult to *control* my weekly expenditure and I always run short at the end of the month.

11   The company's expenditure *went over* its income only slightly last year.

12   I forgot to *demand* my travelling expenses for the last trip I made.

	raise	service	claim
accumulate	lend	exceed	earn

PHOTOCOPIABLE

Unit 1
Writing
1/2

1 a
2 b
3 a
4 b
5 d
6 a
7 d
8 c
9 a
10 c

3 Possible answers

1 There is a clear upward trend in the number of student applications over the period.
2 There is a downward trend in the volume of hits.
3 The numbers of student applications clearly rose during the period.
4 The volume of hits fell.
5 The numbers of drop-outs varied.
6 Numbers of student applications rose.
7 There is no clear overall trend in drop-out numbers.
8 Profits remained steady.
9 There is an upward trend in student application numbers.
10 The overall trend in profits is fairly flat.

4

Generally speaking, Overall, All in all

5

1 Overall, book sales rose over the period.
2 The trend in attendances is/was clearly upward.
3 There was an increase in numbers over the year.
4 Percentages fell overall over/during the past decade.
5 Generally speaking, there was/is an upward trend in the cost of train journeys.
6 Overall, the trend in prices is/was flat.
7 It is clear that the distance covered by shoppers last year declined slowly.
8 Generally, there was/has been a steady rise in the price of grain in recent years.
9 The downward trend in flights abroad is/was clear.
10 There is/was/has been no overall trend in visitor numbers to the various museums in the last few years.

Unit 1
Language focus 1
Possible answers

1 Why did they want you to study English at university? Do they still want you to study English at university?
2 When did you last have to rely on friends? When did things last go wrong for you?
3 What are they planning to do?
4 What did you daydream about? Do you still daydream?
5 Why don't they like travelling?
6 Do you still see them a lot? When was the last time you saw them?
7 Why are you studying English? Do you enjoy studying English?
8 What do you do when you go to parties? When was the last time you went to a party?
9 Why do you get on with people quite well? Do you ever not get on with people?

Unit 2
Word building

1 In your opinion, are practical skills good for your future career?
2 Does television play a significant role in your life?
3 Are computers invaluable tools in your opinion?
4 Is a career in the film industry appealing/ unappealing to you?
5 Do you think that work or studying is exciting?
6 Do you think having a good career is crucial in life?
7 Do you feel that using technology is beneficial or detrimental for young people?

Unit 3
Word building

1 thrilling, thrilled
2 interested, interesting
3 bored, boring
4 exhilarated, exhilarating
5 challenging, challenged
6 excited, exciting
7 motivated, motivating
8 electrifying, electrified
9 stimulating, stimulated
10 irritated, irritating

Unit 4
Language focus 1

Incorrect sentences:

2 Furniture made by hand is more expensive than tables that are machine made.

4 When people are encouraged to keep streets free of waste like litter, then bottles are less likely to cause problems.

5 As more and more people use electronic cards to pay for small items instead of cash, are coins going to become obsolete?

7 Accommodation in cities such as flats and maisonettes doesn't always occupy less space than dwellings like houses do.

9 Uniforms worn at school are one form of clothing that always attracts controversy.

10 Instruments, whether they are wind, percussion or string, are a source of pleasure for people all over the world who are interested in music.

Unit 5
Writing

1 c
2 g
3 h
4 e
5 f
6 d
7 a
8 b

Unit 6
Writing

1

1 First of all
2 is created
3 Secondly
4 is developed
5 Following the prototype stage
6 are manufactured
7 at the same time
8 is also produced
9 After that
10 are put together
11 constructed

2
Possible answer

After the assembly of the parts, the phones are shipped to France, where they are stored in a warehouse for redistribution. Subsequently, they are distributed to the world market. If a phone develops a fault, it is sent to Spain or alternatively, it can be sent to the recycling centre in Poland. From here, it can be repaired and put back onto the world market or the component parts can be used again to make new phones.

Unit 7
Writing

Advantages: 3, 6, 7, 9, 10
Disadvantages: 1, 2, 4, 5, 8

Unit 8
Reading

1 how maps have influenced
2 arises from
3 little need
4 broadly be identified
5 overtones
6 characteristics
7 posterity
8 merged
9 a profound knowledge
10 compiled

Unit 9
Word building

1 overrated
2 undervalued
3 underfunded
4 overrun
5 overcome
6 underestimate
7 underrated
8 overpriced

Unit 10
Language focus

1 The car (that) I bought last year has broken down.

2 My car, which incidentally has just broken down, is apparently worth a lot of money.

3 Lorries that pollute the environment should not be allowed on the roads and their drivers should be fined if they drive them.

4 When I first arrived in this country, I lived in a village, which was a very pleasant experience.

5 I live in a house (,) which has a very large garden at the back.

6 The mobile phone, which was introduced not that long ago, can now be found everywhere.

7 My father, who is a very good musician, taught me how to play the piano as a child.

8 I'd like to talk about a house which I lived in when I was a child.

9 In my opinion, office blocks, which lie empty at the weekend, are better situated outside the centre of towns and cities.

10 Knowing the names of famous people who/that (have) shaped the history of one's own country is essential.

Unit 11
Language focus

1 the government will pay for it
2 If only I had started learning
3 would have fewer
4 needs to be more secure; otherwise,
5 Unless something unexpected happens
6 are
7 If so much money hadn't been
8 Both alternatives are possible
9 If medicine should
10 If people begin

Unit 12
Language focus

1 a The most important b the recognition
2 a a people b a large number
3 a The countryside b the Bolivia
4 a the international importance b the government
5 a a memorable occasion b a radical change
6 a an advice b an area
7 a The United Arab Emirates b the impurities
8 a the books b the culture

Unit 13
Writing

1 an information
2 has went up
3 was accounted for
4 as steadily
5 of evident
6 the nearly three-quarters

7 As to regards
8 money spending
9 the holidays
10 2006 year

Unit 14
Vocabulary

1

1 spendaholic
2 spendthrift
3 spending
4 public
5 R&D
6 Government
7 cuts
8 spree
9 curb

2

1 earned
3 raised
5 service
6 accumulate
8 lend
11 exceeded
12 claim

Progress test 1: Units 1–3

Listening
SECTION 1 Questions 1–10

Questions 1–4

Complete the form below.

Write **NO MORE THAN THREE WORDS AND/OR A NUMBER** for each answer.

<table>
<tr><td colspan="2" align="center">**Casas do Mar**
BOOKING FORM</td></tr>
<tr><td colspan="2"><table><tr><td>*Example*</td><td>*Answer*</td></tr><tr><td>Size of group</td><td>.........6.........</td></tr></table></td></tr>
<tr><td>Villa chosen</td><td>Villa **1** ....</td></tr>
<tr><td>Dates of stay</td><td>19–26th **2** ....</td></tr>
<tr><td>Cost</td><td>£ **3** .... per week.</td></tr>
<tr><td>Deposit payable</td><td>£ **4** ....</td></tr>
</table>

Questions 5–8

Complete the notes below.

Write **NO MORE THAN THREE WORDS AND/OR A NUMBER** for each answer.

To do list
Must **5** .... immediately.
Check Debbie is **6** ....
Ask everyone if they'd like to hire a **7** ....
Pay deposit.
Remember to pay the balance of the cost by **8** .... May.

Questions 9 and 10

Choose **TWO** letters, **A–E**.

Which **TWO** activities would Anna like to do on her holiday?

    A   Lying on the beach

    B   Surfing

    C   Walking

    D   Mountain biking

    E   Dolphin watching

Reading

You should spend about 20 minutes on **Questions 1–13**, which are based on the reading passage below.

Questions 1–5

The Reading Passage below has seven paragraphs, **A–G**.

Choose the correct heading for paragraphs **C–G** from the list of headings below.

> **List of Headings**
>
> **i** How live conversation might even aid a driver
>
> **ii** How the speed of music can affect reaction times
>
> **iii** The effect making calls has on business growth
>
> **iv** A growing problem which needs to be addressed
>
> **v** A comparison of more and less mentally demanding tasks
>
> **vi** The difficulties with preventing people from making calls
>
> **vii** Equipment which could provide a solution to the problem
>
> **viii** Interacting compared with just listening

1   Paragraph **C**

2   Paragraph **D**

3   Paragraph **E**

4   Paragraph **F**

5   Paragraph **G**

A MANY countries have made it illegal to natter into a hand-held mobile phone while driving. But the latest research provides further confirmation that the danger lies less in what a motorist's hands do when he takes a call than in what the conversation does to his brain.

B Melina Kunar of the University of Warwick, in England, and Todd Horowitz of the Harvard Medical School ran a series of experiments in which two groups of volunteers had to pay attention and respond to a series of moving tasks on a computer screen that were reckoned equivalent in difficulty to driving. One group was left undistracted while the other had to engage in a conversation about their hobbies and interests using a speakerphone. As Dr Kunar and Dr Horowitz report in *Psychonomic Bulletin & Review*, those who were making the equivalent of a hands-free call had an average reaction time 212 milliseconds slower than those who were not. That, they calculate, would add 5.7 metres (18 feet) to the braking distance of a car travelling at 100kph (62mph). The researchers also found that the group using the hands-free kit made 83% more errors in their tasks than those who were not talking.

C To try to understand more about why this was, they tried two further tests. In one, members of a group were asked simply to repeat words spoken by the caller. In the other, they had to think of a word that began with the last letter of the word they had just heard. Those only repeating words performed the same as those with no distraction, but those with the more complicated task showed even worse reaction times—an average of 480 milliseconds extra delay. This, the researchers suggest, shows that when people have to consider the information they hear carefully, as they might when making decisions about a business deal, it can impair their driving ability significantly.

D But does chatting to passengers have the same detrimental effect on driving? An earlier study found that it does not. That research, led by Frank Drews of the University of Utah, analyzed the performance of young drivers using a vehicle simulator. Dr Drews found that when using a hands-free phone, a volunteer "drove" significantly worse than he did when just talking to someone playing the role of a passenger. Passengers, the researchers believed, might even help road safety by commenting on surrounding traffic.

E Dr Kunar and Dr Horowitz also explored the effect of simply listening to something—such as a radio programme. For this they played a recording of the first chapter of Bram Stoker's *Dracula*. Even though the test subjects were told to pay attention because they would be asked questions about the story afterwards, it had little effect on their reaction times. Dr Kunar reckons that having to think about responses during a phone conversation competes for the brain's resources in a way that listening to a monologue does not. Dr Drews's work suggests the same thing is true of the idle chatter of a passenger.

F This could mean road-safety advice needs to be revised. America's National Highway Traffic Safety Administration estimates that the use by motorists of hand-held phones is continuing to increase: to 6% of drivers at any given time in 2007, from 5% the previous year. The biggest culprits are aged 16 to 24. People texting while driving, or fiddling with an iPod, also worry safety officials. Now it appears that talking on a phone even when both hands are on the steering wheel is dangerous too.

G Punishing people for using hand-held gadgets while driving is difficult enough, even though they can be seen from outside the car. Stopping people making hands-free calls would probably be impossible—not least because more and more vehicles are now being fitted with the necessary equipment as standard. Persuading people to switch their phones off altogether when they get behind the wheel might be the only answer. Who knows, they might even come to enjoy not having to take calls. And they'll be likelier to arrive in one piece.

Questions 6–12

Do the following statements agree with the information given in the Reading Passage?

Write:

TRUE	if the statement agrees with the information.
FALSE	if the statement contradicts the information.
NOT GIVEN	if there is no information on this.

6 In Horowitz and Kunar's experiments, volunteers drove a specially adapted car.

7 Kunar and Horowitz found that drivers making a hands-free call were more likely to make errors.

8 Non-native speakers found the word-based tasks harder than native speakers.

9 Discussing an important work-related topic could be more dangerous than chatting.

10 Dr Kunar and Dr Drews agree that conversation with a passenger requires more attention than a monologue.

11 People in their 40s are most likely to use a hand-held phone while driving.

12 Increasing numbers of new cars now incorporate everything you need to use a hands-free phone.

Question 13

Choose the correct letter, **A**, **B**, **C** or **D**.

Which of the following is the most suitable title for the Reading Passage?

A Chatting to passengers while driving can be dangerous

B Holding a mobile handset while driving can be dangerous

C Using a hands-free phone while driving can be dangerous

D Listening to the radio while driving can be dangerous

Vocabulary

1 Decide which answer **A**, **B**, **C** or **D** best fits each space and underline it.

1 He always did his homework because he was very ....

  A dynamic   **B** talented   **C** conscientious   **D** respected

2 Unfortunately his sight was .... fast.

  A deteriorating   **B** destroying   **C** harming   **D** improving

3 I can't say I'm very interested .... the environment.

  A with   **B** by   **C** at   **D** in

4 He came from a poor background. .... , he managed to succeed in life.

  A Moreover   **B** In addition   **C** Nevertheless   **D** Although

5 Tennis is a .... sport

  A field   **B** racquet   **C** equestrian   **D** track

6 It wasn't very .... of you to take the last piece of cake.

  A considerate   **B** sociable   **C** reliable   **D** conscientious

7 Flights have recently become much cheaper. .... more people are flying.

  A For example,   **B** However,   **C** As a result,   **D** Nevertheless,

8 I'm really addicted .... chocolate!

  A by   **B** to   **C** with   **D** on

9 I live near the railway station, which is very .... for getting to work.

  A appropriate   **B** necessary   **C** inspiring   **D** convenient

10 When I went horse-riding, I needed ....

  A a rod   **B** an iron   **C** a saddle   **D** a pitch

11 I'm just mad .... old black and white films!

  A about   **B** to   **C** in   **D** with

12 Some people couldn't live without a mobile phone .... I really don't need one.

  A however   **B** in spite of   **C** despite   **D** but

2 Choose the best phrase **i–viii** to describe each graph **A–H** below.

Prices ...

  i fell slightly and then levelled off
  ii remained flat
  iii plummeted
  iv rose gradually
  v fell gradually
  vi soared
  vii dipped
  viii fluctuated

3 Now match the phrases **i–viii** with a description below which has a similar meaning.

1 stayed low

2 took a headlong dive

3 slowly increased

4 took a sharp jump

5 declined over time

6 experienced an insignificant drop before recovering

7 suffered a small drop before stabilizing

8 was erratic

Writing

WRITING TASK 1

You should spend about 20 minutes on this task.

The table below gives information about the spectator sports Americans most enjoyed between 1937 and 2008. Summarise the information by selecting and reporting the main features, and make comparisons where relevant.

Write at least 150 words.

	Football	Baseball	Basketball	Ice hockey	Auto racing	Ice/Figure skating
	%	%	%	%	%	%
2008	41	10	9	4	3	1
2004	37	10	13	3	5	4
2002	37	12	13	3	5	4
1990	35	16	15	3	1	2
1981	38	16	9	2	1	2
1972	32	24	9	4	2	1
1960	21	34	9	3	*	1
1937	23	34	8	2	1	1
* Less than 0.5%						

Copyright© GALLUP. All rights reserved. Reprinted with permission from www.gallup.com.

Grammar

1 Choose the correct verb form for **1–8**.

Meteorite miracle!

A 14-year-old schoolboy **1** (*has been hit/has hit*) by a meteorite – and lived to tell the tale!

Gerrit Blank **2** (*walked/was walking*) to school when he **3** (*has seen/saw*) a ball of light speeding down towards him from the sky. He **4** (*felt/was feeling*) a sharp pain in his hand and **5** (*knocked/was knocked*) off his feet as the meteorite bounced off him. It **6** (*has landed/landed*) a few feet away, creating a large hole in the road. Gerrit escaped with just a burn on his hand.

Meteorites **7** (*will fall/are falling*) to earth all the time, but usually they **8** (*burn up/are burning up*) completely in the atmosphere. This one, the size of a pea when it landed, must have been much bigger originally. The meteorite **9** (*is/is being*) scientifically tested to find out more about where it came from and how old it is. Most meteorites **10** (*date/are dating*) back billions of years.

2 Some of the sentences below contain grammatical errors. Decide which sentences are incorrect and correct them.

1 Fifty years ago, many more people would live in rural areas.

....

2 Twice as much HD television sets were sold this year, compared to last.

....

3 I really can't stand watching soap operas.

....

4 I can't say that I find snowboarding very excited.

....

5 The Burj Dubai is currently highest tower in the world.

....

6 It's much too easy to cheat at exams these days.

....

7 Electronic book readers never will replace real books.

....

8 I would never have spoken to my parents the way that you do!

....

9 Since the beginning of the 21st century, the population doubled.

....

10 I was amazing by the quality of the products on offer.

....

11 Business has been badly effected by the recession.

....

12 He admitted that he had been boring by the lecture.

....

13 Sales are not rising as quickly as we would like.

....

14 The technology is not always a positive thing for humankind.

....

15 Always I am not sure what to do for the best.

....

Progress test 2: Units 4–6

Listening

SECTION 2   Questions 11–20

Questions 11–14

Label the map below.

Write the correct letter, **A–J**, next to questions **11–14**.

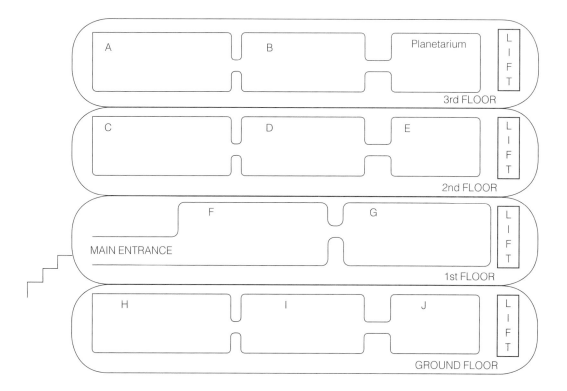

11 Transport Gallery _____

12 People of the Past _____

13 The Human Body _____

14 Refreshments Area _____

Questions 15–18

Choose the correct letter, **A, B** or **C.**

15 When did domestic fridges first start to sell in large numbers?

    A   1934.

    B   1922.

    C   1748.

16 How much did a vacuum cleaner cost in 1900?

    A   £2,000.

    B   £12,500.

    C   £350.

17 Why are the Present Day Galleries particularly suitable for children?

    A   They follow the school curriculum and are very educational.

    B   There are lots of activities the children can take part in.

    C   They use fun, music and lighting designed to appeal to children.

18 What advice does the guide give for children using the water play area?

    A   They should be supervised by an adult.

    B   They should wear protective clothing.

    C   They should not stay longer than 30 minutes.

Questions 19 and 20

Complete the sentences below.

Write **NO MORE THAN THREE WORDS AND/OR A NUMBER** for each answer.

19 The Future Gallery is aimed at children ....

20 Because the Planetarium is managed separately, there is ....

Reading

You should spend about 20 minutes on **Questions 1–13**, which are based on the reading passage below.

Biologists debate the scale of extinction in the world's tropical forests

A rare piece of good news from the world of conservation: the global extinction crisis may have been overstated. This new view of the prospects for biodiversity emerged from a symposium held this week at the Smithsonian Institution in Washington DC, but the controversy over how bad things really are has been brewing since 2006. That was when Joseph Wright of the Smithsonian Tropical Research Institute in Panama and Helene Muller-Landau of the University of Minnesota first suggested that the damage might not be as grim as some feared. They reasoned that because population growth is slowing in many tropical countries, and people are moving to cities, the amount of primary rainforest being felled is dropping and agricultural land is being abandoned, allowing trees to grow. This regrown 'secondary' forest is crucial to the pair's analysis. Within a few decades of land being abandoned, half of the original biomass has returned. Depending on what else is nearby, these new forests may then be colonised by animals and additional plants, and thus support many of the species found in the original forest.

Dr Wright and Dr Muller-Landau therefore reckon that in 2030 reasonably unbroken tropical forest will still cover a third of its natural range, and after that date its area—at least in Latin America and Asia—could increase. Much of this woodland will be secondary forest, but even so they suggest that in Africa only 16–35% of tropical-forest species will become extinct by 2030, in Asia, 21–24% and, in Latin America, fewer still. Once forest cover does start increasing, the rate of extinction should dwindle.

There are, however, two criticisms of this analysis. The first questions whether the raw data about forest cover are a good indicator of biodiversity, at least for big animals. William Laurance, a colleague of Dr Wright's, pointed out to the symposium that birds and mammals are more vulnerable to alterations in their habitat than are insects and other small animals. His data suggest that even in some of the world's best-protected primary forests, these species face severe pressures.

Elizabeth Bennett, of the Wildlife Conservation Society, an American conservation group, agreed and mentioned that for large birds and mammals, uncontrolled hunting for food and for trade is causing a phenomenon known as "empty-forest syndrome". She said that although many forests look healthy when viewed from a satellite, they are actually falling silent because many of their large animals have been removed for subsistence or profit.

Nonetheless, the symposium's participants agreed that the number of species of large animals may no longer be reliable indicators of the status of the millions of other species that live in a forest, and about which far less is known. Most species, as Nigel Stork of the University of Melbourne pointed out, are insects—and these are more resilient and much less threatened.

The second criticism of Dr Wright's and Dr Muller-Landau's view questions their interpretation of the link between a country's population and its rate of deforestation. Dr Laurance suggested this link may not be as strong in the future as it once was. In the past two decades, he said, many parts of the tropics have seen a rise in industrial forms of land use such as soya-bean farming, oil-palm plantations, and oil and gas development, together with the road-building and other construction projects that these bring in their wake. Such activities vary with the demands of international markets, not the size of the local population. In particular, Dr Laurance is worried that the liberalisation of agricultural trade and the rise of biofuels could lead to a huge increase in demand for land in the tropics.

What everyone agreed, though, was that climate change is a threat. Even the optimistic Dr Wright is worried. He warned the meeting that because many tropical species evolved in an environment that has very little temperature variation, they are not equipped to cope with an increase of as little as 3°C, which is the sort of change that many climate scientists predict. Such species may thus have to migrate long distances if they are to survive. He said that by the end of the century, 75% of tropical forests will be warmer than today, and what will remain in these hot, wet places is unknown.

Questions 1–6

Complete the flow-chart below.

Choose **ONE WORD ONLY** from the passage for each answer.

Why the global extinction crisis may have been over-stated.

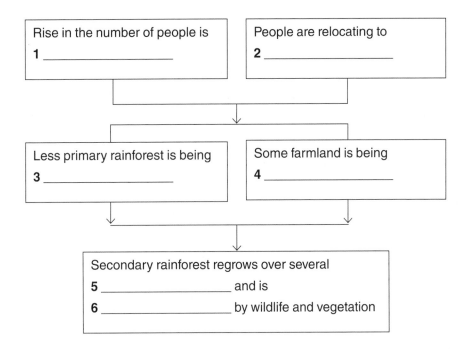

Rise in the number of people is

1 _____

People are relocating to

2 _____

Less primary rainforest is being

3 _____

Some farmland is being

4 _____

Secondary rainforest regrows over several

5 _____ and is

6 _____ by wildlife and vegetation

Questions 7 and 8

Answer the questions below.

Choose **NO MORE THAN TWO WORDS OR A NUMBER** from the passage for each answer.

7 According to Wright and Muller-Landau, how much of its original area will still be covered by tropical rainforest in 2030?

    ....

8 Where do Wright and Muller-Landau predict that the rate of extinction will be lowest after 2030?

    ....

Questions 9–13

Choose the correct letter **A**, **B**, **C** or **D.**

9 Dr Laurance felt that birds and larger animals were in greater danger of extinction because

  A they are more likely to be hunted to extinction by man.

  B they are more likely to suffer from changes to their environment.

  C they do not always live in the best-protected primary forests.

  D they are not really a good indicator of bio-diversity in forests.

10 Satellites may not give the full picture of forest life because they do not show

  A which animals are actually living there.

  B deforestation already planned for the future.

  C whether the trees in the forest are healthy or not.

  D why hunting or trading is taking place.

PHOTOCOPIABLE

11 Everyone at the symposium was in agreement that

    A   both insects and smaller mammals are far more resilient than larger mammals.

    B   analyzing insect species may help us predict the likely fate of other species.

    C   we cannot judge the health of millions of species simply by looking at a few.

    D   the number of species of large animals is comparable with that of smaller species.

12 According to Dr Laurance, population may not be that closely linked to deforestation because

    A   people are learning to use existing farm-land more wisely.

    B   road-building and other construction projects are gradually reducing.

    C   the rise of bio-fuels is reducing the amount of pollution.

    D   large scale exploitation of farm land is driven by the export market.

13 Dr Wright is worried by climate change because tropical species

    A   are not used to rising temperatures.

    B   are not used to migrating seasonally.

    C   are likely to remain in their natural habitat.

    D   are unlikely to cope with a wetter environment.

Writing

WRITING TASK 2

You should spend about 40 minutes on this task.

Write about the following topic.

> *Recently the amount of recyclable material being collected in some countries is more than is being re-used. What do you think are the main causes of this situation? What measures can be used to tackle the problem?*

Give reasons for your answer and include any relevant examples from your own knowledge or experience.

Write at least 250 words.

Vocabulary

1 Complete the gaps with a form of the word in brackets.

Despite a turbulent past and changing borders, Poland has always been an important part of Europe. Perhaps best known in the west for its **1** .... (industry) centres, such as Gdansk, Poland should also be famous for being a **2** .... (beauty) country, with mountains, lakes and forests. Farmland is also important, with a strong **3** .... (agriculture) tradition.

Despite some recent problems, the **4** .... (nation) economy remains relatively successful. **5** .... (technology) developments have created thousands of new jobs. However, a **6** .... (predict) has been made that the population will drop by 18% over the next few decades, which could be **7** .... (danger) for the country's development.

This **8** .... (project) is not based on emigration figures, but on a drop in the birth rate. Even in the most **9** .... (population) areas, the birth rate is already one of the lowest in Europe, perhaps surprising in such a **10** .... (tradition) country.

2 Choose the **TWO** words which best collocate.

1 Be careful not to get yourself into a ..../.................. situation.

(sticky/awkward/adverse)

2 Our 25th wedding anniversary was a ..../.................. occasion.

(effective/memorable/happy)

3 It is sometimes difficult to find the ..../.................. solution.

(perfect/ideal/golden)

4 He saw being made redundant as a ..../.................. opportunity to do what he really wanted to do.

(golden/perfect/happy)

5 The economy is now a ..../.................. issue.

(sticky/burning/serious)

3 Decide which answer, **A**, **B**, **C** or **D** best fits each space.

1 There was a very strange .... on the bus home last night.

   A incident   **B** crisis   **C** outcome   **D** dilemma

2 Since the factory opened, the town has become a .... community.

   A indigenous   **B** governing   **C** dominant   **D** thriving

3 I had the .... that he had not prepared for the exam at all.

   A possibility   **B** impression   **C** opportunity   **D** issue

4 The settlers rarely respected the traditions of the .... people.

   A modern   **B** urban   **C** current   **D** indigenous

5 .... , I didn't believe him, but then he convinced me.

   A Initially   **B** Before   **C** At last   **D** As soon as

Grammar

1 Some of the sentences below contain grammatical errors. Decide which sentences are incorrect and correct them.

1 The police has been blamed for starting the riot.

2 This time next week, we'll just arrive there.

3 You can leave your luggages at reception.

4 I'm planning to go very early tomorrow.

5 The accommodations are terrible!

6 He gave me an excellent piece of advice.

7 He was fined for dropping litters on the street.

8 Be careful or that is breaking.

9 Next June, I'll have worked here for ten years.

10 Small businesses are particularly vulnerable to economic downturn.

11 The length of prison sentences appears to have no effect on levels of crimes.

12 According to informations I recently received, the company is going bankrupt.

13 Something ought be done about pollution.

14 Sorry, I'm being really busy next week.

15 In the past people used to pass furnitures on to their children, not throw it away.

2 Choose the correct form of the verb in brackets.

How chewing gum is made

Chewing gum is made using either a natural rubber, *chicle*, or a synthetic substitute. If chicle is to **1** .... (use), it must first **2** .... (harvest) from the tree. The rubber tapper **3** .... (collect) the chicle by scoring the bark of the tree and **4** .... (catch) the chicle as it **5** .... (flow) down the tree.

The natural or artificial gums are first ground into a coarse kind of flour and then **6** .... (dry) carefully. After a couple of days, the gum base **7** .... (cook) at a very high temperature until it **8** .... (become) a thick syrup. Then it **9** .... (filter) several times.

Next it **10** .... (sweeten) with extremely finely powdered sugar and corn syrup, and flavourings and softeners **11** .... (add). The mixture is then rolled out and cooled before **12** .... (knead) for several hours.

When it is ready, the mixture **13** .... (flatten) and dusted with powdered sugar before being cut into small rectangles, ready for packaging. The sticks **14** .... (wrap) in aluminium foil and paper and **15** .... (seal) into plastic packs ready for shipping.

Progress test 3: Units 7–9

Listening

SECTION 3   Questions 21–30

Questions 21–25

Complete the notes below.

Write **NO MORE THAN ONE WORD AND/OR A NUMBER** for each answer.

<table>
<tr><td colspan="3" align="center">University Skills Certificate</td></tr>
<tr><td></td><td>Lucy</td><td>Jon</td></tr>
<tr><td>Modules taken:</td><td>Preparing for job interviews
Work 21 ....
Personal Development</td><td>Personal Development
Better 22 ....
23 .... Skills</td></tr>
<tr><td>Total credits earned:</td><td>24 .... credits</td><td>25 .... credits</td></tr>
</table>

Questions 26–28

Answer the questions below.

Write **NO MORE THAN TWO WORDS AND/OR A NUMBER** for each answer.

26 How many learning outcomes did the Personal Development Module have?

27 What does Jon say is the first thing to do when you are criticized?

28 According to the questionnaire, what was Jon good at being?

Questions 29 and 30

Choose **TWO** letters from A–E.

Which **TWO** types of coursework are required for the Personal Development module?

A an assignment

B a survey

C a case study

D an online 'blog'

E a literature review

Reading

You should spend 20 minutes on **Questions 1–13**, which are based on the reading passage below.

Learn what you want

A At the Lumiar school in Sao Paulo, there are no classrooms, homework or playtime and in place of teachers, there are full-time mentors to impart "love, wisdom and values", and part-time experts who teach singular skills such as piano, painting or Japanese culture. Learning is based on the Confucian principle: "I listen and I forget, I see and I remember, I do and I learn." The school is the latest project of the unorthodox business guru Ricardo Semler. The Brazilian achieved worldwide fame a decade ago with his million-selling book *Maverick!*, in which he described how he revitalised his family firm by giving employees the power to set their salaries and working hours and to choose their bosses.

B Semler has set about the school system with similar revolutionary gusto. Armed with University of Chicago statistics showing that 94 per cent of what we learn in school is never used in later life, he decided to ditch what he calls the "unsuccessful teaching methods" used in millions of schools around the world. "The fact that kids learnt Ulan Bator was the capital of Mongolia back in school is not making them learn constellations or how to weld or how to use a completely new computer system any faster," Semler says. "We are trying to prove that by giving kids freedom, they will in the end be better educated, with much more residual knowledge than the kids in the disciplined schools. They can have a much happier existence and be much more prepared for life if we don't teach them the stupid things that traditional schools do."

C The realisation that schools were turning out dysfunctional adults came to Semler in 1982, after he took over his father's company and found himself having to "deprogramme" the employees. The 24-year-old expected the workers at the marine pump manufacturer to use their initiative, but few knew how. He fired two thirds of the senior managers on his first day. Although he continued to shake things up, the serious reforms came at the start of the 1990s, when political upheaval almost forced the company to the wall. Redundancies appeared inevitable until the unions presented him with a novel proposal. They agreed to take a wage cut if management did, too, and if they got a larger share of the profits and power of veto over company expenditure. Semler agreed, and when it became clear that the workers were every bit as committed to saving the firm as he was, he gave them more and more responsibility.

D One group of 150 employees branched off to form an autonomous manufacturing unit; it was so successful that Semler split the entire company into small, self-managed divisions. When he went even further and abolished secretaries, working hours and titles, gave employees the freedom to set their own salaries and turned over all decisions to special workers' committees, business experts pronounced him mad and predicted the company would go bust within months. In fact, the opposite happened. The changes helped turn Semco into an agile and modern business whose sales rose from $30 million in 1988 to $212 million last year. The company now has operations in four countries and makes a third of its money from managing the non-core businesses of multinationals such as Wal-Mart and Carrefour. Employee turnover is less than one per cent a year.

E Having satisfied himself that adults thrive on responsibility, Semler set out to show that children would react the same way. "Playing at this age is the fundamental aspect of learning," says Semler. "One of the things that is very silly – and I hear from educators all the time – is that schools essentially teach kids to learn. They don't need school for that. Learning is what they do best. We kill it for them." Although many students spend their first weeks testing the limits of their newfound freedom – Semler admits some do nothing but play video games and eat McDonald's food – the novelty soon wears off and they start demanding to learn new skills.

F Semler wholeheartedly believes the experiment will work – he even sends his four-year-old son to Lumiar – and state schools in nine Brazilian cities have asked him to transform their classrooms into democratic ones, with more toying with the idea. "When we started with the same assumptions at the company, everybody said you can be sure it does not work, and that wasn't our experience at all," he says. "Our assumptions about human beings – that they are basically honest and interested and ready for gratifying work – were not wrong anywhere along the line. We have the same assumptions here and what we've seen so far corroborates what we thought."

Questions 1–5

The reading passage has six paragraphs, **A–F**.

Which paragraph contains the following information?

Write the correct letter, **A–F.**

NB You may use any letter more than once.

1 how Semco's annual sales have increased

2 what often happens when students first attend the Lumiar school

3 the percentage of Semco employees who leave the business each year

4 the impact of traditional schooling on pupils' adult lives

5 Semler's early business decisions

Questions 6–10

Classify the following features as characterizing

A the Lumiar school

B the company 'Semco'

C both the Lumiar school and the company 'Semco'

D neither the Lumiar school nor the company 'Semco'

Write the correct letter **A**, **B**, **C** or **D**.

6 giving people more freedom

7 teaching people how to learn

8 setting up small groups which manage themselves

9 using mentors as role models

10 allowing people to decide on their own rewards and punishments

Questions 11–13

Choose **THREE** letters, **A–H**.

Which **THREE** of the following reforms that Semler made at Semco are mentioned in the text?

A The management led special workers' committees.

B Employees at all levels had their salaries increased.

C The company no longer employed secretaries.

D Employees could decide how much they wanted to be paid.

E The management got a larger slice of the profits.

F Employees could decide who should be made redundant.

G Employees could choose what hours they wanted to work.

H The management were given new responsibilities and job titles.

Writing

WRITING TASK 1

You should spend about 20 minutes on this task.

> The maps below show Sporrington Campus when it was first built in 1978, and in 2008.
>
> Summarise the information by selecting and reporting the main features, and make comparisons where relevant.

Write at least 150 words.

Sporrington Campus 1978

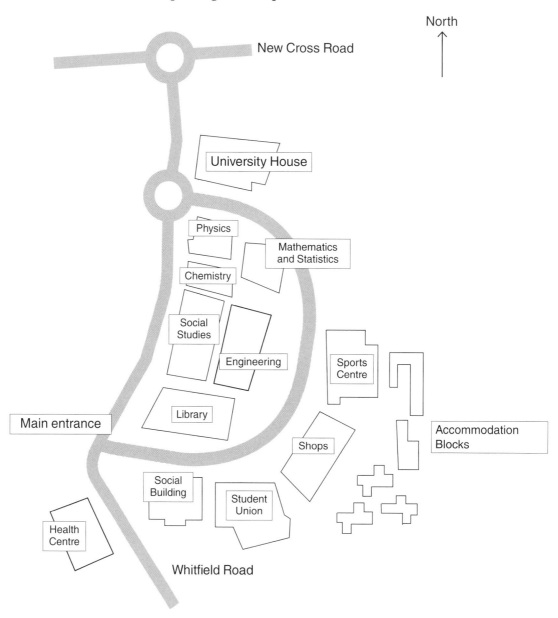

Sporrington Campus, 2008

North

Institute for Education

New Cross Road

Medical School

University House

Main entrance

Physics

Psychology

Mathematics and Statistics

I.T. Services

Chemistry

Archives

Social Studies

Library

Engineering

Sports Centre

Business School

Shops

Accommodation Blocks

Social Building

Student Union

Health Centre

Whitfield Road

Accommodation Blocks

Accommodation Blocks

Vocabulary

1   For each set of three sentences, choose the best word in the box below.

    1   Last year I changed my .... so I didn't have to commute so far.

    2   I really hate having to go to .... at the weekend.

    3   The new supermarket will threaten the .... of the local shop-keepers.

> job   livelihood   work

    4   It is harder to climb the .... ladder, once you have children.

    5   She is a lawyer by .... , but also writes children's books in her spare time.

    6   He went back to college to gain new ....

> profession   qualifications   career

    7   This is a once-in-a-lifetime .... , don't miss it!

    8   The deal could be of financial .... to us in the future.

    9   Making such a good profit was an impressive .... in the current circumstances.

> benefit   opportunity   achievement

  10   The .... is definitely up and coming; house prices have doubled in recent years.

  11   There have been some security issues in the .... of the border.

  12   The house definitely benefits from a central ....

> neighbourhood   location   vicinity

  13   The job is not very well paid, but it has excellent ....

  14   You should take this .... , as you may not get the opportunity again.

  15   Recently, she has enjoyed a great deal of ....

> prospects   success   chance

2   Use the word given in capitals at the end of each sentence to form a word which fits in the gap.

    1   Machu Picchu in Peru is one of the most .... Inca sites.   IMPRESS

    2   We had a .... holiday in the Maldives.   MEMORY

    3   Some of the exhibits in the museum are absolutely ....   PRICE

    4   There are various .... to be found in the National Parks.   ATTRACT

    5   The view was so beautiful I felt quite ....   EMOTION

    6   They are going to build an .... to the museum.   EXTEND

    7   The building has recently undergone a complete ....   TRANSFORM

    8   The house couldn't be in a better .... for local schools.   LOCATE

    9   Returning to my birthplace, after so long, made me very ....   NOSTALGIA

  10   The new house is much more .... than our old one.   SPACE

PHOTOCOPIABLE

Grammar

1 Complete the gaps using the reference words in the box below. You can use the words more than once.

| these | this | they | them | those | its | it |

Ancient trees found using 200-year-old maps

Maps more than 200 years old are being used to help find and protect Britain's natural treasure house of ancient trees. **1** .... maps help reveal how landscapes once looked when vast swathes of the country were covered in forest. As well as showing how much woodland we have lost **2** .... can also help pinpoint the ancient survivors.

The Woodland Trust, the UK's leading woodland conservation charity, launched the Ancient Tree Hunt last summer to record and preserve our oldest trees. **3** .... aims to create a database of at least 100,000 ancient trees by 2011 and is relying heavily on the public to scour their own areas for **4** .... which might be suitable candidates for the Tree Hunt. More than 4,000 ancient trees have been recorded and verified since **5** .... launch six months ago.

Nikki Williams, Ancient Tree Hunt project manager, said: '**6** .... wonderful maps are helping us identify some of the best places to search for remaining ancient trees. People joining the Ancient Tree Hunt can step back in time and see online the former landscapes of parks, gardens and tree-lined avenues. **7** .... also gives people strong clues to follow up as well as a fascinating glimpse of local history. Groups of ancient trees are extremely important habitats, and the old maps show us exactly where **8** .... once stood. We can use **9** .... to target our current searches for remaining clusters of ancient trees.'

Because of its legacy of royal hunting forests established at the time of the Norman Conquest, UK forests have more ancient trees than any other country in Europe. Moreover, **10** .... provide a home to thousands of species of plants and animals, including many rare and threatened species.

2 Choose the best option in each sentence.

1 It is vital to get a good education; .... (unless/otherwise), your employment prospects will be poor.

2 The Student Union .... (used to/would) be in a different building in the 1980s.

3 .... (Was/Were) you to join our company, you would never regret it.

4 .... (Have/Had) I worked a little harder, I would have achieved more.

5 He .... (could be/must be) very wealthy; look at the size of that diamond!

6 .... (Unless/If not) something is done immediately, things will get worse.

7 He .... (must have been /should have been) kinder to her. It was unforgiveable.

8 If universities .... (are not/will not be) properly funded, they will not produce world-class research.

9 If the government invested more in public transport, people .... (had/would) use it more.

10 Hurry up! .... (Unless/If) we leave now, we'll miss the start of the film.

11 If we .... (did/would) not have a housing shortage, house prices would not have risen so sharply.

12 This situation .... (could/could have been) dealt with more effectively.

13 The government .... (should/might) definitely stop subsidizing aircraft fuel.

14 What a fantastic result! You .... (should/must) have worked really hard.

15 Were you .... (offer/to offer) me the vacancy, I would be delighted to accept.

Progress test 4: Units 10–12

Listening

SECTION 4   Questions 31–40

Questions 31–37

Complete the table below.

Write **NO MORE THAN ONE WORD OR A NUMBER** for each answer.

Australian Art

Period	Key artists
Late 18th century	Sydney Parkinson: drew pictures of Australian **31** .... to be taken back to Europe
19th century	John Lewin: settled in Australia in **32** .... As well as nature pictures also painted **33** .... of famous figures Heidelberg School: artists focused on the different kind of **34** .... found in Australia
20th century	Grace Cossington Smith: most famous for her pictures of Sydney Harbour Bridge when not yet **35** .... Emily Kngwarreye: became a professional painter when she was almost **36** .... James Gleeson: surrealist Ian Fairweather: European immigrant who was influenced by Aboriginal and **37** .... art

Questions 38–40

Choose **THREE** letters, **A–G**.

According to the speaker, which **THREE** of the following has John Dalhsen used to make art?

    A   footwear

    B   sand

    C   clothes pegs

    D   plastic bags

    E   shells

    F   seaweed

    G   nylon rope

Reading

You should spend about 20 minutes on **Questions 1–13**, which are based on the reading passage below.

First, middle or last: what's the difference?

Scientists have long believed that birth order plays a large part in determining one's character traits and career choices.

Now we have the proof. Norwegian scientists have released a study that shows that first-borns enjoy on average an IQ advantage of three points over the next in line. The second child in turn, they discovered, is a point ahead of the third. The differences may seem small but the effect, they say, can be enormous. Just two or three IQ points can correlate to a 15-point difference in SATs scores.

And the differences don't stop there. In the Philippines, studies show that last-born siblings tend to be shorter and weigh less than their taller first-born siblings, and tend to go into less prestigious professions.

The statistics seem to suggest that there is more than a little truth in the findings. In a recent poll of 1,583 chief executive officers in America, 53 per cent were first-borns.

This higher achievement is probably caused partly by the amount of attention paid to first-borns by their parents while still an only child, and partly because the eldest devotes time to mentoring their younger siblings.

Dr Richard Woolfson, a Glasgow-based child psychologist, acknowledges that parents put their all into their first child. "By the time the others come along they are more relaxed, knowing what is important and what isn't and, it has to be said, they have less time."

Dr Woolfson is a firm believer in the theory that birth order is partly responsible for certain characteristics. "But this doesn't mean that all first-borns share the same ones," he says. "Only that the tendencies are there."

The challenge for parents, he says, is to ensure that their offspring are not constrained by such tendencies. Some first-borns are brighter because, unconsciously, there are more expectations of them. "Parents need to recognize that each child is individual, with its own strengths and weaknesses. It is about encouraging them to achieve what they can achieve."

He recommends ensuring that each child has a role. For example, if the older child gets to choose an outing, then another should choose the meal out and another is allowed to choose something else. Some parents, who perhaps have a good sense of injustice, do this naturally. Others need to make the effort.

Prof Richard Wiseman, a psychologist at Hertfordshire University, is much more sceptical about the effect of birth order than many of his colleagues.

"If push came to shove, I would say there is something in it, but there are also many other factors at play, for instance a child's attractiveness," he says. "The bottom line is that the relevance of birth order is a very inexact science."

As a youngest child himself, Dr Woolfson recalls readily his most common utterance: "It isn't fair." All of us, he believes, remain very conscious throughout life where we come in the family pecking order.

"Certainly, I do," says Gill Marshall, 43, a mother of three. "I was the eldest and, while my parents were wonderfully supportive, I felt more was expected of me. If I got an A-minus I was told I'd done really well but could have done better. My younger sister, who was generally a B-plus, was told she had done fabulously."

Mrs Marshall has twin boys of nine, Eddie and George, and a six-year-old daughter, Phoebe. Interestingly, Eddie should have been born first, because of his position in the birth canal. But when Mrs Marshall needed an emergency Caesarean, doctors discovered that his twin was trapping his foot and so George arrived five minutes ahead of Eddie.

Yet, astonishingly, the twins divide strictly along who should have been born first lines. Eddie displays all the characteristics of a first-born, while George behaves as a second-born.

Eddie is academic and more mature, but lacks self-esteem. By contrast, George struggles at school, but has a well-developed imagination and is more creative. Eddie obeys every rule at school, while George believes they exist to be broken.

Similarly, while Eddie wants to read what his class list suggests, George is happier with magazines filled with pictures. And that difference is marked in how they play. "If I take them to the woods, George will say: 'Let's play Robin Hood.' Eddie will want to do something much more conventional like run a race.

"Phoebe has benefited from having such vastly different siblings. With George she will play make-believe. With Eddie she is happy to bowl a ball to him." And the mother admits her expectations of her youngest are lower. "I definitely do say: 'You do what you want, love,' more often to Phoebe."

Questions 1–4

Complete the table.

Choose **NO MORE THAN TWO WORDS AND/OR A NUMBER** from the passage for each answer.

Typical features of different birth orders		
First born	**Middle**	**Last born**
IQ is **1** .... higher than middle child. Often have more **4** .... careers.	IQ is **2** .... higher than youngest child.	IQ is lower than older siblings. Often **3** .... and lighter than their siblings

Questions 5–10

Complete the summary using the list of words and phrases, **A–L**, below.

Possible reasons for birth order characteristics

First-born children are the only ones to spend time as only children and usually get **5** .... As siblings arrive, the eldest will also learn from **6** .... them. With younger siblings, parents don't expect such **7** .... Inevitably, parents are now also **8** ....

Dr Woolfson believes in the effect of birth order but not that all first-borns are **9** .... Professor Wiseman thinks that it is **10** ....

A playing with	**B** more material goods	**C** different
D great things	**E** good behaviour	**F** individuals
G teaching	**H** time-poor	**I** more attention
J more complex	**K** more money	**L** the same

Questions 11–13

Look at the following children mentioned in the text and the list of descriptions below.

Match each child with the correct description, **A–F**.

11 Eddie

12 George

13 Phoebe

List of descriptions

A does not like to go against norms

B is far more ambitious and ruthless

C receives less pressure from parents

D has a more attractive personality

E receives more praise from parents

F has more original and unusual ideas

Writing

WRITING TASK 2

You should spend about 40 minutes on this task.

Write about the following topic:

> *Some people think that performing arts should be funded by public money. Others believe that if a play, ballet or opera is good enough it should be able to support itself financially through ticket sales, or corporate sponsorship.*
>
> *Discuss both these views and give your own opinion.*

Give reasons for your answer and include any relevant examples from your own knowledge or experience.

Write at least 250 words.

Vocabulary

Decide which answer, A, B, C or D best fits each space.

1 I was too shy to act in school plays, but enjoyed painting the ....
   A backgrounds   **B** scenes   **C** scenery   **D** screens

2 Many people are extremely .... of art installations, feeling that they are not really art at all.
   A approving   **B** in favour   **C** critical   **D** unfavourable

3 After so many years working closely together, there is a .... relationship between our two companies.
   A specialist   **B** special   **C** specialized   **D** specific

4 Mozart .... his first symphony at the age of eight.
   A designed   **B** showed   **C** composed   **D** expressed

5 London has a very culturally .... population.
   A diverse   **B** different   **C** dissimilar   **D** unusual

6 When politicians retire, they often write their ....
   A mementos   **B** memorabilia   **C** memories   **D** memoirs

7 My uncle is my closest living ....
   A parent   **B** relative   **C** ancestor   **D** sibling

8 *Hamlet* is generally felt to be Shakespeare's best play, his ....
   A masterpiece   **B** piecework   **C** master plan   **D** worktop

9 I am not terribly interested in .... music.
   A nowadays   **B** now   **C** modern   **D** today

10 There's nowhere quite like it anywhere else in the world; it's ....
   A unusual   **B** unique   **C** unexpected   **D** unfamiliar

11 When her husband died, she was left a ....
   A widower   **B** ancestor   **C** descendant   **D** widow

12 My grandfather joined the navy at the age of 12 and experienced considerable ....
   A hardship   **B** hardness   **C** hard shoulder   **D** hardly

13 She .... the whole story! Lies from start to finish!
   A made   **B** fabricated   **C** designed   **D** developed

14 I went to see the play because the .... loved it, but I found it disappointing.
   A criticism   **B** critics   **C** criticizing   **D** critical

15 By discussing issues as they arise, we .... a good relationship.
   A maintain   **B** keep   **C** save   **D** show

Grammar

1 Complete each gap with *a/an, the* or the *zero article*.

Lake Titicaca, which is situated on **1** .... border of **2** .... Bolivia and Peru, is **3** .... largest lake in **4** .... South America and, at 3,812 metres above **5** .... sea level, one of **6** .... highest in **7** .... world. As well as having **8** .... number of **9** .... real islands, **10** .... Lake Titicaca is also home to the Uros, **11** .... group of artificial islands, made from **12** .... floating reeds. **13** .... reeds are tied to **14** .... ropes which are attached to sticks driven into **15** .... bottom of **16** .... lake. The reeds need to be replaced frequently, but, if this is done, **17** .... artificial island could last for about 30 years. Originally, the floating islands were designed this way so that they could be moved if **18** .... danger arose, but nowadays they are **19** .... major tourist attraction, with thousands of visitors **20** .... year.

2 Some of the sentences below contain a grammatical error. Decide which sentences are incorrect and correct them.

   1 The place which I liked it the best was Rio de Janeiro.

   2 If it weren't for my mother, I don't know what I have done.

   3 Exeter University, where I was a student, has a beautiful campus.

   4 If only I hadn't forgotten my key.

   5 That's the town where I used to live in.

   6 Even I had remembered my phone, I didn't have his number.

   7 People which drive to work should car share.

   8 Provided you do the work, you'll pass the exam.

   9 He went to university in Falmouth, where there is good surfing there.

 10 The woman, that was carrying an umbrella, looked at me angrily.

 11 If I were you, I will go straight to the library.

 12 I'll lend you my car if you would drive carefully.

 13 Peter is someone whom I trust completely.

 14 If I had more money, I can buy those shoes.

 15 She said I was someone she would never forget.

Progress test 5: Units 13–14

Listening

SECTION 4   Questions 31–40

Questions 31–35

What does the speaker say about each form of money or barter?

Choose **FIVE** answers from the box and write the correct letter, **A–F**, next to questions 31–35.

Early forms of money and barter in the United States

> **A** used to pay for expensive items
>
> **B** not very long-lasting
>
> **C** used to pay construction workers
>
> **D** temporarily made illegal
>
> **E** used as an offering to the Gods
>
> **F** kept in see-through containers

31 gold dust   ....

32 cocoa beans   ....

33 potlatch   ....

34 wampum   ....

35 tobacco leaves ....

Questions 36–40

Complete the summary below.

Write **NO MORE THAN ONE WORD OR A NUMBER** for each answer.

The development of money in the United States

In 1690 Massachusetts introduced paper money to pay **36** .... Other colonies copied the idea, printing more and more, which resulted in high **37** .... The British government responded by banning paper money in the colonies in **38** ....

In 1790 the dollar first became a **39** .... currency. In those days dollars were always coins. Dollar coins are still legal tender, and until the 1930s, there were also ten-dollar coins, known as **40** ....

Reading

You should spend about 20 minutes on questions 1–13, which are based on the reading passage below.

Car-pooling

We all know the arguments for ditching the car and walking, cycling or using public transport, but for many of us – however strong our green consciences – it simply is not a realistic option. When the distances involved or the lack of bus or train provision makes the car the only solution, then there are ways to make this much maligned form of transport less environmentally damaging. The emphasis has often been on either driving in a more energy-efficient way to minimize petrol use and emissions, or changing your type of car to more eco-friendly forms. Often overlooked, car-pooling – also known as lift-, ride- or car-sharing – offers a flexible method of travel which can dovetail into everyday life while reducing individual carbon footprints.

According to the National Statistics Office, if every person who regularly drives to work alone simply gave another similar driver a lift – even once a week – the number of commuting cars would fall by around 15 percent. The advantages of car-pooling are not just limited to the demands of daily work – trips to particular venues or events also fit well into the same ethos. However, because of the perceived inconvenience of car-pooling and despite its obvious environmental benefits, it is often largely ignored in our thrust towards carbon neutrality.

Environmentally, the nearer to capacity a vehicle is driven, the more fuel-efficient per person it becomes and by the same token, the smaller the individual share of the pollution generated. While the additional weight of passengers in a full "car-pooled" car does mean that more petrol will be burnt, the fact that their own vehicles have been left back in the garage offsets this slightly higher consumption several times over. In addition to the emissions, fewer cars mean less noise pollution, reduced congestion and should help to improve journey times.

From the individual's point of view, the trip can offer a chance to take a break from the inevitable stresses of driving. Formal car-pooling schemes also help to defray some of the expense of running a car – which motoring organizations estimate at around 25p per mile for a small hatchback – with passengers contributing to the petrol and running costs.

For the employer, too, there are benefits to encouraging car-pooling amongst staff. On a practical level, it reduces competition for parking spaces, while at a corporate one, it makes a clear and positive statement of environmental concern. In some areas, the car pool might even be expanded to cover two or more organizations – helpful if a number of different employers occupy an out-of-town Business Park, for instance.

One of the really positive features of the whole idea of car-pooling is that it can be as structured or as informal as the participants involved wish. At one end of the scale, it can be as simple as a "Lift Wanted" advert in the newsagent's window, or a formal scheme administered by any of the facilitator companies which have arisen in response to the growing popularity of the car-pool concept. Formal car-pooling is still in its infancy in the UK, but in other countries the idea has certainly come of age, with town councils in Sweden themselves owning 30,000 pool cars and freeway lanes reserved for "high-occupancy vehicles" in the US. Britain is beginning to catch up though, with the advent of a small number of online car-pool operators, such as National CarShare UK and FreeWheelers. These providers offer a comprehensive matching service, to ensure that the needs and privacy of both drivers and passengers are met, avoiding any potential offence or awkwardness.

If the will is there, almost anyone can car-pool – any two people needing to travel from the same area, to the same area at the same time can share, whether or not they work for the same company. It can also work for shift workers – there are only slightly fewer people commuting outside of the traditional rush hour as travel during it – and scheme providers can arrange lifts with different drivers to cover going in to work and returning if shift patterns are awkward.

With escalating fuel and associated costs, increased congestion and a growing general concern over the environmental damage of road transport, if the Swedish model is anything to go by, car-pooling seems poised to become a major feature of British commuting in the years ahead.

Questions 1 and 2

Choose **TWO** letters, **A–E**.

Apart from car-pooling, what other measures to reduce the environmental impact of using a car are mentioned in the reading passage?

- **A** Driving in such a manner so as to use less fuel.
- **B** Parking outside a town and then cycling in.
- **C** Using bio-fuels rather than petrol or diesel.
- **D** Using a more environmentally friendly car.
- **E** Reducing fuel use by not using a roof rack.

Questions 3–9

Complete the sentences below.

Choose **NO MORE THAN TWO WORDS AND/OR A NUMBER** from the passage for each answer.

3 Car sharing could mean a decline in cars on the road of approximately ....

4 People often dismiss the idea of car-pooling because they think it causes too much ....

5 The fuller a car is, the more .... it becomes for each person in it.

6 Drivers may find it a relief not to have to cope with the unavoidable .... of driving.

7 Persuading employees to use car-pooling makes finding .... easier.

8 In America, shared cars can use specially reserved ....

9 Some companies in the UK now offer an .... service to help people find a suitable car-pooling partner.

Questions 10–13

Do the following statements agree with the views of the writer in the Reading Passage?

Write:

YES	if the statement agrees with the views of the writer
NO	if the statement contradicts the views of the writer
NOT GIVEN	if it is impossible to say what the writer thinks about this

10 Car-pooling needs to be properly administered through a company.

11 The British do not like car-pooling because it affects their privacy.

12 Most people are not in a position to car-pool.

13 Car-pooling is likely to become far more popular in the UK in the future.

Writing

WRITING TASK 1

You should spend about 20 minutes on this task.

> *The chart below shows who married couples thought was responsible for doing a range of household tasks. Summarise the information by selecting and reporting the main features and make comparisons where relevant.*

Write at least 150 words.

Who is most likely to do each of the following in your household? Dec. 6–9, 2007, GPSS Lifestyle Poll Based on 594 adults who are currently married	**Reported by husband** % Saying husband does this chore	**Reported by husband** % Saying wife does this chore	**Reported by wife** % Saying husband does this chore	**Reported by wife** % Saying wife does this chore
Keep the car in good condition	79	6	58	20
Make decisions about savings or investments	49	11	21	60
Wash dishes	21	38	10	20
Do grocery shopping	20	44	12	63
Prepare meals	18	49	10	67
Caring for children on a daily basis	12	45	5	64
Make decisions about furniture and decoration	9	60	3	60

Copyright© GALLUP. All rights reserved. Reprinted with permission from www.gallup.com.

Vocabulary

1 For definitions **1–10** below, write a noun beginning with the letters given. You should write one letter for each space. All the words are connected to the topic of systems.

1 I _ _ _ _ _ _ _	a computer system that allows access to websites and email
2 v _ _ _ _ _ _	a long bridge on high posts, often across a valley
3 s _ _ _ _ _	a computer that controls all the computers in a network
4 p _ _ _ _	a tall metal structure which holds wires carrying electricity
5 s _ _ _ _ _ _ _ _	an object sent into space to send and receive information
6 g _ _ _	a network, such as one that supplies electricity
7 t _ _ _ _ _	an underground passage through which vehicles travel
8 w _ _ _	a deep hole dug in the ground to access oil or water
9 c _ _ _ _	a thick plastic-covered wire used for carrying electricity
10 r _ _ _ _ _ _ _	a factory where a natural substance is purified

2 Match each word in the left-hand column with a word in the right-hand column to make three compound nouns in each box.

1–3

money	creation
cash	crops
wealth	laundering

4–6

savings	tax
income	account
spending	power

7–9

debt	spree
credit	mountain
spending	reserves

10–12

currency	war
consumer	spending
price	conversion

13–15

ethical	customs
traditional	code
mineral	wealth

PHOTOCOPIABLE

Grammar

1 Rewrite the sentences using a modal verb.

1 You are not allowed to smoke here.

You .... smoke here.

2 The car parking situation is likely to improve with more car-pooling.

The car parking situation .... improve with more car-pooling.

3 Visitors are obliged to wear an ID Pass at all times.

Visitors .... wear an ID Pass at all times.

4 You are allowed to see a doctor even if you don't have medical insurance.

You .... see a doctor even if you don't have medical insurance.

5 It was a bad idea to wait so long before going to the dentist.

You .... waited so long before going to see the dentist.

6 It isn't essential for them to build a new runway at Heathrow.

They .... build a new runway at Heathrow.

7 It would have been possible for you to help me, if you had wanted to.

You .... helped me, if you had wanted to.

8 The conductor stopped the train, even though it wasn't necessary.

The conductor .... stopped the train.

9 The new skyscraper is predicted to be the tallest in the world.

The new skyscraper .... the tallest in the world.

10 The best thing for you to do is to write to the prime minister.

You .... write to the prime minister.

2 For each gap decide if you need to add the words in brackets or not. If not, leave the space blank.

Study shows happiness 'is contagious'

'Hell is other people,' wrote the French existential philosopher Jean Paul Sartre. Half a century later, research has shown exactly the reverse **1** (of this) .... may be true.

In a study of 4,739 adults **2** (whose) .... happiness was monitored over 20 years from 1983 to 2003, doctors found that close physical proximity was a key factor in the spread of happiness; it is, in effect, contagious. A friend who becomes happy and **3** (who) .... lives within a mile increases your own likelihood **4** (of happiness) .... by 25 per cent. But if **5** (they) .... live more than a mile away there is no effect **6** (on you) .... Previous research has shown that people can 'catch' each other's moods through copying facial expressions or **7** (through copying) .... other bodily activities. Students **8** (who are) .... assigned to share with a depressed room-mate become **9** (depressed) .... themselves, while waiters who provide 'service with a smile' see the benefits **10** (of smiling) .... in the size of their tips. In the study, researchers found the biggest boost to happiness **11** (in the study) .... came from living next door to a happy neighbour, increasing the chances of happiness by 34 per cent. **12** (This) .... was much greater than the effect of other **13** (people) .... in the same block. But spouses have a smaller effect on happiness than friends **14** (do) .... ; you have an eight per cent higher likelihood of being happy if your partner is **15** (happy) ....

Final test

Listening

SECTION 1   Questions 1–10

Questions 1–4

Complete the notes below.

Write **NO MORE THAN THREE WORDS AND/OR A NUMBER** for each answer.

Notes on St Martin's Leisure Centre

> *Example*
>
> Facilities: Swimming Pool, Gym and <u>Fitness Classes</u>

Classes available evenings and weekends: Pilates, circuit training, **1** ....

Gym opening hours: Mon–Sat **2** .... am to .... pm

Induction session: Instructor tests members' fitness, creates a **3** ....
and shows them how to use equipment.

Personal training available but at an **4** ....

Questions 5–8

Complete the table below.

Write **NO MORE THAN THREE WORDS OR A NUMBER** for each answer.

Contract Options

Option	Details	Price
Active Wellness	Unlimited use Only available for Students, unemployed and those **5**	£25.00 a month
Club Wellness	Six-month contract	£ **6** .... a month or 'pay as you go' £ **7** .... a session
Casual Member	Pay each time you visit	Joining fee: £ **8** .... Annual membership fee: £20.00 £4.50 per visit.

Questions 9 and 10

Complete the sentences below. Write **NO MORE THAN TWO WORDS** for each answer.

9 The man is booked for an induction on .... at 1pm.

10 For the induction, he should NOT wear ....

SECTION 2   Questions 11–20

Questions 11–13

Choose the correct letter, **A**, **B** or **C**.

11 According to the speaker, a gap year is

    A   viewed with suspicion by employers.

    B   a good way to become more mature.

    C   usually not very well organized.

12 The speaker says that work experience can help people

    A   find out what they really want to do.

    B   get a better job.

    C   get a good place at university.

13 Steve decided

    A   to study Media Studies.

    B   not to go to university.

    C   to go to university as a mature student.

Questions 14 and 15

Choose **TWO** letters **A–E**.

What **TWO** activities make up the gap-year trip to Argentina?

   A   Teaching kids to swim

   B   Learning Spanish

   C   Teaching English

   D   Working with animals

   E   Working with street children

Questions 16 and 17

Answer the questions below.

Write **NO MORE THAN THREE WORDS OR A NUMBER** for each answer.

16 How much could it cost approximately to be airlifted to one's own country?

....

17 If travelling with friends, what should people decide on before they leave?

....

Questions 18–20

Choose **THREE** letters **A–G**.

Which **THREE** safety measures does the speaker advise?

   A   Make sure your family know what your itinerary is.

   B   If there is a hotel safe, keep your valuables there.

   C   Use travellers' cheques, rather than carrying cash.

   D   Don't leave your bag on the back of a chair.

   E   Use a holdall or suitcase rather than a backpack.

   F   Don't travel alone, especially if you are a woman.

   G   Always keep money and cards on your person.

SECTION 3 Questions 21–30

Questions 21–27

Complete the summary below.

Write **NO MORE THAN THREE WORDS AND/OR A NUMBER** for each answer.

Summary of findings on campus tours
Data was collected using a **21**...................... after the tour.
First, people were asked about the information they had received **22** .... – if it had arrived **23** .... and if it was helpful.
The content of the tour had an average score of **24** .... on the scale, but there was a problem with the **25** .... of the tour.
The tour guide was considered **26** .... and people really appreciated the **27** ....

Questions 28–30

Which suggestions does each person make for improving the research?

Choose **THREE** answers from the box and write the letters, **A–F**, next to questions 28–30.

A Use more yes/no questions.
B Ask people to grade aspects of the tour 1–10.
C Ask for immediate feedback.
D Leave more room on the form for comments.
E Interview visitors in person.
F Provide a freepost envelope.

28 Saira ....

29 Marco ....

30 Dr Khan ....

SECTION 4 Questions 31–40

Questions 31–36

Complete the sentences below.

Write **NO MORE THAN THREE WORDS AND/OR A NUMBER** for each answer.

31 According to the 'short chronology' theory, people settled in the New World no more than .... ago.

32 The 'landbridge' theory has been generally accepted since ....

33 The people who came over the landbridge are thought to have been ....

34 According to the 'pacific coastal model' people arrived by boat from ....

35 There is no .... that people came to America from Australia.

36 DNA in a tooth found in Alaska suggests that people spread .... around 10,000 years ago.

Questions 37–40

Choose FOUR answers from the box and write the correct letter, **A–C**, next to questions 37–40.

Which Californian tribe can be described in the following ways?

A The Chumash
B The Tongva
C Both the Chumash and the Tongva

37 have a sea-faring tradition

38 have two different names

39 have a name which means 'people of the earth'

40 have been in California for at least 8,000 years

Reading

READING PASSAGE 1

You should spend about 20 minutes on **Questions 1–13**, which are based on reading passage 1 below.

Can the can

A place that is covered in graffiti and festooned with rubbish makes people feel uneasy. And with good reason, according to a group of researchers in the Netherlands. Kees Keizer and his colleagues at the University of Groningen deliberately created such settings as part of a series of experiments designed to discover if signs of vandalism, litter and low-level lawbreaking could change the way people behave. They found that they could, by a lot: doubling the number who are prepared to litter and steal.

The idea has been around for a while. In the late 1980s George Kelling, a former probation officer who now works at Rutgers University, initiated what became a vigorous campaign to remove graffiti from New York City's subway system, which was followed by a reduction in petty crime. This idea also underpinned the "zero tolerance" which Rudy Giuliani subsequently brought to the city's streets when he became mayor.

Many cities and communities around the world now try to get on top of anti-social behaviour as a way of deterring crime. But the idea remains a controversial one, not least because it is often difficult to account for other factors that could influence crime reduction, such as changes in poverty levels, housing conditions and sentencing policy—even, some people have argued, the removal of lead from petrol. An experimental test of the "broken windows theory", as Dr Kelling and his colleague James Wilson later called the idea, is therefore long overdue.

Dr Kelling's theory takes its name from the observation that a few broken windows in an empty building quickly lead to more smashed panes, more vandalism and eventually to break-ins. The tendency for people to behave in a particular way can be strengthened or weakened depending on what they observe others to be doing. This does not necessarily mean that people will copy bad behaviour exactly, reaching for a spray can when they see graffiti. Rather, says Dr Keizer, it can foster the "violation" of other norms of behaviour. It was this effect that his experiments set out to test.

His group's first study was conducted in an alley that is frequently used to park bicycles. As in all of their experiments, the researchers created two conditions: one of order and the other of disorder. In the former, the walls of the alley were freshly painted; in the latter, they were tagged with graffiti. In both states a large sign prohibiting graffiti was put up, so that it would not be missed by anyone who came to collect a bicycle. All the bikes then had a flyer attached to their handlebars. This needed to be removed before a bicycle could be ridden.

When owners returned, their behaviour was secretly recorded. There were no rubbish bins in the alley, so a cyclist had three choices. He could take the flyer with him, hang it on another bicycle (which the researchers counted as littering) or throw it to the floor. When the alley contained graffiti, 69% of the riders littered compared with 33% when the walls were clean.

The other experiments were carried out in a similar way. In the second one, a temporary fence was used to close off a short cut to a car park, except for a narrow gap. Two signs were erected, one telling people there was no throughway and the other saying that bicycles must not be left locked to the fence. In the "order" condition (with four bicycles parked nearby, but not locked to the fence) 27% of people were prepared to trespass by stepping through the gap, whereas in the disorder condition (with the four bikes locked to the fence, in violation of the sign) 82% took the short cut.

Nor were the effects limited to visual observation of petty criminal behaviour. It is against the law to let off fireworks in the Netherlands for several weeks before New Year's Eve. So, in a third experiment, two weeks before the festival the researchers randomly let off firecrackers near a bicycle shed at a main railway station and watched what happened using their flyer technique. With no fireworks, 48% of people took the flyers with them when they collected their bikes. With fireworks, this fell to 20%.

The most dramatic result, though, was the one that showed a doubling in the number of people who were prepared to steal in a condition of disorder. In this fourth study, an envelope with a €5 ($6) note inside (and the note clearly visible through the address window) was left sticking out of a post box. In a condition of order, 13% of those passing took the envelope (instead of leaving it or pushing it into the box). But if the post box was covered in graffiti, 27% did. Even if the post box had no graffiti on it, but the area around it was littered with paper, orange peel, cigarette butts and empty cans, 25% still took the envelope.

The researchers' conclusion is that one example of disorder, like graffiti or littering, can indeed encourage another, like stealing. Dr Kelling was right. The message for policymakers and police officers is that clearing up graffiti or littering promptly could help fight the spread of crime.

Questions 1–5

Do the following statements agree with the information given in Reading Passage 1?

In boxes **1–5** on your answer sheet, write:

> **TRUE**   if the statement agrees with the information
>
> **FALSE**   if the statement contradicts the information
>
> **NOT GIVEN**   if there is no information on this.

1 Dr Kees Keizer discovered that seeing litter and grafitti caused twice as many people to break the law.

2 Rudy Giuliani served two terms as Mayor of New York.

3 The 'broken windows theory' has been universally accepted.

4 A reduction in the proportion of lead in petrol could bring down the incidence of crime.

5 According to Dr Keizer, people who observe bad behaviour, such as smashing windows, will be more likely to do precisely the same thing themselves.

Questions 6–10

Complete the flow-chart below.

Choose **NO MORE THAN THREE WORDS OR A NUMBER** from the passage for each answer.

First experiment by Dr Keizer's team

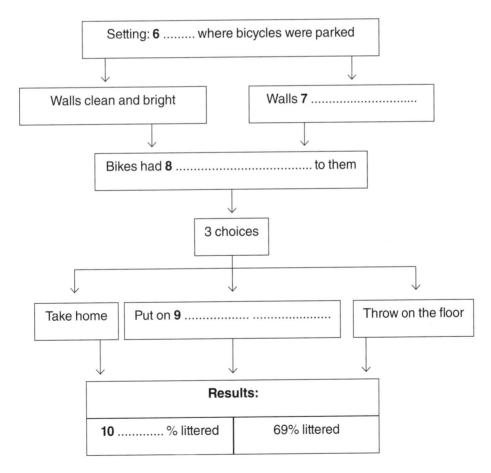

Questions 11–13

Complete the table below.

Choose **NO MORE THAN TWO WORDS OR A NUMBER** from the passage for each answer.

Further experiments by Dr Kelling's team		
Study No.	**Research question**	**Results**
2	Would people ignore a **11** .... sign if they saw other people ignoring a 'no-locked bikes' sign?	Yes, 55% more people ignored the sign.
3	Would people litter more if they saw fireworks being let off illegally?	Yes, only **12** .... of people took litter home with them in these circumstances.
4	Would more people steal money from a **13** .... if the surrounding area was dirty?	Yes, almost twice as many.

READING PASSAGE 2

You should spend about 20 minutes on **Questions 14–27**, which are based on the reading passage below.

The legacy of Krakatoa

A One hundred and twenty-five years ago this Wednesday occurred the biggest bang the inhabited world has ever known. Indonesia's Krakatoa volcano erupted. It did so with the force of 13,000 Hiroshima atom bombs, propelled a trillion cubic feet of rock, pumice and ash into the air, and made a noise loud enough to be heard 1,930 miles away in Perth. The explosions, fallout and resulting tidal wave (130 feet high in places) killed 36,417 people in Java and Sumatra, destroyed 165 villages and towns, and two-thirds of the island. Wind streams blew the fine ash as far away as New York; sea levels were raised in the English Channel, and over the following year, global temperatures were reduced by 1.2C.

B Today, the remains of one of Indonesia's most active volcanoes continue to spit and bubble. Now part of Ujung Kulon national park, it is known as Anak Krakatoa, or Krakatoa's child, a post-collapse cone which has emerged from within the caldera of the original volcano over the past half-century and now stands about 600ft above sea level.

C This Wednesday, the anniversary of the 1883 eruption, locals and tourists will remember the catastrophe when they visit Anak during the annual Krakatoa Festival – not exactly a celebration, more of a cultural memorial dedicated to one of history's most momentous natural disasters.

D Richard Arculus, a professor of geology at the Australian National University in Canberra, will be sorry not to be there. He is among what he calls a "specialized gang" that traverses the world in search of the Earth's more unstable crusts and underwater volcanoes. Anak Krakatoa is a must. "It's got a kind of status. You can go to the lip and sometimes, if it's not erupting, you will see an active vent with smoke and steam coming out of it," he said. While it is not the most orthodox of tourist attractions, it pulls a steady stream of visitors excited by the Hollywood version of events, immortalised by the 1969 film *Krakatoa, East of Java*.

E What they see is that there is very little greenery on Anak Krakatoa itself apart from some stunted vegetation around the perimeter. Professor Arculus added, "If it stopped erupting, if ash stopped coming out of it, it would be colonised by tropical vegetation very quickly." But at the moment, it appears to be more of a barren rock.

F The national park it is part of, roughly the size of Bedfordshire, is home to Java's largest remaining area of lowland rainforest, and became a Unesco World Heritage Site in 1992. It is known for its Javan one-horned rhino, the rarest large animal on Earth with only 50 left, 250 species of birds, and, possibly, the Javan tiger, although this has not been sighted since 1950.

G Krakatoa has provided writers and film-makers with a feast of stories. There is the account of the steamship thrown nearly two miles by the giant tidal waves that engulfed many nearby islands. But the most extraordinary tale involved a German quarry manager who told how he was swept off the roof of his three-storey office, only to be saved by a passing crocodile. As he cascaded through the jungle propelled by the giant wave, he spotted the croc beside him and leapt on its back. Safely aboard, he dug his thumbs into the creature's eye sockets and was carried along for the next few miles until he was dumped on the jungle floor.

H Myth or not, it is part of the folklore of Krakatoa, which sits astride the same faultline responsible for the 2004 earthquake off the coast of Sumatra. Surprisingly, the volcanic eruption of 1883 was not as severe as this more recent seismic movement. Professor Arculus said the total amount of water displaced by the Krakatoa volcano was much less. "The problem around Krakatoa was that there was a big population living around the Sumatran and Javan shores, and because they were only a few kilometres away they copped a lot of it, but the tsunami was relatively trivial in size."

I Professor Arculus also corrects the misspelling of the volcano's name, which is officially Krakatua. "It was wrongly spelt on the telegraph when the news was sent to London and it's been corrupted by the Brits ever since," he pointed out. While Anak Krakatua – or Krakatoa – is largely dormant, tourists can still witness wisps of smoke erupting from the emerging cone. But there is no real reason to worry, at least for the moment. It'll take several thousands of years before it gets to the same size and has the potential to erupt and collapse again.

Questions 14–19

Reading Passage 2 has nine paragraphs, **A–I**.

Which paragraph contains the following information?

Write the correct letter, **A–I**, in the boxes **14–19** on your answer sheet.

NB You may use any letter more than once.

14 a bizarre story of how a wild animal saved someone's life

15 a reference to a misspelling

16 details of the effects the eruption had around the world

17 the wildlife that can be found near the volcano site

18 when the volcano is likely to become dangerous once more

19 why people still want to visit Anak Krakatoa

Questions 20–27

Complete the sentences below.

Choose **NO MORE THAN THREE WORDS** from the passage for each answer.

Write your answers in boxes **20–27** on your answer sheet.

20 Many people died in Java and Sumatra as a result of the eruptions at Krakatoa and the subsequent enormous ....

21 What is left of Krakatoa is now called Anak Krakatoa, which translates as ....

22 Anak Krakatoa has little plant life on it because it has not yet ....

23 No-one has seen .... for over half a century.

24 The German quarry manager held onto the crocodile by its ....

25 The 2004 earthquake was more .... than the famous eruption of 1883.

26 Krakatoa caused a heavy deathtoll because of the size of the nearby ....

27 Although the volcano is now dormant, ... can still be seen coming out of it.

READING PASSAGE 3

You should spend about 20 minutes on **Questions 28–40**, which are based on the reading passage below.

A | It was once accepted currency among neuroscientists that the physical development of the brain stopped in very early childhood – save for a gradual loss of brain cells. However, in recent years all that has changed. Scientists now realise that the teenage brain undergoes the same sort of radical re-development seen in the rest of the body. The appearance of adult characteristics during puberty, such as facial hair in boys, appears to be paralleled inside the head with some equally dramatic changes in the physical structure and layout of the brain. It was not until the advent of brain scans – which allowed scientists to study the living brain in real time – that the true scale of the changes in teenage brain circuitry became fully apparent.

B | Two main changes are now known to take place during adolescence. The first involves the growth of fatty insulation around the electrically charged neurons – the message-transmitting cells of the brain. This extra insulation increases the speed of transmission a hundredfold. The second change concerns the growth and then deliberate pruning back of the synapses, which link neurons to one another. This re-shaping of the brain is considered a critical part of intellectual maturity. Tests show that there is a marked change in the way the adolescent brain handles information and deals with problems – a sign of growing maturity. "There seems to be a qualitative shift in the nature of thinking such that adolescents are more self-aware and self-reflective than prepubescent children," says Dr Blakemore. "Adolescents develop a capacity to hold in mind more multi-dimensional concepts and are thus able to think in a more strategic manner."

C | It was a 1999 study that laid much of the groundwork for the recent reappraisal of the teenage brain. Judith Rapoport, a child psychiatrist at the US National Institute of Mental Health in Washington DC, studied the brain development of 145 children using magnetic resonance imaging. Dr Rapoport found a phase of overproduction of grey matter in the frontal cortex – the 'thinking' part of the brain – just prior to puberty. The brain's grey matter is made of nerve cells, or neurons, and their connections. It was already known that an earlier growth of grey matter in the womb was followed by a general pruning back of cells in the first few years of life. Now it became apparent that there was a second wave of growth and pruning during puberty.

D | Even more interesting was the discovery that this time it was focussed primarily on the brain's pre-frontal cortex, the part of the outer cortex responsible for 'higher' functions such as decision-making, planning, the control of emotions, empathy and the understanding of other people's facial expressions. One of the key roles of the pre-frontal cortex, for instance, is understanding and interpreting the facial expressions of others. Adults rely on the frontal cortex to interpret faces. Teenagers are not very good at this, or at least they seem to be not very good. Take the expression of fear. When taking part in psychological tests young teenagers are notoriously bad at detecting fear in the faces of others. Brain scans show why. In early adolescence, teenagers use a part of the brain called the amygdala to interpret fear in a facial expression. This is an evolutionary ancient part of the brain and it forms part of the primitive 'gut reactions' – instincts that do not involve much thought. During adolescence, possibly because of the reshaping of the brain, adolescents shift from relying on the amygdala to using the pre-frontal cortex.

E | It may, at first glance, seem rather odd that cutting back on nerve connections is a critical part of achieving intellectual maturity. But in fact it is not a good thing to have too much grey matter. "We need to prune it back, to get rid of the excess," Dr Blakemore explains. It seems then that teenagers go through a period when their pre-frontal lobes are 'learning' to work more efficiently. This is the part of the brain that distinguishes man from the rest of the animal kingdom. It's what makes us – and teenagers – human. So the next time a teenager behaves badly, spare a thought for the 'work in progress' still taking place between their ears.

Questions 28–33

Complete the summary of paragraphs A and B below.

Choose **NO MORE THAN THREE WORDS** from paragraphs A and B for each answer.

Write your answers in boxes 28–33 on your answer sheet.

It used to be thought that, except for a steady shedding of **28** .... , the brain did not continue to grow and develop after **29** .... This perception has been challenged, thanks to the use of **30** .... As a result, scientists have discovered that it is not only the body which changes physically during **31** .... , but also the structure and layout of the brain.

The first change is that the neurons become more insulated, something which dramatically **32** .... the speed of the messages being transmitted. The second change is that the brain once again produces new **33** .... , before pruning them back.

Questions 34–39

Classify the following descriptions as relating to

  A the brain in adulthood.

  B the brain in early adolescence.

  C the brain in early childhood.

Write the correct letter, **A**, **B** or **C**, in boxes 34–39 on your answer sheet.

34 It is difficult for the brain to think strategically.

35 Excess nerve connections are cut back primarily from the frontal cortex.

36 Excess nerve connections are cut back from the whole brain.

37 It is difficult for the brain to 'read' other people's emotions effectively.

38 The brain uses the frontal cortex to interpret expressions.

39 The brain relies quite heavily on the amygdala to understand emotions.

Question 40

Choose the correct letter, **A**, **B**, **C** or **D.**

Write the correct letter in box 40 on your answer sheet.

40 Which of the following is the most suitable title for Reading Passage 3?

    A   The teenage brain: how it differs from the child's brain

    B   The teenage brain: why teenage behaviour may be down to more than hormones

    C   The teenage brain: the potential dangers of brain scans

    D   The teenage brain: how it distinguishes man from the animals

Writing

WRITING TASK 1

You should spend about 20 minutes on this task.

The table below gives information about the amount of different materials in thousands of tonnes collected from households in Britain for recycling over a four-year period.

Summarise the information by selecting and reporting the main features, and make comparisons where relevant.

Write at least 150 words.

Different materials in '000s of tonnes collected for recycling

	Year 1	Year 2	Year 3	Year 4
Paper and card	600	811	934	973
Glass	311	349	397	429
Compost	279	455	798	941
Cans	18	26	26	26
Plastics	6	8	13	8
Total	**1,214**	**1,649**	**2,168**	**2,377**

WRITING TASK 2

You should spend about 40 minutes on this task.

Write about the following topic:

Flying impacts upon the climate far more than any other action people can take as an individual. How can people be encouraged to stop or cut down on flying? What can the government do to help?

Give reasons for your answer and include any relevant examples from your own knowledge or experience.

Write at least 250 words.

Speaking

PART 1

The examiner asks the candidate about him/herself, his/her home, work or studies and other familiar topics.

EXAMPLE

Media

- Do you enjoy watching television? Why/Why not?
- Do you prefer to obtain your news from a newspaper or the television? Why?
- What kind of programmes are most popular in your country? Why?
- Would you like to appear on television? Why/Why not?

PART 2

You will have to talk about the topic for one to two minutes. You have one minute to think about what you are going to say. You can make some notes to help you if you wish.

EXAMPLE

> Describe a place you like to visit in your leisure time.
>
> You should say:
> - where the place is
> - who you go there with
> - what kind of things you do there
> - and explain why you like to go there.

PART 3

Discussion topics:

Hobbies

EXAMPLE

How have hobbies changed since you were a child?

What differences are there in your country between hobbies popular with men and hobbies popular with women?

Why do you think people have hobbies?

Sport

EXAMPLE

Do you think that sports are too commercialized these days? Why/Why not?

How can playing team sports help people to work better in a team at work or school?

Why do you think people take part in extreme sports (such as bungee jumping)?

Progress test 1

Listening

Section 1

1 Rosa
2 June
3 750
4 150
5 book (the) flights
6 insured
7 (private) chef
8 (the), 15th
9 and 10 C, E, in any order

Listening script 3.1
Section 1

V = villa owner; A = Anna

V: Hello? How can I help you?

A: Well, I'm looking to book a villa for a short holiday for myself and five other friends.

V: How many bedrooms would you want?

A: Three would be fine – we don't mind sharing.

V: Well, there's Villa Margarida, that has three bedrooms, or Villa Rosa, which has two bedrooms that can both take three people. That one's obviously a bit cheaper.

A: Oh, I think the cheaper one, Villa Rosa, please. How do you spell that?

V: R–O–S–A

A: And how much is that for a week?

V: That depends when you want to come.

A: Say the beginning of July, or end of June?

V: Well, up to the 26th June is mid-season, and after that is high season.

A: What about 19th–26th June then?

V: Yes, the villa is free then at the moment.

A: And how much would that be?

V: That would be £750 for the week, for the villa, not per person.

A: That sounds fine. Can I book that then?

V: Yes, of course. You'd need to pay a twenty per cent deposit to secure the booking, so that's £180.00. Oh no, sorry, it's £150.00 of course. You can send a cheque in euros or make a direct transfer …

....

A: I wonder, could you give me some advice about organizing the flights and so on?

V: Well, the first thing is to make sure you book the flights straightaway. Faro is a very popular destination and flights can get booked up very quickly.

A: OK, yes, I'll look into that.

V: And are you going to hire a car?

A: Yes, my friend Debbie's quite happy to drive. She's driven on the continent before.

V: Well, just make sure she's insured.

A: Good point, I'll check that.

V: What are you planning to do about food?

A: Does the villa have a decent kitchen?

V: Oh yes, but you don't want to be doing too much cooking on holiday, do you? We can offer you a private chef at a very reasonable rate. It won't cost any more than going out to eat, and you can have it in the comfort of your own place.

A: That sounds interesting, I'll talk to the others and see if they'd like to hire a chef. Can I get back to you on that?

V: Of course. Just don't forget that you need to pay the balance of the cost, that's £600, by the 15th of May.

A: No, I will … Oh, just one more thing. Are there any particular places or activities you'd recommend?

V: Well, if the weather's good, I expect you'll just want to lie on the beach.

A: Well, actually we quite like active holidays.

V: Well, if you like walking, there is some beautiful countryside just away from the coast. Or you could go mountain biking …

A: I think we'd rather go walking than biking. More chance to admire the scenery.

V: Do you play golf?

A: Oh no, not at all.

V: You could go out on a boat dolphin watching. There are usually lots of schools of dolphins around.

A: Really? That sounds great, how would we arrange that …

Reading

1 v
2 i
3 viii
4 iv
5 vi
6 FALSE
7 TRUE

8   NOT GIVEN
9   TRUE
10 TRUE
11 FALSE
12 TRUE
13 C

Vocabulary

1

1   C
2   A
3   D
4   C
5   B
6   A
7   C
8   B
9   D
10 C
11 A
12 D

2

A   vi
B   iv
C   vii
D   viii
E   iii
F   ii
G   v
H   i

3

1   ii
2   iii
3   iv
4   vi
5   v
6   vii
7   i
8   viii

Grammar

1

1   has been hit
2   was walking
3   saw
4   felt
5   was knocked

6   landed
7   are falling
8   burn up
9   is being
10 date

2

1   Fifty years ago, many more people **used to** live in rural areas.
2   Twice as **many** HD television sets were sold this year, compared to last.
3   Correct
4   I can't say that I find snowboarding very **exciting**.
5   The Burj Dubai is currently **the** highest tower in the world.
6   Correct
7   Electronic book readers **will never** replace real books./**Never will** electronic readers **replace** real books.
8   Correct
9   Since the beginning of the 21st century, the population **has** doubled.
10 I was **amazed** by the quality of the products on offer.
11 Business has been badly **affected** by the recession.
12 He admitted that he had been **bored** by the lecture.
13 Correct
14 **Technology** is not always a positive thing for humankind.
15 I am not **always** sure what to do for the best.

Progress test 2

Listening

11 H
12 J
13 C
14 A
15 A
16 C
17 B
18 B
19 over 12/twelve
20 an extra charge

Listening script 3.2
Section 2

Hello, everyone. Welcome to the Time Capsule, a brand-new kind of interactive museum. Why is it called the Time Capsule? Well, because we don't just look at things from the past, but also explore the present and the future. We have four floors of exhibits, and ten different galleries, so first of all, let's orientate ourselves. We are currently standing at the main entrance, which is actually on the first floor. If you look at your map, you'll see that the first gallery houses an exhibition called 'Technology Today'. Passing through that gallery you'll find yourself in the Communications Gallery, opposite the lifts. In this area we look at lots of different forms of communication, particularly new types of communication. If you then take the lifts down to the ground floor, there are three galleries. The furthest one from the lifts is the transport gallery, where we have a fine collection of old trams and buses, next is the gallery devoted to Great Inventions, this is a very interactive area, where you can try all sorts of things out, and finally, on the far right as you look at the map, is the gallery called 'People of the Past.' The ground floor is, as you can see, completely given over to an exploration of our past, while the first and second floors concentrate on the present. Looking at the second floor, as you come out of the lift there is a gallery about Life on Earth, and on the far left as you look at the map is a fascinating exhibition about the human body. In between these two exhibitions is our interactive children's area, aimed particularly at the under-eights.

If you get hungry or thirsty, you just need to go up to the top floor, where the refreshments area is to the left of the futures gallery, which is next to the Planetarium.

....

OK, now you've got your bearings, let me tell you a little more about the galleries and exhibits. As I mentioned, our exhibitions divide into past, present and future. Starting with the past, perhaps the most interesting exhibition is Great Inventions. This focuses on everyday inventions, such as the fridge. Did you know that although the first refrigerator was invented in 1748, and domestic fridges were first launched in the 1920s, they didn't become a popular household item until 1934, when it was so hot that people found they couldn't otherwise keep their food fresh … . Or, that one of the first vacuum cleaners on the market, around 1900, would have cost about £350.00, that's about £12,000 in today's money. Time Capsule also has plenty of emphasis on the present day, with exhibits which are directly relevant to our lives today. These Present Day galleries are particularly suitable for younger children, as they are very interactive. For example, you can walk through a reconstruction of different habitats in our Life on Earth exhibition, experiencing the jungle, or the polar regions. Or in the Human Body, you can play with a giant digestive system and see exactly what does happen to your food mm … The play area is extremely innovative, and if you have children, you may find it hard to get them out of

there again! A particular favourite is the water play area – just make sure you borrow an apron!

On the top floor, you can find our future gallery and the Planetarium. The future gallery looks at developments in space and technology, and is particularly suitable for those over 12. Younger children can of course visit as well, though. I should point out that there is an extra charge for the Planetarium, as it's run separately from the Time Capsule.

Ok, I hope that covers it. Er … any questions?

Reading

1 slowing
2 cities
3 felled
4 abandoned
5 decades
6 colonised
7 a third/one-third/$\frac{1}{3}$
8 Latin America
9 B
10 A
11 C
12 D
13 A

Vocabulary

1

1 industrial
2 beautiful
3 agricultural
4 national
5 Technological
6 prediction
7 dangerous
8 projection
9 populous
10 traditional

2

1 sticky/awkward
2 memorable/happy
3 perfect/ideal
4 golden/perfect
5 burning/serious

3

1 A
2 D
3 B

4 D

5 A

Grammar

1

1 The police **have** been blamed for starting the riot.

2 This time next week, we'll **be** just **arriving** there/we'll **have** just **arrived** there.

3 You can leave your **luggage** at reception.

4 Correct

5 The **accommodation is** terrible!

6 Correct

7 He was fined for dropping **litter** on the street.

8 Be careful or that **will break**.

9 Correct

10 Correct

11 The length of prison sentences appears to have no effect on levels of **crime/crime levels**.

12 According to **information** I recently received, the company is going bankrupt.

13 Something ought **to** be done about pollution.

14 Sorry, **I will be/am/'m** really busy next week.

15 In the past people used to pass **furniture** on to their children, not throw it away.

2

1 be used

2 be harvested

3 collects

4 catching

5 flows

6 (are) dried

7 is cooked

8 becomes

9 is filtered

10 is sweetened

11 are added

12 being kneaded

13 is flattened

14 are wrapped

15 (are) sealed

Progress test 3

Listening

21 experience

22 teamwork

23 communication

24 20/twenty

25 30/thirty

26 5/five

27 listen carefully

28 team worker/teamworker

29 and 30 A, D, in any order

Listening script 3.3
Section 3

T = tutor; L = Lucy; J = Jon

T: Hello, everyone. Jon and Lucy, it's your turn to feed back to us on how you've been getting on with the University Skills Certificate. Could you tell us which modules you decided to take and why, and which of these you found most useful, and why? Lucy?

L: Well, I really wanted to focus on skills that I might need after I graduate, so I mostly opted for business-oriented modules. I took the module on 'preparing for job interviews' as I thought that might be useful, and also the one on 'work experience'. And I also had to take the core module on 'personal development'. Bit of a waste of time, that one …

J: I can't agree with that. I took the personal development course along with 'Better Teamwork', and they were both really useful. And I think they'll make me more employable.

T: So, you did Personal Development and Better Teamwork. Jon … , what was your third option?

J: Communication Skills.

T: And how many credits did you earn? Did you get the full certificate?

L: Well, I would have done, if it hadn't been for the Personal Development course. You see, it was a core module, which meant I had to complete it to finish the course. I didn't though, so I only got 20 credits. I might go back and do a different core module though and get my 30 that way.

J: Each of my modules was 10 credits, so I had 30 credits in total, which gave me the certificate.

T: And did you feel the modules were worthwhile? You seemed to disagree somewhat on the Personal Development module. Can you tell us a bit more about it?

. . . .

J: Yes, well, I thought it was really useful. There were four main learning outcomes, er, no actually five, I think. Defining assertive behaviour, understanding how that is expressed, dealing with criticism, drawing up personal development plans and improving our own interpersonal behaviour.

T: Which of those did you personally find most useful?

J: Oh, I think maybe dealing with criticism. I used to find it really hard when people criticized me for anything, but they gave us some strategies for dealing with it better.

T: Such as?

Jon: <u>Well, first of all really listen carefully to the criticism,</u> rather than being too defensive. It sounds obvious.

L: Well, it is obvious, isn't it? That's what I didn't like about the course. It was all really obvious. I just didn't feel I was learning anything.

T: Was there anything positive you felt you got out of the course?

L: Well, I did enjoy doing the personality questionnaire. I found out some useful things about my style as a member of a group. Apparently I'm a good 'shaper'.

T: What does that mean?

L: That I'm a high achiever.

T: And what about you, Jon?

Jon: <u>The questionnaire showed I was a good team worker.</u>

T: What did the coursework consist of?

L: Well, I thought we might need to do a lot of reading, you know, read round the subject and then produce a review of the literature, but it wasn't like that at all.

Jon: No, that's right, it was more personal than that. <u>We had to keep a 'blog', a kind of online diary,</u> and the tutors read it and wrote comments.

T: Wasn't there any kind of formal assessment? A case study or something?

Jon: <u>It was formally assessed through an assignment.</u> We had to write about assertive behaviour and how it is expressed, looking at things like body language.

T: Oh right, that sounds interesting …

Reading

1 D
2 E
3 D
4 B
5 C
6 C
7 D
8 B
9 A
10 D
11–13 C, D, G, in any order

Vocabulary

1

1 job
2 work
3 livelihood
4 career
5 profession
6 qualifications
7 opportunity
8 benefit
9 achievement
10 neighbourhood
11 vicinity
12 location
13 prospects
14 chance
15 success

2

1 impressive
2 memorable
3 priceless
4 attractions
5 emotional
6 extension
7 transformation
8 location
9 nostalgic
10 spacious

Grammar

1

1 These
2 they
3 It
4 those
5 its
6 These
7 This
8 they
9 them
10 they

2

1 otherwise
2 used to
3 Were
4 Had
5 must be
6 Unless
7 should have been
8 are not
9 would
10 Unless
11 did

12 could have been

13 should

14 must

15 to offer

Progress test 4

Listening

31 wildlife

32 1800

33 portraits

34 light

35 completed

36 80/eighty

37 Asian

38–40 A, D, G, in any order

Listening script 3.4

Section 4

In the first of this series of talks on Australian culture, I'd like to give you an overview of Australian Art. We will mostly be concentrating on the period after the first settlers arrived, looking at Aboriginal Art in a separate lecture.

As you know, James Cook first charted the coastline of Australia in 1770, and on board his ship was perhaps Australia's first non-Aboriginal artist, Sydney Parkinson, a botanical illustrator. The drawings he made of Australian <u>wildlife</u> were taken back to Europe, where they were not always taken very seriously. Famously, a great many people thought that his drawing of a platypus was a hoax, … that such a creature could not really exist!

Further expeditions in the early nineteenth century also carried professional illustrators and the first resident professional artist was John Lewin. He settled here in <u>1800</u>, although he had originally intended to return to England, using the proceeds he made from his paintings of wildlife. Unfortunately for him, the fashion for this had passed, so he also set up a business as a painter of <u>portraits</u> of well-known people in Sydney.

The nineteenth century is all about the move from a more European perspective, towards developing a uniquely Australiian vision. Artists such as Tom Roberts and Arthur Streeton were part of the so-called Heidelburg school, which focused on the very different Australian <u>light</u>, representing the much brighter, vibrant colours of our land. Incidentally, the school wasn't named after the German city, but after a farm near Melbourne where the painters met to paint.

By the 1850s art exhibitions had begun to be popular and the first art gallery, the National Gallery of Victoria as it's now known, was founded in 1861.

It isn't until the twentieth century that the first well-known women artists began to emerge. At the beginning of the century one well-known female artist was Grace Cossington Smith, the subject of a recent exhibition at the National Gallery. Cossington Smith is perhaps best known for her paintings of Sydney Harbour Bridge, before it was <u>completed</u>. She was drawn to the image of the two sides straining to meet in the middle.

More recently, Emily Kngwarreye, an Aboriginal artist who didn't begin painting professionally until she was nearly <u>eighty</u>, has become one of the most commercially successful Australian artists ever. One of her last paintings recently sold for over a million dollars.

Other notable artists and movements of the twentieth century would have to include James Gleeson, Australia's foremost surrealist, and Ian Fairweather, a Scottish expatriate, whose paintings were an amazing mixture of Aboriginal and <u>Asian</u> art.

....

And now we reach the present day. Of course artists continue to be influenced by the great movements of the past, but there are some peculiarly twenty-first century influences too. The digital age is making quite an impact, as is the increasingly urgent question of the environment. One artist who is particularly well known for his eco-art is John Dalhsen. Dalhsen makes his art from things found on the beach, but not the seaweed and seashells you might expect. About ten years ago, Dalhsen, who loved walking on the beach, started to notice quite how much rubbish was being washed up. He started picking it up to bring home and noticed how, sorted into different colours, it could seem almost beautiful. In 2000, he won the Wynne Prize for his work, *Totems*, tall totem poles made entirely of <u>rubber beach sandals</u> that he had found washed up on the sand. Another more recent work, *Blue Rope*, has layers of different colours, blue and green. It looks like the sea, but is made from old <u>nylon rope</u>, fishing nets and <u>plastic bags</u>. Not surprisingly, the environmental movement has taken him to their hearts, as not only is he actually picking up a great deal of rubbish, he is also doing a lot to raise awareness of the problem …

Reading

1 3/three points

2 a point

3 shorter

4 prestigious

5 I

6 G

7 D

8 H

9 L

10 J

11 A

12 F

13 C

Vocabulary

1 C
2 C
3 B
4 C
5 A
6 D
7 B
8 A
9 C
10 B
11 D
12 A
13 B
14 B
15 A

Grammar

1

1 the
2 zero article
3 the
4 zero article
5 zero article
6 the
7 the
8 a
9 zero article
10 zero article
11 a
12 zero article
13 The
14 zero article
15 the
16 the
17 an
18 zero article
19 a
20 a

2

1 The place which I **liked the best** was Rio de Janeiro.
2 If it weren't for my mother, I don't know what I **would** have done.
3 Correct
4 Correct
5 That's the town where I used to **live**.

6 Even **if** I had remembered my phone, I didn't have his number.
7 People **who** drive to work should car share.
8 Correct
9 He went to university in Falmouth, where there is good **surfing**.
10 The woman, **who** was carrying an umbrella, looked at me angrily.
11 If I were you, I **would** go straight to the library.
12 I'll lend you my car if you **drive** carefully.
13 Correct
14 If I had more money, I **could/would** buy those shoes.
15 Correct

Progress test 5

Listening

31 F
32 A
33 D
34 C
35 B
36 soldiers
37 inflation
38 1764
39 national
40 eagles

Listening script 3.5

Section 4

Today I'm going to talk to you about the early history of money in the States. Let's start by looking at how people traded before the early settlers arrived. Most people agree that there wasn't actually money in the sense we understand it today. Mostly there were different sorts of barter systems. However, we know that in Mexico the Aztecs did sometimes use gold as a kind of currency. Basically they would barter, but use the gold dust, which was kept in transparent quills so you could see how much was in there, to make up the difference if one item was worth significantly more than another. Another form of payment was cocoa beans – chocolate was very popular! They would use sacks with thousands of beans as a way of making very large payments. In North America and Canada, the native Americans had a system called potlatch. Essentially, a potlatch was a kind of party where the host would show how wealthy he was by giving away as much as possible. People took it in turns to host the potlatch and competed to give stuff away, so in the end everyone in the community was provided for. Potlatch was actually banned in Canada for a while as it was not thought to contribute to the work ethic. Actually, banning

---

it had a detrimental effect on the work ethic because it removed a lot of the motivation to earn.

Wampum was also adopted as a currency by the settlers, but it wasn't a currency to begin with. Wampum are beads made from seashells, and they were certainly very valuable among the American Indians. The right shells were hard to find and the beads were time consuming and difficult to make, so this gave them a commodity value. They would certainly have been used in bartering. The settlers, however, used them as a kind of money. In fact the workers who built the city of New York were paid in Wampum. There were a lot of alternative currencies about in those days. Another one was tobacco. Tobacco leaves were used as currency in and around the colony of Virginia for about 200 years. They were not the most practical of currencies though, they tended to fall apart quite quickly, and gradually certificates representing tobacco held in warehouses started to be used instead – in effect the first paper money.

....

In the colonies' later years, other forms of paper currency started to be issued. In 1690, Massachusetts was the first colony to issue notes to pay soldiers. The notes could be redeemed for gold or silver, but were also accepted as legal tender. Other colonies followed suit. As time went on, the British government started to try and prevent the colonies from issuing paper money.

That was partly because they didn't want to lose control, but also because some colonies were issuing so much that it was causing very high inflation. This obviously worried the British government and, in fact, it culminated in the complete banning of all colonial paper money in 1764 – this was one of the main reasons behind the American Revolution. During the revolution, America produced a flood of paper money, which was worth less and less, and although in the short-term it did finance the revolution, it inevitably led to hyperinflation. By the end of the war, American finances were in chaos and in 1790, the dollar was established for the first time as a national currency. The hope was that by replacing all the different states' currencies, some stability could be achieved. However, there was a great shortage of gold and silver and the government was forced to accept the use of foreign gold and silver coins, particularly Spanish dollars, as legal tender as well. Gradually these were phased out, but American silver dollars are still legal currency, though you don't see many of them around these days. Did you know that there were also ten dollar coins, known as eagles because of the bird printed on them? These were in circulation right up until the 1930s …

Reading

1 and 2   A and D
3 15 percent
4 inconvenience
5 fuel-efficient
6 stresses
7 parking spaces
8 (freeway) lanes
9 online
10 NOT GIVEN
11 NOT GIVEN
12 NO
13 YES

Vocabulary

1

1 Internet
2 viaduct
3 server
4 pylon
5 satellite
6 grid
7 tunnel
8 well
9 cable
10 refinery

2

1 money laundering
2 cash crops
3 wealth creation
4 savings account
5 income tax
6 spending power
7 debt mountain
8 credit reserves
9 spending spree
10 currency conversion
11 consumer spending
12 price war
13 ethical code
14 traditional customs
15 mineral wealth

Grammar

1

1 You **can't** smoke here.
2 The car parking situation **should** improve with more car-pooling.
3 Visitors **must/have to** wear an ID pass at all times.
4 You **can** see a doctor even if you don't have medical insurance.
5 You **shouldn't have** waited so long before going to see the dentist.

6 They **don't have to/don't need to** build a new runway at Heathrow.

7 You **could have** helped me, if you had wanted to.

8 The conductor **needn't have** stopped the train.

9 The new skyscraper **will be** the tallest in the world.

10 You **should/ought to** write to the prime minister.

2

1 –
2 whose
3 –
4 of happiness
5 they
6 –
7 –
8 –
9 depressed
10 –
11 –
12 This
13 people
14 –
15 –

Listening

Section 1, Questions 1–10

1 exercise to music
2 8, 8
3 programme/program
4 extra cost
5 over 60
6 32.00
7 10.00
8 35.00
9 Saturday
10 outside shoes

Listening script 3.6
Section 1

R = receptionist; C = customer

R: Good morning, St Martin's Leisure Centre. Can I help you?

C: Hi, I was wondering if you could give me some information about your fitness facilities.

R: Sure. We have a pool with sauna and spa area, a gym with fitness equipment and various fitness classes. What do you think you might be interested in?

C: Well, er … probably not the pool, I'm not too keen on swimming. Probably the gym, or maybe some of the classes. What classes do you offer?

R: Quite a range. Pilates, yoga, circuit training, exercise to music, Aquafit … . But some of these are only available during the day.

C: Oh, I could only come evenings or weekends.

R: Well, there's a pilates class on a Monday evening and circuit training on Tuesday and Thursday. Oh, and there's exercise to music on Saturday mornings. I have to say, it's mostly ladies at that one though …

C: What about the gym? What are the opening hours?

R: That's open during our normal opening hours – 8am to 8pm Monday to Saturday, 9 to 6pm on Sundays.

C: And would I get any instruction in how to use the gym?

R: Well, you would have to have an induction session with an instructor. He or she sees how fit you are and then creates a programme to suit you and show you how to use the gym.

C: And then I'm on my own?

R: Well, we do offer one-to-one personal training, but at an extra cost.

....

Final test key

C: How much does it cost to join the gym then?

R: Well, we offer different packages. The cheapest one is Active Wellness. This entitles you to unlimited use of the gym, plus swim, sauna and fitness classes. But you need to be <u>over 60</u>, a student or unemployed. It's £25 a month

C: Well, that's no use. What packages are available to me then?

R: Well, the next cheapest is Club Wellness, with a six-month contract. That's <u>£32</u> a month.

C: That doesn't sound too bad.

R: Or you can join Club Wellness on a pay as you go option at <u>£10</u> each visit to the gym.

C: Why is that option more expensive?

R: Well, you can cancel it any time you like, whereas with the cheaper one, you're locked in for six months.

C: Oh, OK, I see.

R: Or you can be a casual member and pay a joining fee of <u>£35</u> and an annual membership fee of £20 and then you can just pay £4.50 every time you come. That's a good option if you don't think you'll use the gym that often.

C: Oh, I think I'll be more likely to come if I pay monthly – I want to get my money's worth! I think I'll go for the six-month membership.

R: OK, well, if you want to book an induction session, you can do all the paperwork at the same time. When would be a good time?

C: Do you have anything on Saturday?

R: No, sorry, we're really busy … perhaps Sunday at 3pm? Ah, no we do have a slot at 1 o'clock.

C: On Sunday?

R: No, <u>Saturday</u>. Would that be OK?

C: Yes, great, thanks. And what should I wear?

R: Oh, a T-shirt, shorts or tracksuit trousers, nothing special. Oh, but you must wear some indoor trainers, not <u>outside shoes</u> of any kind. That's really quite important …

Section 2, Questions 11–20

11 B

12 A

13 B

14 and 15 B, D, in any order

16 £70,000/seventy thousand pounds

17 (some) ground rules

18–20   A, D, G, in any order

Listening script 3.7
Section 2

Hi, my name's Susan Morris and I'd like to talk to you all today about taking a gap year. Many of you will have been making applications to university, but perhaps have thought about doing something else first, taking a year out of formal education to travel, to work or volunteer.

<u>Gap years used to be viewed with a certain amount of suspicion by universities and employers. This is certainly not the case anymore. Increasingly it's being recognized that a well-organized gap year can help young people to develop their independence and maturity</u>.

You don't have to go abroad to have a good gap year. <u>Work experience in this country can be very valuable, and can help you decide if a particular career or university course is really what you'd like to do</u>. For instance, I recently met a young man, Steve, who had applied for a Media Studies course at university. In his gap year he volunteered for the local hospital radio. This led to paid work with a local radio station where he is now a top presenter. <u>He decided against going to university at all</u>, though, as he says, if it all goes wrong, he can still go as a mature student.

Or during your gap year, you could also choose to volunteer abroad. For example, if you're a good swimmer, you could go and teach kids to swim in Fiji. You could work with primary and secondary school kids, coaching in PE lessons and after-school clubs. <u>Or you could go to Argentina for a four week Spanish course, followed by a voluntary job at Cordoba zoo, working with jaguars, pumas and other exotic animals.</u>

For many people, however, the idea of a gap year is synonymous with travelling the world, taking a road trip across America, or travelling by train across Europe or exploring Asia or South America. It sounds wonderful, but it can involve a lot of planning …

....

Firstly, you really need to prepare a budget. A round-the-world ticket costs on average a thousand pounds. However, it's thought that the average gap year costs about £5,000. The extra goes on such things as food, accommodation, Internet access and telephone calls and, very importantly, travel and medical insurance. Never travel without proper insurance; it is simply not worth the risk. The cost of being airlifted to hospital could be £20,000, and <u>almost £70,000</u> if you need to be airlifted back home.

Then consider if you want to travel alone or with friends. Travelling can be frustrating, so try to choose a friend who you know can manage money and be relied on in a time of crisis. Ideally, choose someone you have already travelled with successfully. Before you leave it's very important for you to set <u>some ground rules</u>, to make sure you're both in agreement about how to manage things.

Finally, I'd like to talk a little about safety. This is particularly important if you decide to travel on your own. <u>Always keep</u>

your money, cards and passport on you. In crowded areas it can be a good idea to wear your backpack on your chest rather than your back. This makes it harder for pickpockets to operate. Never leave your bags dangling on the back of a chair. Keep them on your lap, ideally looped round your wrist. If you are planning to travel alone, it's particularly important to keep in touch with relatives and friends, so that everyone is aware of your plans.

Planned properly, a gap year can be a wonderful experience, and I hope I've given you some food for thought. Any questions?

Section 3, Questions 21–30

21 feedback/feed-back form
22 before the tour
23 in good time
24 four/4
25 length
26 (very) knowledgeable
27 free gifts
28 E
29 D
30 C

Listening script 3.8
Section 3

D = Dr Khan; S = Saira; M = Marco

D: Hi, come in. How are you Saira? Marco?

S: Hello, Dr Khan. Fine thanks.

M: Yes, fine.

D: So, you looked at the impact of the new campus tours that have recently been set up for people who are thinking of coming and studying here.

S: Yes, we thought it would be good to do something where our findings could have a tangible benefit for the university and help to improve the service offered.

D: Yes, it's a relatively new idea taking groups of people round the campus regularly to give an overview of what we offer. So, how did you go about collecting data?

M: We put together a feedback form to give people to fill in after they'd taken the tour. First of all, we asked some questions about the information which had been sent out before the tour. We had been told that a lot of people don't actually turn up for the tours and we wanted to know why.

D: So, what did you ask them?

S: If they had received information about the tour in good time before the visit.

D: That's a good question.

S: And if they had found the information helpful.

D: Hmm.... I think there's a bit of a problem with that question.

M: Quite a lot of people said no, but although we knew there was a problem, we still didn't know what the problem was.

S: Yes, we should have asked a more open question, like: 'What did you find most helpful or least helpful about the information?' Most people said they had received the information in time though.

D: Who did you give the feedback form to?

M: People who'd been on the tour.

D: So actually, they were the people who had turned up. Maybe you'd need to think about talking to the people who didn't turn up?

S: I suppose so, but that could be difficult though. Anyway, then we asked them about the content of the tour itself. We asked people to rate various things on a scale of 1–5, with 1 being the lowest and 5 the highest.

M: The content of the tour generally came out quite high, about 4 on average, so we know that people are seeing what they need to, though I guess we could find out a bit more about this ... However, the length was marked down at an average of 2. We're not sure though if this means the tour was too short or too long.

D: Or both!

M: Yes, I suppose so. Everyone thought the person leading the tour was very knowledgeable.

S: Oh ... and er ... people were very pleased with the em ... free gifts they were given at the end.

....

D: So, how do you think you could improve the research methodology and find out a bit more? Saira?

S: Well, I think it would be a good idea to move away from the yes/no questions and even the grading 1–5 and ask more open questions. Perhaps we could actually talk to people face to face? What do you think, Marco?

M: I think that might be quite difficult to set up. I agree with you about the open questions, but I think we should just leave more spaces on the feedback form for people to write comments on. We could ask people to answer why/why not.

D: I think both approaches are possible, but if you do what Saira's talking about, it will inevitably reduce the number of people you can get feedback from.

S: Well ... yes, but we might get some much more detailed information. I don't think people like writing pages and pages on a feedback form.

D: I think you also need to think about when you ask for feedback. You might get more responses if you ask for the feedback straightaway, rather than asking people to post it back to you. Even with a freepost envelope, a lot of people won't bother.

Section 4, Questions 31–40

31 16,000/sixteen thousand years
32 the 1930s/nineteen thirties
33 nomadic hunters
34 north-east Asia
35 genetic evidence
36 down the coast
37 C
38 B
39 B
40 C

Listening script 3.9
Section 4

Hello, everyone. Today, I'd like to give you a brief overview of the different theories and models of migration to the New World, or the Americas. I should start by saying that the question of how people first came to and colonized the Americas has by no means been settled, and I won't be giving you the answer, just a number of popular theories.

First of all, there are two general schools of thought. One thinks that the first people arrived in the New World no longer than 16,000 years ago. This idea, believe it or not, is known as 'short chronology'. The other school of thought, 'long chronology', believes that it was much longer ago than that, perhaps as much as 40,000 years ago.

There is also some argument as to how the first people reached the Americas. Perhaps the longest standing theory, widely accepted since the 1930s, is the 'landbridge' theory. This suggests that people migrated from Siberia into Alaska, across the Bering Strait, which then contained a landbridge linking the two continents. According to the theory, the people migrating would have been nomadic hunters. Spearheads of a particular shape have been found all over North and Central America, supporting this theory and putting the migration at between 17,000 and 10,000 years – a short chronology.

The long chronology school of thought would argue that although people undoubtedly did cross the Bering Strait at that time, they were not the first people to arrive. There is some evidence of earlier inhabitation, especially in the south of the United States and Central and South America.

The big question is where they came from. A number of theories have been put forward. The Pacific coastal model suggests that people arrived by boat from north-east Asia, following the coastline. However, other anthropologists suggest that the first people crossed from Australia or Polynesia. There are some apparent similarities between the Australian Aborigines and some of the tribes of Southern Patagonia. However, genetic evidence does not bear this theory out.

Genetic evidence is actually starting to really make some headway into understanding migration patterns. Recently the DNA was extracted from a 10 300-year-old tooth which had been found in a cave in southern Alaska. Researchers discovered descendants with the same DNA all along the Pacific coast from California to Tierra del Fuego. This strongly indicates that some of the first inhabitants may have dispersed down the coast, though it is thought that this was no more than about 10,000 years ago.

....

Several of the descendants found by this study were descendants of Chumash Indians, living in California. Similarities have been found between their DNA and that of people living in Japan and north-east Asia, perhaps supporting the Pacific coastal model.

The history of the Chumash and other neighbouring Californian tribes is interesting and may provide further evidence of their ancestry. Along with the Tongva, a tribe found to the south, they regularly went out onto the ocean fishing. This is unusual amongst New World peoples, and may indicate that this is how their ancestors originally arrived. The boats used by the Chumash are called 'tomols' and there may be a linguistic link with a similar word used by the Polynesians. Tongva boats are called 'ti-ats'

The Tongva are also known as Gabrielenos, after the tradition of naming tribes after nearby Spanish missions. The original name of the Tongva means 'people of the earth'. Plenty of Chumash and Tongva places names are still used in California, such as 'Malibu' in Los Angeles County.

Settlements prove that the Chumash were in the area at least 10,000 years ago, and archeologists have uncovered a prehistoric Tongva site, estimated to be 8,000 years old. This, of course, still fits very comfortably within the 'short chronology' theory I mentioned earlier.

READING

Reading Passage 1, Questions 1–13

1 TRUE
2 NOT GIVEN
3 FALSE
4 NOT GIVEN
5 FALSE
6 (an/the) alley
7 tagged with graffiti
8 (a) flyer attached
9 another bicycle
10 33
11 no throughway
12 20%
13 post box

Reading Passage 2, Questions 14–27

14 G
15 I
16 A
17 F
18 I
19 D
20 tidal wave
21 Krakatoa's child
22 stopped erupting
23 the Javan tiger
24 eye sockets
25 severe
26 population
27 wisps of smoke

Reading Passage 3, Questions 28–40

28 brain cells
29 very early childhood
30 brain scans
31 puberty
32 increases
33 synapses
34 C
35 B
36 C
37 B
38 A
39 B
40 B

WRITING

Task 1

Model answer

The table shows how much of a range of materials was collected for recycling in a four-year period in Britain.

Overall, the amount of material being recycled has nearly doubled over the period, from 1,214 thousand tonnes to 2,377. Paper and card have remained the items most often recycled, though the quantity has increased from 600 thousand tonnes to 973 thousand tonnes. By far the biggest increase has been in the amount of compost collected for recycling, rising steadily from 279 thousand tonnes to 941 thousand tonnes over the four-year period. This means that far more compost is now collected than glass, which has risen only slightly over the period. In contrast to these increases, the amount of plastics and cans being sent for recycling has hardly changed at all. There was a small increase in cans in the first year, but since then it has remained level. The amount of plastics being recycled has actually dropped in the fourth year, after previous small increases.

Task 2

Model answer

Just one long-distance flight a year can use as much carbon as all our other activities for the year. Clearly, something needs to be done about the increasing number of flights being taken.

More and more people are flying, largely because flights have become cheaper and more accessible. People need to change their mind-set, so that jetting off to another country for the weekend is no longer an acceptable thing to do. Business travellers as well, should try to use modern technology such as web-cams and video-conferencing before they step on a plane to go to a meeting.

Ultimately, though educating people may reduce demand, the government will also have to make some changes in policy. Firstly, instead of constantly opening new airports and runways, they should be looking to close them down. Of course, they will then need to provide people with good alternatives. Some countries around the world already have excellent high-speed rail networks; these could be expanded to provide people with a comfortable and reasonably fast option.

At the moment, fuel for aircraft is not taxed. This is the main reason why flights remain so affordable.

If tax had to be paid, people would think very carefully about the cost of each flight. Of course, some people will argue that this is just ensuring that only the rich can fly, but it is the very poorest of the world, in flood- and drought-prone countries, who will truly suffer if we continue to destroy the atmosphere through frequent flying.

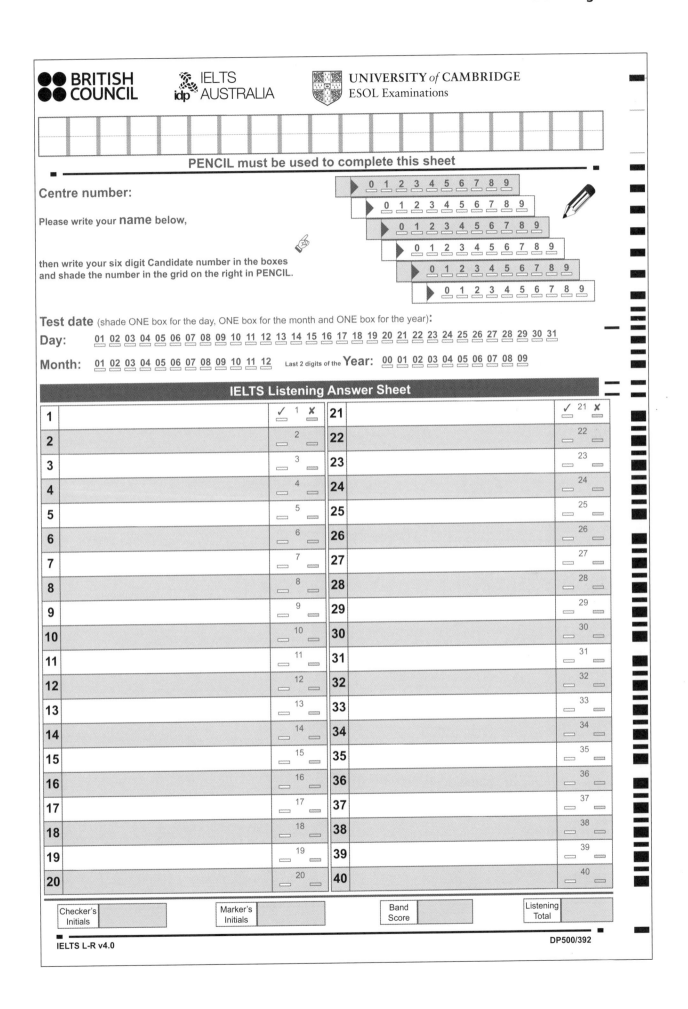

Reading answer sheet

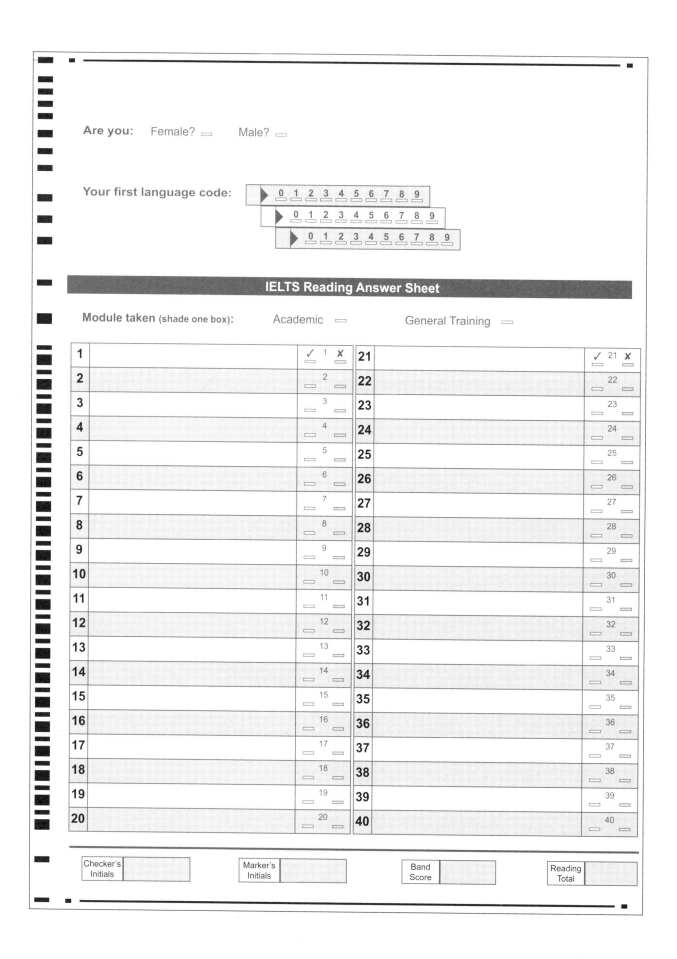

Are you: Female? ⬚ Male? ⬚

Your first language code:

0 1 2 3 4 5 6 7 8 9
0 1 2 3 4 5 6 7 8 9
0 1 2 3 4 5 6 7 8 9

IELTS Reading Answer Sheet

Module taken (shade one box): Academic ⬚ General Training ⬚

1		21	
2		22	
3		23	
4		24	
5		25	
6		26	
7		27	
8		28	
9		29	
10		30	
11		31	
12		32	
13		33	
14		34	
15		35	
16		36	
17		37	
18		38	
19		39	
20		40	

| Checker's Initials | | Marker's Initials | | Band Score | | Reading Total | |

IELTS Material from Macmillan Education

READY FOR IELTS

Our new IELTS course combines the successful elements of the Ready For series and an experienced author team to ensure students aiming for IELTS bands 5-6.5 are ready for success.

ISBN: see www.macmillanenglish.com

CHECK YOUR VOCABULARY FOR IELTS

Contains a range of activities to help build, improve and revise English vocabulary for the IELTS examination.

ISBN: 9780230033603

IELTS TESTBUILDERS

Designed to help improve exam performance, the IELTS Testbuilders each contain four complete practice tests reflecting a full range of exam task types.

IELTS Testbuilder 1: 9781405014045
IELTS Testbuilder 2: 9780230028852

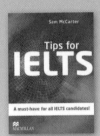

TIPS FOR IELTS

All the information you need to know for the IELTS exam. Includes hints on how to tackle specific question types, strategies for increasing speed and accuracy and common mistakes to avoid.

ISBN: 9780230033603

IMPROVE YOUR IELTS SKILLS SERIES

These three preparation courses develop language, skills and techniques to help students achieve a higher IELTS score Aimed at bands 4.5-7.5.

Reading: 9780230009455
Writing: 9780230009448
Listening and Speaking: 9780230009486

IELTS FOUNDATION

Provides a motivating package of material to meet the needs of students training towards IELTS band 4-5.5.

ISBN: 9781405096164

IELTS GRADUATION

A comprehensive course for students aiming at bands 5.5-7.5. Contains a wide range of activities to help improve students' IELTS score.

ISBN: 9781405080750

IELTS FOUNDATION STUDY SKILLS

Self-study books for students aiming at IELTS band 4-6. Provides practical information and teaches the skills needed to succeed in the exam.

Academic Module: 9781405017220
General Module: 9781405082013

IELTS GRADUATION STUDY SKILLS

Can be used alongside IELTS Graduation Student's Book or as a stand-alone self-study book. Aimed at bands 5.5-7.5.

ISBN: 9781405080781

MACMILLAN

www.macmillanenglish.com/exams

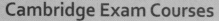

MACMILLAN **EXAMS**

Cambridge Exam Courses

Testbuilders

IELTS Materials

Exam Courses for Younger Learners

Grammar and Vocabulary

www.macmillanenglish.com/exams